Homosexuality, Which Homosexuality?

International Conference on Gay and Lesbian Studies

Dennis Altman
Carole Vance
Martha Vicinus
Jeffrey Weeks
and others

Uitgeverij An Dekker/Schorer Amsterdam

GMP Publishers, London

The *Homosexuality, Which Homosexuality? Conference* was a joint venture
of the Research Group Gay and Lesbian Studies of the
Interdisciplinary Centre for the Study of Science, Society and
Religion, Free University of Amsterdam and the Schorer Foundation,
a gay and lesbian social service agency.

Organizing committee:
Rudolf Bevaart
Wim Haan
Nettie van Heezik
Marty P.N. van Kerkhof
Anja van Kooten Niekerk
Thijs Maasen
Theo van der Meer
Hans Meij
Riek Stienstra

This conference was organized with financial assistance from:
Algemeen Cultureel Centrum, Free University
Interdisciplinary Centre for the Study of Science, Society and
Religion, Free University
The British Council
City of Amsterdam
Free University
Free University Chaplain
Koningin Juliana Fonds
Koninklijke Nederlandse Academie van Wetenschappen
Mama Cash
Ministery of Education and Science
Ministery Welfare, Health and Cultural Affairs
Ministery of Employment and Social Security
Nationaal Fonds Geestelijke Volksgezondheid
Schorer Foundation
University of Siegen, West-Germany

Published by GMP Publishers, London and
Uitgeverij An Dekker/Schorer, Amsterdam 1989
© Jhr. Mr. J.A. Schorerstichting, Amsterdam, 1988
© Individual articles the author
Typeset by Vidicom-Vidiset bv, The Hague
Printed in The Netherlands by Krips Repro bv, Meppel
ISBN 0 85449 091 4 (Great Britain)
ISBN 90 5071 057 3 (The Netherlands)

TABLE OF CONTENTS

HOMOSEXUALITY, WHICH HOMOSEXUALITY?

INTRODUCTION

It was Tuesday, 15 December 1987. Some 500 men and women from 22 countries assembled in Amsterdam at the Free University for the Conference called *Homosexuality, Which Homosexuality?* Following more than two years of preparation, the Gay and Lesbian Studies Group of the Free University and the Schorer Foundation, could at last welcome participants to the largest gay and lesbian studies conference ever held. Inspired by Carole Vance's keynote address, participants went on to discuss for three days some 200 papers in 100 workshops. And on the fourth and final day of the Conference, internationally known scholars delivered public lectures. These we are proud to present, together with Carole Vance's opening address, in this book.

BACKGROUND TO THE CONFERENCE

In 1978, students and faculty at the University of Amsterdam undertook the first successful initiative in the Netherlands toward developing a gay and lesbian studies programme. Similar initiatives later resulted in gay and lesbian studies programmes at the Universities of Utrecht and Nijmegen.

In 1984 an Initiative Group of Gay and Lesbian Studies was set up at the Free University in Amsterdam, the Netherlands' Protestant university. This marked a turning point in the history of the university itself, as one of its founding fathers, former prime minister Abraham Kuyper, at the turn of the century had launched a notoriously vehement attack in the Dutch Parliament on the early homosexual rights campaign in Holland.

To stimulate interest in this new academic field within the university, the members of the group decided to organize a major international meeting. Together with the Schorer Foundation, the Dutch social service agency for homosexuality, which proposed to celebrate its 20th anniversary by co-organizing the conference, the first plans were made in 1985. The organizers followed the precedent of their colleagues at the University of Amsterdam, who had organized the first international lesbian and gay studies conference *Among Men, Among Women* in 1983; and of the organizers of the *Sex and the State* Conference in Toronto in 1985.

For a decade there has been a growing controversy among gay and lesbian scholars centring around two rival scientific theories and their implications for homosexuality: *essentialism* and *constructionism*. The organizers of *Homosexuality, Which Homosexuality?* chose this controversy as their theme, calling on participants to confront the dilemmas raised by this debate and to dwell upon its consequences for their own research and for mental health practice.

Stimulated by their predecessors, the organizers went to great lengths to make the Conference into the academic event of the year (or maybe even the decade). The knowledge that only forty kilometres from Amsterdam the gay and lesbian studies group of the Univerity of Utrecht had decided to organize an international meeting immediately preceding *Homosexuality, Which Homosexuality?* proved an extra stimulus to turn the Conference into a successful enterprise.[1] That in one country two international gay and lesbian conferences can be held within one week's time typifies that peculiarly Dutch phenomenon known as the 'pillarization' of society. Each sect or interest group traditionally organizes its own facilities for education, communication, and other endeavours. This tradition may well have had enduring influence on scholarly life in the Netherlands, for there also exist two rivalrous camps in gay and lesbian studies: the so-called Amsterdam and Utrecht 'schools'. Ideally this could be a stimulus for academic debate. Unfortunately, however, the schism has created a 'battleground' where, more often than not, personal ambitions and rivalries abound.

ON THE CONFERENCE THEME

For centuries, same-sex acts between men and between women have been liable to interventions by clerical and secular authorities, who called them sins and crimes. Contemporaries perceived such acts not as behaviours immanent in personality structures, but as *deeds* betraying religious and social heterodoxy. As such they were part of a hotchpotch of 'unnatural acts' that also included masturbation, anal intercourse between men and women and bestiality.

Not till the second half of the 19th century would *systematic* interference with homosexuality come to pass. In 1864 Karl Heinrich Ulrichs (initially under the pseudonym of Numa Numantius) began publication of a series of booklets on same-sex behaviour. He claimed, employing (from our point of view) a curious mixture of medical, political, and poetical arguments, that same-sex behaviour between men resulted from an inborn condition: *anima muliebris virili corpore inclusa*, a female soul enclosed in a male body. Ulrichs coined the terms 'urning' and 'dioning', the former of which survived well into the 20th century.[2] Unlike the Hungarian writer and translator Kertbeny (alias Benkert), who some five years later introduced the term 'homosexual', Ulrichs fought a lonely battle with legal authorities and the medical profession over his ideas.[3] The latter was certainly quick to pick up Ulrichs's ideas on the innateness of the condition, but whereas Ulrichs took this condition to be proof of the naturalness of *Urningtum*, for writers like Westphal (who called it 'contrary sexual feeling') and Krafft-Ebing it became sexual or even moral pathology, usually a symptom of degeneracy. Not everyone underwrote the biological background of homosexuality. Some considered it to be an *acquired* condition, even prior to the appearance of Freud's ideas on the polymorphous sexuality of children. (Meanwhile it was not Kertbeny but most notably Jäger who was responsible for the gradual ascendancy of the term 'homosexual' over other words.) Neither Ulrichs nor Kertbeny were members of the medical profession. Yet it would be medicine, biology, psychology, and sexology that were to create a new frame of reference, converting same-sex behaviours into biologically or psychologically based dispositions and subsuming all sexual arrangements between members of the same sex under them.[4] The biological sex of 'the homosexual' was not considered important. Though most writings were mainly or exclusively about men, it seemed then easy enough to establish corresponding processes in women as well.

Until the late 1960s, the 19th-century concept of homosexuality as a *sexual identity* (whether inborn or acquired), which was constant throughout history and over different cultures, remained unchallenged. It was Mary McIntosh's landmark article 'The Homosexual Role' (1968) that questioned the notion of homosexuality as a universal condition of a minority. McIntosh not only saw that the propagation of such a condition as a means of control to keep the bulk of society pure, but she also argued that instead of a condition (or identity) one should speak of a homosexual *role*, a historical phenomenon, whose origins in England she traced back to the 17th century.[5] Like others, most notably Simon and Gagnon, she applied labelling theory, with all its inadequacies, to homosexuality.[6] But it was Michel Foucault, writing in the mid-70s, who would be most influential on the modern debate on homosexuality. Against the claim of biology and sexology to have furnished a description of a universal and continuous category of homosexuality, and against their ongoing quest for an aetiology of it, Foucault boldly asserted that in their 19th-century compulsion to categorize sexual *acts* these disciplines had themselves constructed sexual *categories*. Hence the term *social constructionism* applied to the current of thought which strives to expose the processes by which sexual categories and identities are created. One of these processes came to be known as the 'medicalization of homosexuality'.[7] A firmer basis for these theories was provided by the work of Ken Plummer and Jeffrey Weeks,[8] the latter of whom has contributed to this volume as well. With rather the same ease with which 19th-century scientists deemed their theories and descriptions to be applicable to lesbianism, the emergence of a lesbian identity would later be ascribed to a process of medicalization as well. Yet this assertion is questioned by Martha Vicinus in her contribution to this book.

As is usually the case in such debates, many more voices were to be heard than those mentioned here, and within the past decade the intricacies of the constructionism debate have given cause for fundamental reflection. Not only the concept of homosexuality, but that of sexuality and even of sexual desire as unchanging, god-given, or natural phenomena have been questioned, and have been claimed to be shaped according to historical and cultural need.

THE BIRTH OF A CONTRADICTION

Using the word 'debate' implies that with the introduction of this new thesis a contradiction was born between two approaches which are now often called essentialism and constructionism. Essentialism embraces explicitly or implicitly the 19th-century medico-biological concept, assuming historical and cultural continuity: homosexuals and lesbians have always and everywhere existed. In contrast to the continuity suggested by essentialism, constructionism stresses discontinuity. In this view homosexuality is a historical, Western construction. In its most radical form, constructionism assumes that a break took place in the 19th century. Constructionism also points to the multiformity of homosexuality in other cultures to demonstrate the inadequacy of the medico-biological concept.

In the *Among Men, Among Women* congress in 1983, primary emphasis was placed on research perspectives deriving from a constructionist approach. To this end, the term 'homosocial arrangements' was adopted, referring to all those same-sex constellations that could produce homosexuality. But this conference did not focus on the debate between essentialism and constructionism. Neither did the *Sex and the State* conference, but, willy-nilly, the debate emerged quite emotionally during the final session. Academic and political arguments were confounded, and the impasse the debate had arrived at became exposed.

The organizers of *Homosexuality, Which Homosexuality?* questioned when announcing the Conference the way in which essentialism and constructionism are viewed within scholarly debate on homosexuality as mutually exclusive approaches. They posed the question of whether historical and cultural *continuities* could exist alongside discontinuities (or vice versa) and asked contributors to address this issue in their papers. Implicitly this could mean they could go beyond the limits on frame of reference and interpretation which a debate like this one seems to set.

In each of the five sections of the Conference – History, Literature and Arts, Social Sciences, Theology, Current Issues – scholars dealt in the mode of their own disciplines with the issue, sometimes questioning the appropriateness of the debate for their own field. Perhaps most prominently of all, historians seem to have outgrown the sharp opposing views usually represented in the debate. Historians formerly known as constructionists were found discussing continuities in the history of homosexuality. Likewise, former essentialists were discussing the many faces of homosexuality in the past. In a provocative lecture on the history of homosexuality, offered in this volume, Randolph Trumbach addressed issues like family, gender, periodicity, the use of anthropological concepts – thus building cross-cultural bridges and leaving the original questions of the debate far behind.

Not only historians dealt with the issue in this way. Jan Schippers, for instance, member of the therapy staff of the Schorer Foundation, tried in his lecture to reach a synthesis between both theories. While a constructionist approach does restrain therapists from presenting their clients with a too simplistic concept of homosexuality as a matter of mere identity, Schippers maintains on the other hand that homosexual *identities* in this day and age are a necessity for the development of homosexual lifestyles.

The organizers of the *Homosexuality, Which Homosexuality?* Conference have never entertained the pretension that they could end the debate once and for all. Indeed there are many fields, such as social work and legislation, where the question of *which* homosexuality is only now emerging. That is to say, dominant essentialist beliefs are just starting to be challenged there. Moreover, the political implications of one position or the other are now beginning to dawn on us.

Although constructionism has had significant influence on social and historical research on lesbianism and homosexuality, it has by no means succeeded in eliminating essentialism. Social constructionism was the target of much criticism at its emergence, and it still is.

A ROOM OF ONE'S OWN

Gay and lesbian studies originated out of gay and lesbian politics. In the wake of a decade of academic research and writings, gay and lesbian scholars now see themselves confronted with questions about political responsibilities as opposed to academic ones, about fundamental versus politically opportune research, about working in an ivory tower versus accepting benefits offered in the form of governmental and private subsidies.

The dilemmas of the debate between essentialists and constructionists may seem an academic problem at first glance. Moreover, activists often accuse constructionists of undermining the gains of the gay and lesbian movement and depoliticizing it. Yet the ongoing medicalization of homosexuality *and* repressive measures directed at lesbians and gays (witness the recent adoption of the notorious Clause 28 in Britain) remain a matter of concern for activists and academicians alike. Both groups continue to hold important responsibilities; both have a profound need for 'a room of one's own'. They will meet in their alertness to societal repression, as well as in their quest for intellectual freedom. The organizers of *Homosexuality, Which Homosexuality?* took pride in being able to strengthen a young tradition of gay and lesbian scholarship. We hope we have encouraged scholars as well as activists to critically examine existing concepts of homosexuality and to find new ways of broadening academic research.

Anja van Kooten Niekerk
Theo van der Meer
on behalf of the Conference Organizing Committee

NOTES

1 *Homosexuality Beyond Disease* Conference, 10-12 December 1987.
2 Hubert Kennedy, *Ulrichs. The Life and Works of Karl Heinrich Ulrichs, Pioneer of the Modern Gay Movement.* Boston: Alyson Publications, 1988.
3 Manfred Herzer, 'Kertbeny and the Nameless Love'. *Journal of Homosexuality* 12:1 (Fall 1985).
4 Gert Hekma, *Homoseksualiteit, een medische reputatie. De uitdoktering van de homoseksueel in negentiende-eeuws Nederland.* Amsterdam: SUA, 1987.
5 Mary McIntosh, 'The Homosexual Role'. *Social Problems* 16 (1968) pp. 182-91. Reprinted in Kenneth Plummer (ed.), *The Making of the Modern Homosexual.* London: Hutchinson, 1981.

6   Kenneth Plummer, 'Building a Sociology of Homosexuality'. In Plummer, *op.cit.*

7   Michel Foucault, *La volonté de savoir. (Histoire de la sexualité*, Vol. 1.)* Paris: Gallimard, 1976. (English translation *The History of Sexuality*, Vol. 1. New York: Random House, 1978; London: Allen Lane, 1979.)

8   Kenneth Plummer, *Sexual Stigma: An Interactionist Account.* Boston: Routledge & Kegan Paul, 1975;
Jeffrey Weeks, *Coming Out: Homosexual Politics in Britain from the 19th Century to the Present.* London: Quartet, 1977.

SOCIAL CONSTRUCTION THEORY: PROBLEMS IN THE HISTORY OF SEXUALITY

Keynote Address
Carole S. Vance

Social construction theory in the field of sexuality proposed an extremely outrageous idea. It suggested that one of the last remaining outposts of the 'natural' in our thinking was fluid and changeable, the product of human action and history rather than the invariant result of the body, biology, or an innate sex drive.

Empirical and theoretical work on the history of sexuality has grown dramatically in the last twenty years, for which social construction approaches plus the invigorating questions raised by social movements like feminism and lesbian and gay liberation are largely responsible. Indeed, the links between social construction theory and gay activism run very deep. Efforts to transform society inevitably raised questions about the past and the future, as they also called into question prevailing ideological frameworks for examining the 'facts' about sex and gender.

This attempt to historicize sexuality has produced an innovative body of work to which historians, anthropologists, sociologists, and others have contributed in an unusual interdisciplinary conversation. Social construction theory has become the influential, some charge orthodox, framework in the new sex history. Its advantages (lest you've forgotten) can be immediately recognized through comparison with contemporary mainstream literature in sexology and biomedicine, seemingly archaic kingdoms in which the body and its imperatives still rule.

The very real advantages of social construction theory, however, and the enthusiasm it has generated make it all the more necessary to identify and explore current problems in social construction. In doing so, this paper attempts to differentiate between problems which are generated by common misunderstandings of social construction theory – and thus which are more easily resolved – and intellectual problems embedded in the social construction framework for which no quick and easy solution can be found.

TRUE CONFESSIONS OF A SOCIAL CONSTRUCTIONIST

In the sometimes heated debates that have gone on about essentialism and social construction, the word 'essentialist', to some ears, sounds increasingly pejorative – a dirty word, a contemptuous put-down, a characterization of being hopelessly out of date. Yet we need to start this discussion by recognizing that we have all been brought up to think about sexuality in essentialist ways.

Essentialism can take several forms in the study of sexuality: a belief that human behavior is 'natural', predetermined by genetic, biological, or physiological mechanisms and thus not subject to change; or the notion that human behaviors which show some similarity in form are the same, an expression of an underlying human drive or tendency. Behaviors that share an outward similarity can be assumed to share an underlying essence and meaning.

The development of science and social science in Euro-America in the past century can be characterized by a general movement away from essentialist frameworks toward perspectives that, although called by various names, are constructionist. These new frameworks have challenged the 'natural' status of many domains, presenting the possibility of a truly *social* inquiry as well as suggesting that human actions have been and continue to be subject to historical forces and, thus, to change. Gender and sexuality have been the very last domains to have their natural, biologized status called into question. For all of us, essentialism was our first way of thinking about sexuality and still remains the hegemonic one in the culture.

The novelty of constructionist approaches in sexuality explains several things: the volatile reaction to it (among heterosexuals, too, not just lesbians and gays); the residual essentialism in all of us, even those trying to work in a social construction frame; and the difficulty in adopting a consistent rather than a partial constructionist approach. Some use the words 'social construction', yet their analytic frames show – unbeknownst to them – many remaining essentialist elements. This leads to the phenomenon of somewhat unattractive, if triumphant, 'essentialist tendencies' in their colleagues' work. Seen in a more generous light, this scrutiny is an attempt to clarify the assumptions we use in doing our work and make them explicit.

The dominance of essentialist approaches also explains why there are few self-proclaimed essentialists. Only those who depart from the dominant system have cause to label themselves; those who work within it remain more unselfconscious. For the same reasons that heterosexuals do not classify themselves or have a developed awareness of 'heterosexual identity', essentialists have had less reason to name themselves and reflect on their practice than social constructionists.

The chief virtue of social construction theory is the new questions it encourages us to ask. Social construction is not a dogma, a religion, or an article of faith. If and when in the course of these discussions it becomes reified, its value is lost. Social construction theory does not predict a particular answer: whether something we call 'gay identity' existed in the 17th or 19th century, in London or in Polynesia, or whether 19th-century female romantic friendship or crossing-women are properly called 'lesbian', is a matter for empirical examination. Contemporary gay identity might exist in other times and cultures or it might not; its construction could be the same as we know it now, or radically different. Construction theory does not have a stake in the answer, but it is committed to asking the questions and to challenging assumptions which impair our ability to even imagine these questions. Construction theory is against premature closure, and its price is tolerating ambiguity.

UNHELPFUL CRITICISMS OF SOCIAL CONSTRUCTION THEORY

The ways in which social construction theory intersects with sexual politics and our daily social and personal lives gives the discussion surrounding it a special volatility and charge, often disguised in more intellectual, though still legitimate, concerns. It is evident that many problems with social construction theory remain to be worked out. However, there is a class of criticisms of social construction theory which is based on a misunderstanding and even possibly intentional misreading of it. These criticisms do not advance the development of our discussion, because they set up false problems and draw attention from legitimate questions. Before moving on to genuine problems in social construction theory, I would like to identify unhelpful and misguided ways of phrasing the issues.

Some critics contend that social construction theory implies that sexual identity, or more to the point, lesbian and gay identity is somehow fictional, trivial, unimportant, or not real, because it is socially constructed. The punch line 'it's *only* socially constructed' is a characteristic remark of these critics, revealing their belief that only biologically determined phenomena could have any significance in human social life. This is an odd position for historians and social scientists to take. Social construction approaches call attention to the paradox between the historically variable ways in which culture and society construct seemingly stable reality and experience: here, the ways in which the prevailing sexual system seems natural and inevitable to its natives, and for many individuals the expression of some deeply-felt essence. To explain how reality is constructed does not imply that it is not real for the persons living it – or trivial, unimportant, or ephemeral, though it is also true that the insight of construction, when absorbed by the natives (that is, us) has the potential to subvert the natural status of the sexual system and cause us to question and rethink our experience of essential identity.

Other variants of this misreading suggest that individual sexual identity is easily changeable, much like a new outfit plucked from the closet at whim; that individuals have conscious control over sexual identity; and that large scale cultural formations regarding sexuality are easily changed. Since social constructionists have said nothing of the kind, one is at first puzzled by the enormity of this misunderstanding, but the explanation for it is perhaps to be found in the special status of sex in our culture and our thought.[1]

An analogy from anthropology is useful here. It is commonplace for anthropologists to say that human behavior is socially or culturally constructed, by which we mean that human behavior is learned and not intrinsic or essentially determined. But to suggest that any feature of human life, for example, national or ethnic identity, is socially constructed is not to say that it is trivial. Nor is it to say that entire cultures can transform themselves overnight, or that individuals socialized in one cultural tradition can acculturate at whim to another.

This criticism of social construction confuses the individual level with the cultural level: that sexuality is constructed at the level of culture and history through complex interactions which we are now trying to understand does not mean that individuals have an open-ended ability to construct themselves, or to reconstruct themselves multiple times in adulthood. (This is not to deny individuals' experiences of sexual malleability and change, which are probably considerably more extensive than our cultural frames and our own biographical narratives admit.) The specialness of sex is highlighted by this comparison, since a quite ordinary and accepted insight about cultural construction in most areas of human life seems very difficult to understand without distortion when applied to sexuality. When we come to sex, our minds grind to a halt: normal distinctions become incomprehensible, and ordinary logic flies out the window.

A third major misreading of construction theory concerns continuity and change. In contrast to essentialism's assumption of continuity in behavior and subjective meaning, social construction appears much more receptive to the possibility of change, discontinuity, and rupture. Some critics have exaggerated this characterization, claiming that constructionist theory predicts only discontinuity and, thus, any demonstration of historical or social continuity proves that construction theory is wrong.

The openness to recognizing difference in behavior and subjective meaning, however, in no way commits the researcher to always finding it, nor does it rule out the discovery of similarity. The very nature of historical and cultural change makes it likely that peoples closely related by time and space will show many continuities.

We should be especially attentive to these types of criticisms of social construction theory (especially signaled by the comment 'it's *only* socially constructed'), because the continual demand to address misreadings of the theory is unhelpful and needs to be put to rest. Energy would be better spent in exploring three genuine and difficult theoretical issues: 1) degrees of social construction theory; 2) the instability of sexuality as a category; and 3) the role of the body.

DIFFERENT DEGREES OF SOCIAL CONSTRUCTION

The widespread use of social construction as a term and as a paradigm obscures the fact that constructionist writers have used this term in diverse ways. It is true that all reject transhistorical and transcultural definitions of sexuality and suggest instead that sexuality is mediated by historical and cultural factors. But a close reading of constructionist texts shows that social construction spans a theoretical field of what might be constructed, ranging from sexual acts, sexual identities, sexual communities, the direction of sexual desire (object choice) to sexual impulse or sexuality itself.

At minimum, all social construction approaches adopt the view that physically identical sexual acts may have varying social significance and subjective meaning depending on how they are defined and understood in different cultures and historical periods. Because a sexual act does not carry with it a universal social meaning, it follows that the relationship between sexual acts and sexual identities is not a fixed one, and it is projected from the observer's time and place to others at great peril. Cultures provide widely different categories, schemata, and labels for framing sexual and affective experiences. The relationship of sexual act and identity to sexual community is equally variable and complex. These distinctions, then, between sexual acts, identities, and communities are widely employed by constructionist writers.

A futher step in social construction theory posits that even the direction sexual desire itself, for example, object choice or hetero/homosexuality, is not intrinsic or inherent in the individual but is constructed. Not all constructionists take this step; for some, the direction of desire and erotic interest are fixed, although the behavioral *form* this interest takes will be constructed by prevailing cultural frames, as will the subjective experience of the individual and the social significance attached to it by others.

The most radical form of constructionist theory[2] is willing to entertain the idea that there is no essential, undifferentiated sexual impulse, 'sex drive' or 'lust', which resides in the body due to physiological functioning and sensation. Sexual impulse itself is constructed by culture and history. In this case, an important constructionist question concerns the origins of these impulses, since they are no longer assumed to be intrinsic or, perhaps, even necessary. This position, of course, contrasts sharply with more middle-ground constructionist theory which implicitly accepts an inherent sexual impulse which is then constructed in terms of acts, identity, community, and object choice. The contrast between middle-ground and radical positions makes it evident that constructionists may well have arguments with each other, as well as with essentialists. Each degree of social construction points to different questions and assumptions, possibly to different methods, and perhaps to different answers.

The increasing popularity (perhaps even faddishness in some circles) of the term 'social construction', however, made it appear that social construction is a unitary and singular approach and that all social construction writers share the same paradigm. But a review of social construction literature, which makes its first distinct appearance in the mid-1970s, as well as its forerunners in the 1960s, shows a gradual development of the ability to imagine that sexuality is constructed. The intellectual history of social construction is a complex one, and the moments offered here are for purposes of illustration, not comprehensive review.[3]

Intellectual precursors to constructionist approaches, for example, include anthropologists doing cross-cultural work on sexuality in the 1960s.[4] They assumed that culture encouraged or discouraged the expression of specific sexual acts and relationships. Oral-genital contact, for example, might be a part of normal heterosexuality in one group but taboo in another; female homosexuality might be severely punished in one tribe yet tolerated in another. However, these anthropologists accepted without question the existence of universal categories like heterosexual and homosexual, male and female sexuality, and sex drive. Culture shaped sexual expression and customs, but the basic material to work with – a kind of sexual Play Doh – was the same everywhere, a naturalized category and thus never open to investigation. Although we can recognize this work as a precursor to social construction theory, it clearly contains many essentialist elements.

The struggle to move away from essentialist and naturalizing ways of thinking about sexuality was a difficult one. Mary McIntosh's 1968 essay on the homosexual role appears to us as a landmark article, offering many suggestive insights about the historical construction of sexuality in England.[5] But her observations vanished like pebbles in a pond, until they were engaged with by mid-1970s writers, clearly motivated by the questions of feminism and gay liberation. An identifiably constructionist approach dates from this period, not before.

Early work in lesbian and gay history attempted to retrieve and revive documents (and lives) which had been lost or been made invisible. These lives were first conceived of as lesbian or gay, and the enterprise akin to a search for historical roots, an attempt to document the existence of gay people and experience. This was history against the grain, against the heterosexist narrative: in short, activist history and history as political work. To their credit, researchers who had started this enterprise from a firm point of fixed sexual categories began to consider other ways of looking at their material and more expansive questions to ask. Jonathan Katz's work is one example of this process, since his first book, *Gay American History*, is very much in the 'gay ancestors' tradition.[6] In the course of researching his second book, *Gay/Lesbian Almanac*, he began to consider that sexual acts reported in American colonial documents from the 17th century, for example sodomy, might not be equivalent to contemporary homosexuality.[7] Sodomy – then understood as any unnatural, nonreproductive sexual act – was a temptation and sin to which anyone, male or female, could fall victim, as to envy or theft. Although the documents amply show discovery and punishment, colonial society did not seem to conceive of a unique type of person – a homosexual – who engaged in these acts, nor did it provide a homosexual identity on a cultural level or anything resembling a homosexual subculture on a social level.

Katz's second book marks a sharp departure from the first, in that records or accounts that document same-sex emotional or sexual relations are not taken as evidence of 'gay' or 'lesbian' people, but are treated as jumping off points for a whole series of questions about the meanings of these acts to the people who engaged in them and to the culture and time in which they lived.

The intellectual development reflected in Katz's work is not unique to him, but appears in many others' as well. And from this work came an impressive willingness to imagine: had the category 'homosexual' or 'lesbian' always existed? And if not, what was its point of origin and the conditions for development? If identical physical acts had different subjective meanings, how was sexual meaning constructed? If sexual subcultures come into being, what leads to their formation? In these and other questions, they imagined what has become the foundation of lesbian and gay history.[8]

The intellectual history of social construction is a complex one. The point of briefly noting a few moments in its history here is simply to illustrate that social construction theorists and writers differ in their willingness to imagine *what* was constructed. For us, their differences suggest that we should avoid using 'social construction' in such an undifferentiated way. As readers we should try to be clear about what each theorist or author imagines to be constructed. As writers and speakers, we should try to indicate more exactly what we mean by social construction in our own work.

THE INSTABILITY OF SEXUALITY AS A CATEGORY

Because they were tied to essentialist assumptions which posited biological and physiological factors as influential in determining the contours of sexuality, sexological and biomedical paradigms of sexuality nevertheless offered one advantage: sexuality enjoyed the status of a stable, ongoing, and cohesive entity. The constructionist paradigm more flexibly admits variability in behavior and motive over time and place. But to the extent that social construction theory grants that sexual acts, identities and even desire are mediated by cultural and historical factors, the object of study – sexuality – becomes evanescent and threatens to disappear. If sexuality is constructed differently at each time and place, can we use the term in a comparatively meaningful way? More to the point in lesbian and gay history, have constructionists undermined their own categories? Is there an 'it' to study?

We have attempted to address the problem of false universalism by exercising more care in our terminology and conceptual categories: thus, in examining fellatio among Sambia adult men and teenage boys in the New Guinea highlands[9], it may be more appropriate to speak of 'same-sex' rather than 'homosexual' acts or relations. The first term attempts to describe sexual behavior without assuming that its social and affective meaning is equivalent to that of contemporary society: New Guinea is not Amsterdam or Greenwich Village. This term and others like it encourage openness rather than premature closure in our thinking about the historical and cultural meaning of diverse sexual acts and identities. However, even with my care, I've already called these acts 'sexual'.

Here we may detect, despite genuine efforts toward conceptual and definitional openness, that even the new sex history has an ambivalent and more complex relationship to the idea of sexuality as a coherent category. Some social constructionists explicitly encourage the total deconstruction of the category of the sexual, for example, Foucault. Others have not taken this theoretical position, though it remains implicit in their work. For, if sexuality is constituted differently in different times and places, it follows that behaviors and relations seen as sexual by us (contemporary Euro-Americans) may not be by others, and vice versa.[10]

Questioning the very category of sexuality, however, proves difficult. A student of mine agreed that it would be incorrect to call Sambia male initiation rites involving fellatio between older men and younger boys 'homosexuality', but he was nevertheless convinced that this was experienced as a sexual act by those engaging in it. How did he know it was sexual, I asked? 'Their cosmology posits that young boys grow to adulthood only through the ingestion of semen,' he replied, 'but you don't see them eating it with a bowl and a spoon.' The move to question the category 'sexuality' remains counterintuitive, therefore, and thus often results in an intellectual stance that can only be inconsistently or unconvincingly maintained. The attempt to deconstruct sexuality as a meaningful universal construct has also generated considerable backlash for reasons we will describe later.

Many other social constructionists assume, as perhaps it is easier to, that specific, core behaviors and physical relations are reliably understood as sexual, even though they occur in diverse cultures or historical periods. The knowledge or assumption that behavior is indeed sexual serves as a guide to what must be studied of what might be safely ignored. To give up this assumption considerably widens the field of what might be the object of study, with both good and bad results. The often implicit assumptions about the sexual nature of physical acts or relations depend in turn on deeply embedded cultural frameworks that we use to think about the body.

THE ROLE OF THE BODY

Social construction's greatest strength lies in its violation of our folk knowledge and scientific ideologies that would frame sexuality as 'natural', determined by biology and the body. This violation makes it possible, indeed compels us to raise questions that a naturalizing discourse would obscure and hide. Social constructionists have been even-handed in this endeavor, dethroning the body in all fields – in heterosexual history as well as in lesbian and gay history. At first, we greeted this development with good cheer, happy to be rid of the historical legacy of 19th-century spermatic and overian economies, women's innate sexual passivity, and the endless quest to find the hormonal cause of homosexuality. Yet the virtue of social construction may also be its vice.

Has social construction theory, particulary variants which see 'sexual impulse', 'sex drive', or 'lust' as created, made no room for the body, its functions, and physiology? As sexual subjects, how do we reconcile constructionist theory with the body's visceral reality and our own experience of it? If our theory of sexuality becomes increasingly disembodied, does it reach the point of implausibility, even for us? And if we wish to incorporate the body within social construction theory, can we do so without returning to essentialism and biological determinism?

Let me discuss these points more concretely by giving an example from my own work on female circumcision. Although not a specifically lesbian or gay topic, it illuminates the difficulty of thinking about the relationship of sexuality to the body and has much to offer for other body issues.

Briefly, female circumcision[11] is an umbrella term for traditional customs carried out in various Middle Eastern and African countries. These customs involve the surgical alteration and removal of female genital tissue, usually performed by midwives and female kin. The procedures vary in severity and range from removing part or all of the clitoris (simple circumcision) to removing the labia (excision). In infibulation, the most radical form of surgery, the clitoris and labia are excised, and the vaginal opening is sutured to reduce its circumference, making heterosexual penetration impossible and thus guaranteeing virginity. These operations are done at different ages and for different reasons – to promote hygiene and fertility, to render women aesthetically more feminine and thus marriageable, and to promote virginity. It is important to understand that these procedures are widespread and in local terms thought to be required by religion or custom.[12]

In the past ten years, an intense conversation has developed between Western and Third-World feminists over these practices. It is not my goal here to thoroughly describe this debate, or to suggest, by examining Western views, that we enjoy a privileged vantage point or right to intervene. What interests me here is how we think about these practices and the body in less guarded moments.

First, we tend to think about the effect of these customs, particularly on sexual functioning. We draw on a physiological model of Masters and Johnson, which places the clitoris at the center of female sexual response and orgasm.[13] We reason that removal of part or all of the clitoris interferes with orgasm, perhaps making it impossible. That is, we are universalizing a physiological finding made on American subjects without much thought.[14] Could Sudanese women's responses be different?

If we are willing to consider that sexual response is more than physiology, we might ask what is known about female sexual experience in these cultures. The answer is not clear cut, in part due to the small number of studies done and the difficulty of doing them. A Sudanese gynecologist compared women with different degrees of circumcision in Khartoum, finding that women with milder degrees of circumcision reported orgasm whereas women with severe degrees did not.[15] But even this inquiry depends on eliciting a response to terms like 'orgasm', whose subjective meaning is what is at issue. A highly-educated Sudanese woman who had been infibulated mused on this problem during our conversation in New York. Familiar with the Masters and Johnson framework which would suggest orgasm was unlikely, she asked me if she had experienced an orgasm. But how could I know?, short of resorting to the clearly inappropriate American adage: 'if you have to ask, you haven't.' She struggled to navigate the boundaries of culture and language, saying that perhaps she did, since she enjoyed sex with her husband and found the experience pleasurable.

Our response is complicated: still tied to a physiological frame, we think about different degrees of tissue removed, the possible nerves remaining under the excised clitoris, the transferral of sexual response from one body zone to another. We strain to imagine a different scenario of pleasure, still plausible within our framework. Western feminists also think of what is familiar to us: women's accommodation to the lack of sexual pleasure and even active displeasure – rationalizations, protestations of satisfaction, low expectations. In viewing these customs, we oscillate between imagining the sexually familiar and the unfamiliar. Nor are we alone in our efforts to compare and contrast: another Sudanese woman familiar with Western culture found her situation far from unique. 'You circumcise women, too,' she said, 'but you do it through Freudian theory, not through surgery. You are not so different from us.'

If we give up physiological frames of thinking about circumcision and acknowledge that in these countries it is a culturally normative practice, we begin to entertain unsettling questions. Is female orgasm constructed? What are the conditions for it? Is it necessary? Is it a physiological potential, whose expression may be facilitated or curtailed? If curtailed, is that repression and injustice? Or is the construction of female orgasm open-ended, with no imperative for it to happen? Can sexual pleasure be constructed totally without orgasm for women? (And here I

mean, can women in an entire culture experience sexual pleasure, though they rarely or never experience orgasm?, not the
more customary question we might ask in our own culture: can
a single sexual episode be pleasurable, even though the woman
has not experienced orgasm? These are very different questions.)

By now, even social constructionists, particularly women, are
disturbed and upset. Abandoning or even detaching from a physiological frame makes us feel – to the extent that we questioned
this practice – that we are now losing ground to object to it. It
points up the tendency, even among social constructionists, to
defend sexuality and sexual pleasure in terms of an essential right
and the functioning of the body. More importantly, the discomfort we experience as the body slips away, or threatens to, in this
particular case suggests that we need to explore the limitations
of sexual theory which has no room for the body. As we consider
restoring the body to social construction theory, we wonder if it
is possible to be a materialist without sliding into essentialism?
Are there ways to integrate bodily sensation and function into a
social construction frame, while still acknowledging that human
experience of the body is always mediated by culture and subjectivity, and without elevating the body as determinative? The
answer will not be found in a return to essentialism, whether frank
or disguised, but in exploring more sensitive and imaginative
ways of considering the body.

As difficult as these problems may be, social constructionists
do not grapple with theoretical issues about degrees of social
construction, the object of study, or the meaning of the body in
a vacuum. The new sex history is indebted to feminism and gay
liberation for many of its insights, for non-academic settings
which nurtured this work during the early stages of its development when the university disapproved, and for its intellectual
urgency. These popular political movements created an
audience of activist and self-reflective individuals who very much
wanted to know and to use the knowledge to inform their activism. I mention this because some of the problems in social construction theory, particularly the critical reaction to it in the last
few years in lesbian and gay political circles, originate in the
meaning of this theory to members of oppressed groups in the
contemporary sexual hierarchy.[16]

THE SEXUAL SUBJECT'S DESIRE FOR HISTORY

A common motivation for fans of lesbian and gay history was a desire to reclaim the past and to insist on lesbian and gay visibility in every place and at every time. But the discoveries of the new sex historians have sometimes proved disturbing, as researchers gave up their initial certainty about the existence of 'gay people' and embarked on a more complicated discussion about the origins of gay identity in the 17th to 19th centuries. In these discussions, sexual acts could not be read as unproblematic indicators of homosexuality; and rather than an unchanging essence which defied legal and religious prohibitions, homosexuality increasingly came to be seen as a variable experience whose boundaries and subjectivity were shaped through complex negotiations between state institutions, individuals, and subcultures.

Variability, subjectivity, negotiation and change often violated the wish for a continuous history. If the point of gay history was to document an ancestry, a gay *Roots*, then for many activists this kind of gay history was frustrating, even a failure. The disappointment and anger at not being able to see oneself reflected in the mirror of history has fueled some of the criticism of social construction theory in the belief that a more essentialist perspective would permit the development of group history and solidarity.

In addition, it is common for mainstream lesbian and gay political and lobbying groups in the United States to use essentialist argument and rhetoric in advancing their case. Lesbians and gays are deserving of civil rights, they say, much like women, ethnic, and racial groups. This argument derives less from a self-conscious theoretical commitment to essentialism and more from the pervasiveness of essentialist frames in American culture, particularly in regard to race and ethnicity. In an ideological system that defines these groups as natural, real, and organized according to relatively unchanging biological features, one obvious and powerful symbolic strategy is to claim an equal status for lesbians and gays. In this ideological and political context, it is to the advantage of all groups struggling for resources to stress not only group unity and historical privilege (buttressed by and documented through histories of the ancestors), but their status as an essential group to which members have no choice in belonging. Fundamentalists and conservatives are fond of ridiculing the analogy between gay rights and minority rights: minorities are 'real' groups to which members can't help but belong through their racial features, whereas no one has to be gay, if he or she simply refrains from sin and lust. Gays and lesbians do not constitute a natural group, right-wingers insist; they are just a bunch of perverts.

In such an arena, gay politicos and lobbyists find it helpful in the short run to respond with assertions about gays through the ages, to assert a claim to a natural group status, and to insist that being gay is an essential, inborn trait about which there is no choice. And, indeed, essentialist arguments about sexual identity can be extended to heterosexuals and used to good advantage: if sexual identity is inborn, or at least fixed by age three, then lesbian or gay schoolteachers pose no threat to students in terms of influencing their identity or development (in an undesirable way, the argument would seem to concede). By dint of repetition, ideas about gay essentialism were reinforced in the contemporary gay movement (though they were hardly unknown in American culture) and, more importantly, linked to group advancement, success, and self-affirmation. Therefore, arguments which opposed or undercut essentialist rhetoric about gay identity were increasingly unfamiliar and heretical, even perceived as damaging to gay interests. Within the lesbian and gay community's internal discussions and self-education, the failure to make a distinction between politically expedient ways of framing an argument and more complex descriptions of social relations promoted an increasingly rigid adherence to essentialism as an effective weapon against persecution.

THE RELATIONSHIP OF MARGINAL GROUPS TO DECONSTRUCTION

In a similar vein, it is ironic to note that in the war of ideas against heterosexual hegemony social construction theory has become most influential only in the intellectual circles of oppositional groups. Social construction theory may be the new orthodoxy in feminist, progressive, and lesbian and gay history circles, but it has made a minimal impact on mainstream authorities and literatures in sexology and biomedicine. These groups continue their investigation and theorizing from the assumption that sexuality is essential. At most, the deviant status of homosexuality calls for inquiry into its etiology (whether hormonal, psychological, or sociological), but the causes of heterosexuality have attracted little interest. In traditional sexual science, heterosexuality remains an unexamined and naturalized category, and little in popular culture causes heterosexuals to consider their sexual identity or its origins and history.

In contrast, the social constructionist framework common in lesbian and gay history has become disseminated to a larger lesbian and gay public. Some wonder whether this constructionist perspective is helpful. What are its implications? Why should lesbians and gays have a developed consciousness that their sexual identities have been 'constructed', when heterosexuals do not? Does this intellectual sophistication lead to a sense of group frailty instead of robustness? And does any history of construction inevitably pose the theoretical possibility of a future deconstruction, even disappearance, which is alarming and uncomfortable? The retorts of Dorothy Allison and Esther Newton at recent conferences – 'deconstruct heterosexuality first!' and 'I'll deconstruct when they deconstruct' – reflect in their immediacy and robustness both anxiety about group dissolution and the improbability of such a development.

The tension here is identical to a tension felt within feminism, which simultaneously holds two somewhat contradictory goals. One goal is to attack the gender system and its primacy in organizing social life, but the second goal is to defend women as a group. Defending women or advancing their interest (in equal pay, abortion rights, or child care, for example) emphasizes their status as a special group with a unique collective interest, distinct from men, thus replaying and perhaps reinforcing the very gender dichotomy crucial to the system of gender oppression.

The same irresolvable tension exists within the lesbian and gay movement, which on the one hand attacks a naturalized system of sexual hierarchy which categorizes and stabilizes desires and privileges some over others, and on the other hand defends the interest of 'lesbian and gay people', which tends to reify identity and essential nature in a political process I've described. There is no solution here, since to abandon either goal for the other would be foolish. Real, live lesbians and gays need to be defended in an oppressive system, and the sexual hierarchy, which underlies that oppression, needs to be attacked on every level, particularly on the intellectual and conceptual levels where naturalized systems of domination draw so much of their energy. There is no easy solution here, but even an awareness of this tension can be helpful, since it powerfully contributes to the larger political and emotional climate in which social construction theory is received, and rightly so.

CONCLUSION

Social construction theory offered many radical possibilities in theorizing about sexuality. To take the next steps, we need to continue and deepen our discussion about its very real problems. These problems will not be resolved through theoretical discussion alone, though such discussions offer clarification, but through the course of continued research and investigation.

To the extent social construction theory strives for uncertainty through questioning assumptions rather than seeking closure, we need to tolerate ambiguity and fluidity. The future is less closed than we feared, but perhaps more open than we hoped. All movements of sexual liberation, including lesbian and gay, are built on imagining: imagining that things could be different, other, better than they are. Social construction shares that imaginative impulse and thus is not a threat to the lesbian and gay movement, but very much of it.

Clearly, the tension between deconstructing systems of sexual hierarchy and defending lesbians and gays will be an ongoing one. In that case, we need to find a way to acknowledge more openly and respond more appropriately to the emotional responses social construction theory engenders, deeply felt responses about identity, community, solidarity, politics, and survival – in short, our lives.

NOTES

I am pleased to acknowledge my debts in writing this paper, most especially to the researchers, writers, and activists (too many to acknowledge by name) whose work in the past twenty years originated and refined social construction approaches in sexuality.

This paper was originally given as a keynote address at the International Scientific Conference on Gay and Lesbian Studies in Amsterdam, December 15, 1987. I've remained faithful to the talk format rather than convert my remarks into a formal paper. Many thanks to those responsible for this stimulating and productive conference: the hard-working Conference Organizing Committee; the Schorer Foundation; and the Research Group for Gay and Lesbian Studies of the Interdisciplinary Centre for the Study of Science, Society, and Religion, Free University of Amsterdam. I am especially grateful to Anja van Kooten Niekerk and Riek Stienstra for their dedication and vision. Thanks also to participants in the conference for their helpful comments and criticisms.

While writing and revising this paper, I benefitted from the comments and conversation of Alan Berube, Frances Doughty, Lisa Duggan, Jeffrey Escoffier, Janice Irvine, Jonathan Katz, Lou McDonald, Esther Newton, Gayle Rubin, Ann Snitow, David Schwartz and Gilbert Zicklin. I appreciated the encouragement of Lisa Duggan, Frances Doughty, and Alan Berube at crucial moments. Thanks also to my students at Columbia University School of Public Health for their comments in our seminar on 'Sexuality, Health Issues, and Public Policy'.

Portions of this paper were first presented at the Berkshire Conference on the History of Women, Wellesley College, June 20, 1987.

1   Gayle Rubin, 'Thinking Sex'. In Carole S. Vance (ed.), *Pleasure and Danger: Exploring Female Sexuality*. London: Routledge & Kegan Paul, 1984, pp. 267-319.

2   There is no suggestion here that the most radical forms of social construction theory are necessarily the best, although the exercise of totally deconstructing one of the most essential categories, sexuality, often has an electrifying and ener-

gizing effect on one's thinking. Whether this degree of deconstruction can be plausibly maintained is another question, explored in a later section of this essay.

3   A more comprehensive account is offered in my review 'An Intellectual and Political History of Social Construction Theory'. Unpublished manuscript.

4   For typical examples of this approach, see:
      Robert C. Suggs, *Marquesan Sexual Behavior*. New York: Harcourt, Brace, & World, 1966;
      Marvin K. Opler, 'Anthropological and Cross-Cultural Aspects of Homosexuality'. In Judd Marmor (ed.), *Sexual Inversion*. New York: Basic Books, 1965, pp. 108-23;
      William Davenport, 'Sexual Patterns and their Regulation in a Society of the Southwest Pacific'. In Frank A. Beach (ed.), *Sex and Behavior*. New York: Wiley & Sons, 1965, pp. 164-207.

5   Mary McIntosh, 'The Homosexual Role'. *Social Problems* 16 (1968) pp. 182-91. Reprinted in Kenneth Plummer (ed.), *The Making of the Modern Homosexual*. London: Hutchinson, 1981.

6   Jonathan Katz, *Gay American History*. New York: Thomas Y. Crowell, 1976.

7   Jonathan Katz, *Gay/Lesbian Almanac*. New York: Harper & Row, 1983.

8   One interesting question concerns the differential manifestation of social construction theory in lesbian versus gay male history. The most contentious battles between essentialists and social constructionists have been conducted in gay, not lesbian history. At first glance, one might think this is so because social construction theory has had less impact on lesbian history and, indeed, there is less self-conscious invocation of constructionist frameworks in some of this work.
      An examination of the actual content, however, suggests widespread adherence to constructionist approaches in lesbian history. And essentialism, when it appears, often takes a different form, focusing less on the universality of sexual acts, as is the case in gay male history, and more on the universality of emotion and interpersonal relations. The

reasons for these differences would be interesting to explore.

9   For an ethnographic account of these practices, see Gilbert Herdt, *Guardians of the Flutes*. New York: McGraw Hill, 1981.

10 We have been sensitized to the dangers and limitations of imposing our categories and systems of meaning. The commitment to avoid ethnocentric readings of non-Western behavior, however, encounters another problem: the tendency in the cross-cultural literature to withhold and dismiss data about homosexuality, from combined motives of sexual reticence and homophobia. Similar problems occur in history. Knowing this, the alert reader is reluctant to accept the glib and formulaic dismissals that the behavior in question does not constitute homosexuality, and instead leaps at suggestive evidence, treating data which can only be seen as clues as definitive evidence instead. We need to chart a course between these extremes.

11 Although 'female circumcision' is perhaps the most common Western term for these practices, many researchers in the field prefer the terms 'female genital surgery' or 'female genital operations'. Female circumcision too easily suggests an analogy to male circumcision, whereas the procedures performed on women are usually far more serious in terms of the degree of bodily tissue removed and in the physical and psychological consequences.

12 For more detailed description and discussion of female circumcision, see:
    Asma El Dareer, *Women, Why Do You Weep? Circumcision and Its Consequences*. London: Zed Press, 1982;
    Olayinka Koso-Thomas, *The Circumcision of Women: A Strategy for Eradication*. London: Zed Press, 1987;
    A. Verzin, 'Sequelae of Female Circumcision'. *Tropical Doctor* 5 (1975) pp. 163-69;
    World Health Organization, Eastern Mediterranean Regional Office, *Traditional Practices Affecting the Health of Women and Children*. Khartoum, February 1979;
    R. Cook, *Damage to Physical Health from Pharaonic Circumcision (Infibulation) of Females: A Review of the Medical Literature*. World Health Organization, Office for the Eastern Medi-

terranean, 1976;
Fran P. Hosken, *The Hosken Report: Genital and Sexual Mutilation of Females*, 3rd rev. ed. Lexington, Mass.: Women's International Network News, 1982.

13   William Masters and Virginia Johnson, *Human Sexual Response*. New York: Bantam Books, 1966.

14   Constructionists might well question whether the sexual response among even American women should be viewed as a function of physiology.

15   Ahmed Abu-el-Futuh Shandall, 'Circumcision and Infibulation of Females: A General Consideration of the Problem and a Clinical Study of the Complications in Sudanese Women'. *Sudan Medical Journal* 5 (1967) pp. 178-207.

16   For a discussion of the concept of sexual hierarchy, see Gayle Rubin, *op.cit.*, pp. 279-83.

AIDS AND THE RECONCEPTUALIZATION OF HOMOSEXUALITY

Dennis Altman

(This paper is dedicated to the memory of James Baldwin, whose writings helped many of us to understand that is was society, not us, which was the problem.)

The starting point of this paper is the historic accident that AIDS appeared as a new disease, first diagnosed among male homosexuals, at a time of rapid change in social and cultural attitudes to homosexuality itself in most Western countries. There has already been considerable discussion on the way in which the gay connection affected the conceptualization of AIDS. Equally important is the way in which the link with AIDS has affected the social construction of homosexuality.

AIDS has not altered the fundamental reality of homosexuality (although it may have meant some people are less willing to adopt a gay identity; evidence on this point remains scanty). On balance it seems that AIDS has strengthened the growth of gay identity and community already evident in most Western countries before its onset. Indeed, it seems likely that the response to AIDS by both the gay community and the larger society is largely a function of the extent to which gays had carved out some degree of political legitimacy for ourselves in the 1970s. Where a gay movement had succeeded in establishing some official recognition (e.g. the Netherlands, Scandinavia, California, parts of Australia) this affected the response of governments in the fight against AIDS. Where there had been less success in establishing a gay movement this was also reflected in official attitudes towards AIDS (as in almost every authoritarian society and not a few allegedly democratic ones).

The most dramatic impact of AIDS on concepts of gay identity is in the area of sexuality; the epidemic has severely strained the mores of sexual adventure and experimentation that seemed an integral part of gay male life until the early 1980s. In so doing, it has made clear that gay community is based on more than a shared set of sexual arrangements; indeed, AIDS itself has become part of the common experience of gay men, which may further isolate us from both lesbians and non-gays, while strengthening our own communal organizations.

In writing this lecture I have drawn heavily on my own experience, first while I was researching my book, *AIDS In The Mind Of America*[1] on both coasts of the United States in 1984/5, and subsequently back in Australia, where I have been both a government advisor and vice-president of the Victorian AIDS Council (a juxtaposition that already says something about the approach adopted by the Australian, in contrast to the United States federal government). Over the past few years I have briefly visited Canada, Sweden, France, Britain, and New Zealand, but any references I make to the situation outside my immediate experience need be tentative and exploratory. What is clear, however, is that wherever there exists a self-conscious gay community and identity AIDS has become an overwhelming preoccupation, which hangs over all of us.

My own career suggests to me that the distinction between 'academic' and 'activist' is a false one. But it is striking how little work on politics has gone on under the rubric of gay/lesbian studies, and this conference is no exception. We badly need comparative studies of the gay movement and of specific campaigns, many of which (e.g. the two major referenda in California on gay-related topics) have virtually been ignored by gay scholars.[2] My own ignorance was sharply brought home to me in the discussion following this paper, particularly in light of comments from participants from Mexico and Brazil.

AIDS AND THE QUESTION OF GAY IDENTITY

Early in the epidemic I speculated whether the fear and stigma associated with AIDS would lead to a decline in the number of men who chose to identify themselves as gay, or at least adopt homosexual behaviour as an integral part of their life. That I can pose this in terms of choice suggests that I still adhere to a constructionist view of homosexuality, despite the strength of some of the criticisms made of this theory recently.[3]

At this point it seems to me that there exists no evidence to suggest that such a decline has occurred, although it is true that I am working almost entirely on the basis of impressionistic data. My feeling is that at least as many teenagers are adopting a gay identity and/or homosexual behaviour pattern as was true ten years ago, and that in most Western countries of which I have first hand knowledge they are able to integrate an awareness of AIDS into this identity or behaviour. (This feeling is reinforced by one New Zealand study which claimed: 'The personal psychological awareness of sexual orientation reported by young people now is quite consistent with what was reported by the previous generation. But the social experience of these people, and their patterns of sexual activity, have changed quite radically.'[4]) It may also be true that some men are seeking to change their sexual identity in response to AIDS – as Brendan Lemon wrote in a recent short story: 'Somewhere toward the end of the AIDS decade, Paul decided to go straight.'[5] I doubt if this is the experience of significant numbers of men.

Thus at one level the title of this paper is somewhat misleading, for AIDS has not apparently affected the incidence nor the fundamental meaning of homosexuality in Western societies. It has, however, meant very real changes in the ways in which we experience homosexual identity, both at an individual and a collective level.

Some observers have claimed that since the onset of AIDS gay men have been less likely to define themselves in sexual terms. Certainly it is true that not inconsiderable numbers of men are remaining celibate for long periods of time, without this affecting their sense of gay identity. But it seems to me that it makes any concept of gay identity quite meaningless if we try to deny it is an identity clearly based upon sexual preference, even if this preference is not always acted upon.

It is true that a particular style of gay life, closely linked to a constant search for sexual adventure and excitement, a world depicted in novels such as *Faggots*, *Tricks*, or *Dancer for the Dance*, has declined, at least in the major centres of gay America. Bathhouses and backroom clubs have been closed down due to the epidemic in both New York and San Francisco, and have lost clients in those cities where they have been permitted to stay open. There is some evidence that gay businesses have declined in at least those cities most affected by the epidemic.

Even allowing for this it is my impression that the sort of gay world created by the twin engines of cultural change and commercialization during the 1970s has been largely untouched by AIDS. Indeed, outside the United States new saunas have opened in the past two years in Melbourne, Montreal and Paris, and in the United States Randy Shilts's title of his book on AIDS – *And the Band Played On* – is still an appropriate description of much of gay life. On my last trip to the U.S. I was struck by the sheer size and verve of gay life in cities such as Dallas and Boston.

GROWTH OF COMMUNITY ORGANIZATIONS

In many of the countries represented at this conference, the AIDS epidemic has seen the development of large gay community organizations concerned with providing education, support services, and counselling to both those with AIDS and to the much larger group who are threatened by it. Almost everywhere AIDS organizations arose out of and remain closely linked to the gay community, although the first and the largest, New York City's Gay Men's Health Crisis remains one of the few to so declare itself. Indeed, a number of AIDS organizations have quite specifically sought to include and represent other groups than gay men, both as a reflection of medical realities and political desirability.

In some cases it may be that AIDS organizations have developed to a point where it is no longer accurate to think of them as gay community organizations. Indeed, AIDS makes the definition of gay community problematic in a new way. Now it is not merely the traditional division between homosexual identity and behaviour, and the argument as to whether lesbians and gay men constitute one or two communities, that are involved. There are numbers of people who, without being homosexual in any sense, have committed themselves to working with gay communal organizations, just as there are men who regard themselves as feminists. I don't know what term to use for them, but I do know that they are more a part of my community than those homosexual men and women who support politicians such as Reagan and Thatcher whose policies oppress us.

AIDS has undoubtedly created a strong sense among many gay men and women that we have a responsiblity to do something about this disease, not just on an individual level but also as members of a community. 'We have to look after other gay men, because nobody else gives a damn' was a feeling encountered very often, at least in the United States, in the early years of the epidemic. This feeling was evident in the outpouring of hundreds of thousands of gay women and men, and their supporters, at the recent march on Washington, where anger at federal inaction on AIDS was clearly a major driving force.[6]

My own experience with the Victorian AIDS Council suggests that voluntary AIDS organizations become important community resources, through which people, in addition to the work they are directly involved with, also develop very deep ties of friendship and support. In Melbourne we have had the luxury of a low case load and considerable government support – the state government responded to the epidemic by financing the establishment of a Gay Men's Community Health Centre – and our situation is a much easier one than in American cities of similar size such as Houston or Miami-Fort Lauderdale. Our experience suggests, however, that with proper resources the gay community can generate impressive organizational responses to the epidemic.

In addition to such straightforward arguments about the ways in which AIDS has strengthened gay community we need consider two other areas: the paradox that more overt homophobia based on AIDS has also served to strengthen gay identity/community, and the ways in which the gay community has produced a large body of cultural reflection upon the meaning of the epidemic, thus unintentionally reinforcing the perception of AIDS as a specifically gay disease.

While it is true that AIDS is not in any intrinsic sense a gay disease, it is the gay communities of the Western world who have produced cultural images and reflections on the meaning of the epidemic, through films, novels, theatre, art works – think of the 800 square-foot Quilt memorializing those dead from AIDS that was part of the Washington protests. (The Quilt disproved Edmund White's suggestion that AIDS has 'tilted energies away from the popular arts ... and redirected them towards the "solitary" high arts.'[7]) It is hardly accidental that theatre, far more immediate an art form than either the novel or the cinema, has proven a particularly appropriate forum to canvass the emotions and issues raised by AIDS, as other papers have demonstrated; Larry Kramer's *The Normal Heart* was as important a commentary for the politics of its time and place as earlier *cris du coeur* such as Arthur Miller's *The Crucible*.

There is little doubt that AIDS has given new energy to our opponents, which in turn has led to a marked increase in anti-gay violence and attempts to repeal legislative gains of the past two decades. *Newsweek* considered these developments so striking, at least in Britain, that it ran one story headed 'An Ugly Anti-Gay Backlash', and in the United States there have been Congressional hearings which have demonstrated the recent rise in homophobic violence. As AIDS has provided a new pretext for right-wing fundamentalists, whether of the religious kind like Jerry Falwell or secular like Jean le Pen and the British Tories, to attack homosexuals, the response, at least in the United States, has been to mobilize gays to fight back. Large-scale political action by the gay community on AIDS-related issues began with the campaign waged in late 1986 to defeat the LaRouche-initiated referendum in California which would have introduced quarantine for anyone testing HIV-positive. A strong campaign, and support from many politicians and health authorities, defeated the measure by almost 2 to 1.[8] Since then there has been a marked rise in direct gay political action, as in the rise of groups like ACT UP (in New York) or ACTING OUT (San Francisco) and in the civil disobedience actions that accompanied the March on Washington and subsequent events in the U.S..

Examples from elsewhere are harder to find. In the spring of 1987 a rally of 10,000 Germans protested proposals for harsh measures by the Bavarian Land government. And in both Sydney and Melbourne antibody-positive activists have organized rallies in protest at the expense and limited availability of AZT.

This discussion has been largely restricted to gay men, although in some countries lesbians have played an important part within AIDS movements. In my own city of Melbourne the great majority of women who participate in AIDS work have been straight, and I suspect that one consequence of AIDS has been to increase separateness between gay women and men, not least because the official perception of 'the gay community' as male acts so as to reinforce the already male-centredness of that movement. This is emphatically not the case in the United States, where AIDS has quickly moved from being perceived as a gay male issue to one that has provided new unity between lesbians and gay men. In the United States lesbians have provided considerable leadership in the AIDS battles, from early on in the epidemic (think for example of the role of the 'Blood Sisters' in offering support to gay men) to the March on Washington where a majority of those arrested for direct action were women.[9] I would hope this renewed sense of a common community between gay women and men, so apparent at this Amsterdam conference, extends to other countries.

I do not want to offer too rosy a view of gay community and support as the response to AIDS. There is another side to this which is the considerable amount of fear, paranoia, and unfocused anger that is also evident in some of the gay world. For some the reaction to the epidemic has been irrational anger or apathy – irrational not in the sense that it is not understandable, or in the case of anger, unjustified, but irrational because it does little to meet the challenge. (A good example of this sort of anger is the way in which a once great paper, the *New York Native* has denouced some of the most hard-working supporters of the gay community, such as Mathilde Krim and Jeff Levi, when they in any way disagreed with the increasingly eccentric line taken by that paper.) While many of us have found a way of coping with fear and loss by our participation in communal and support organizations, others have retreated to a sort of emotional autism, so scared – and scarred – by the prospect of the disease that they avoid any form of emotional contact. As Paul Reed wrote recently: 'It would seem that our community is becoming increasingly fractured and useless, that there is no reason for self-improvement, for spiritual nourishment, for emotional maturity.'[10]

AIDS AND GAY LEGITIMACY

One of the paradoxes of AIDS is that it has forced governments to deal with gay movements and openly gay individuals to an unprecedented extent. Whereas the response of all but a handful of governments has been to demand greater surveillance and repression of homosexuality, a demand not unheard in even the most progressive of societies, most liberal democracies have seen the necessity to establish contact with their gay communities to better respond to AIDS. On a global scale the countries in which a meaningful gay community/movement exists form a minority; one can only fear the worst as fear of AIDS adds to official homophobia and authoritarianism in the countries of Eastern Europe and much of the Third World, and applaud the efforts of the World Health Organization to persuade governments of the need to recognize their gay populations.

I can best illustrate the progress of gay legitimation through AIDS by reference to Australia, possibly the first country to accord official recognition of the gay movement's stake in determining AIDS policy. In late 1984 the Federal government established the National Advisory Committee on AIDS, chaired by Australia's best known woman journalist, and appointed two gay leaders to its membership. Since then the Federal government has facilitated the establishment of a Federation of AIDS Organizations, made up of the predominantly gay state AIDS Councils; and it recently funded a conference of educators and researchers into gay/bisexual behavioural change. The opening session of that conference, where a woman psychologist lectured an audience which included government officials on fisting, water sports, and other 'exotic sex practices', was a vivid mark of how AIDS has made the previously unmentionable the subject of official discourse and helped legitimize (and, let it be acknowledged, control) gay sex as well as the gay movement.

In a number of Western European countries there has been some consultation with gay groups, though in very few has it been institutionalized and publicly recognized to the extent in Australia. The United States is a special case, because of the importance of local governments; while San Francisco included gay representatives in city policy making from very early on in the epidemic – the City already had an Office of Gay and Lesbian Health when AIDS hit – elsewhere gay AIDS organizations have been totally ignored. When President Reagan finally established a Presidential Commission on AIDS in mid-1987 he reluctantly included one openly gay man, but one who was there for his medical expertise, rather than his links to the gay movement. Even this degree of recognition seems unlikely in countries such as Mexico, Brazil, the Philippines, or Japan, in all of which there are gay organizations which are almost totally unacknowledged by the authorities.

Nonetheless, it is undoubtedly the case that in almost every Western country – though least so, as far as I know, in southern Europe – AIDS has meant a new visibility for gays, and increased access to governments. One of the consequences of this is the creation of a new class of gay leaders, people who sit on government committees, hold government-financed jobs, and travel at government expense to international conferences. As one of these people I know only too well the risks of becoming alienated from the people we seek to represent.

AIDS AND THE CONSTRUCTION OF SEXUALITY

There are few examples in history to match the dramatic changes in sexual behaviour which have occurred among homosexual men since the onset of widespread safe-sex advice. (There are, of course, few comparable times when sexual behaviour has been so closely scrutinized and monitored, which itself raises some real questions: Is gay behaviour, even identity, changed by the enormous attention that has been paid to it by both professionals and the media as a consequence of AIDS? When does legitimacy and representation become control and co-option?)

Considerable numbers of epidemiological surveys and reports from sexually transmitted disease clinics in a number of countries all point to a sharp decrease in unprotected anal intercourse in the homosexual population. It is not merely that tens of thousands of men have incorporated condoms into the act of intercourse; there is considerable anecdotal evidence that anal intercourse itself has been abandoned by very many gay men (which makes the term 'sodomite' even less appropriate than previously as a synonym for homosexual).

At the same time AIDS had led to the creation of new forms of sexual expression, of which the American 'jack-off clubs' are the most obvious. The ability of many thousands of men to eroticize forms of behaviour once thought of as mere preludes to 'real' sex – most obviously mutual masturbation – is a strong indication of the elasticity of sexual desire. It is important to note, however, a point which reinforces my earlier arguments: that what is involved is a change in specific *behaviour* but not in the *object* of desire.

For some, AIDS has become a reason to argue against sexual adventure and erotic experimentation; AIDS is being used by many prominent forces in our society to argue for a return to 'traditional values', by which they seem to mean heterosexual monogamy and homosexual celibacy. Within the gay world, debate about what sort of sexual behaviour is appropriate since AIDS is often marred by bitter and irrational arguments, in which wild accusations of either puritanism or irresponsibility are thrown back and forth. Thus Randy Shilts's otherwise excellent book is marred by his total inability to accept that not everyone who thought it wrong to close the bathhouses in San Francisco was irresponsible and unconcerned by the spread of AIDS (just as those on the other side of the debate saw everyone who believed in closure as homophobic and probably fascist).[11]

Outside several cities in the United States, government enforced closures of sex venues has, in fact, occurred much less than one might have predicted several years ago. In a number of Western countries, as has been true here in Amsterdam for some years, there has been a recognition of the value of such venues as places within which men can be encouraged to change risky behaviour; and in Australia, after some initial decline, it is my observation that sex venues are once again flourishing – but with new practices, above all the almost automatic acceptance by most patrons of the use of condoms for anal sex.

The most interesting changes are, however, not in sexual behaviour but in patterns of interaction and intimacy, where we can only venture guesses based on necessarily very limited personal experience. More gay men are, I think, developing close friendships and affectionate relationships in which genital sexuality plays a lesser role, and affection and shared commitment to community a greater. Writing before the onset of AIDS, Edmund White suggested that: 'The current notion of hot sex in New York [may] be a mere transition, a new recuperation of old oppression, and we would expect this period to be followed by a sweeter, calmer one in which romance and intimacy and sustained partnership between lovers would emerge again.'[12] There are those who would argue that this is now happening because of AIDS.

AIDS AND THE RETURN TO GAY LIBERATION

Over the past year it has struck me that AIDS is leading gay men and our organizations towards some of the practices associated with the gay liberation movements of fifteen years ago. Consciousness-raising is now referred to as workshopping, and gay pride as self-esteem, but the basic premise that internalized self-hatred can only be overcome by empowering people to overcome social stigma is being rediscovered as a central plank of attempts to alter sexual behaviour patterns. (Research evidence at this point is rather inconclusive, but it does seem that gay men who have low self-image and little contact with a 'gay community' find behavioural change more difficult than others.[13])

During the late 1970s and early 1980s it became fashionable to dismiss earlier gay liberation ideals and structures as unrealistic and utopian. The gay movement sought a new respectability, summed up in the establishment of groups like the American National Gay Task Force and Gay Business Associations, and their counterparts elsewhere.[14] To some extent AIDS has meant a strengthening of this tendency, in the already discussed entry into advisory groups and government bureaucracies. But it has also meant a new militancy and a new stress on grassroots organizing. In the United States the new gay bureaucrats were among those arrested (by police wearing yellow gloves) in protests against government inactivity in Washington, D.C., and calls for civil disobedience have come from formerly mainstream leaders such as Los Angeles's Duke Comegys, co-chair of the Human Rights Campaign Fund.[15] In Australia, where we have far less reason to protest government response, AIDS has brought a new population into gay organizations, where newcomers are re-learning some of the basic precepts of the gay liberation movement of fifteen years ago.

It is difficult for those of us who have not lived in the major centres of the epidemic to recognize the extent to which it has devastated our community. A friend of mine in New York tells of going to the funeral of someone who had died of AIDS, and commenting on how small the attendance was. That's because, he was told, most of those who would have come are already dead. In New York, San Francisco, Los Angeles, and a growing number of other cities anyone – gay or straight, woman or man – with ties to the gay community is experiencing the sort of devastation that Andrew Holleran catches in this interchange in his wonderful story 'Friends at Evening':

> 'So you think nothing will ever, ever be the same?' said Ned.
> 'Nothing,' said Mister Lark, screwing the cap on his jar of face cream. 'We're all going in sequence at different times. And will the last person please turn out the lights?'[16]

The long-term implications of this amount of death and suffering for those who survive AIDS are as yet hard to determine. We know something of the psychological costs in the short term; we have yet to come to grips with the full extent of the longer-term effects. Large numbers of gay men in their thirties and forties are dealing with the constant presence of death several decades before they would otherwise expect it. Even if medicine finds ways of curing and preventing this disease, a whole generation of gay men will bear its scars for the rest of our lives.

When AIDS first hit there was an understandable reaction which claimed it invalidated the sexual liberationist struggles of the previous decade. Some went further and prophesied that it meant the end of gay life as we had come to understand it in the past two decades. This, after all, was not an impossible scenario – gay life in Germany, which had seemed fairly well established in the 1920s, was very quickly wiped out by Hitler. But six years into the epidemic I think we can be fairly sure that while the losses have been enormous, and the grief of those of us who survive will stay with us for the rest of our lives, gay life, gay identity, and gay community will not disappear. As Paul Berman wrote in the *Village Voice*: 'The sexual revolution of the last twenty years can be reined in, it can be redirected, but it can't be repealed.... Naturally the plague will cause changes in sexual behaviour and imagination, both in the immediate present as emergency measures and in the post-emergency long run. But those long-run changes will be an evolution towards something new, not a return to something old. Neither utopia nor conservation will be the future.'[17] However horrible the devastation caused to our people by AIDS, the gay communities constructed in the last two decades, will survive and grow.

NOTES

1   Published in Britain under the title *AIDS and the New Puritanism*. London: Pluto, 1986.

2   One of the few exceptions is Barry Adam, *The Rise of a Gay and Lesbian Movement*. Boston, 1987.

3   See Frederick Whitam and Robin W. Mathy, *Male Homosexuality in Four Societies*. New York, 1986; and S. Epstein, 'Gay Politics, Ethnic Identity: the Limits of Social Constructionism'. *Socialist Review* 93/94 (1987).

4   Phil Parkinson, 'Stigma and Risk'. Unpublished paper. Wellington, 18 september 1987, p. 7.

5   B. Lemon, 'Female Trouble'. *Christopher Street* 116, p. 48.

6   See 'The March on Washington'. *The Advocate*, 10 November 1987, pp. 11-35; and L. Cagan, 'More Than a March'. *Zeta Magazine*, January 1988, pp. 35-36.

7   E. White, 'Esthetics and Loss'. *Artforum*, January 1987.

8   'LaRouche Initiative Stopped Dead'. *New York Native*, 17 November 1986.

9   Cindy Patton, 'No Turning Back'. *Zeta Magazine*, January 1988, pp. 67-73.

10 P. Reed, *Serenity*. Berkeley, 1987, p. 17.

11 R. Shilts, *And the Band Played On*. New York: St. Martins Press, 1987.

12 E. White, *States of Desire*. New York, 1979, p. 279.
13 The Macquarie University AIDS Research Project (Sydney) is producing evidence which strongly supports this conclusion.
14 I develop this argument in my *The Homosexualization of America*. Boston, 1983.
15 See Mark Vandervelden, 'Civil Disobedience'. *The Advocate*, 29 September 1987.
16 A. Holleran, 'Friends at Evening'. In G. Stambolian (ed.), *Men on Men*. New York, 1986, p. 95
17 P. Berman, 'Culture Shock'. *Village Voice*, 23 June 1987.

BLOOD FURIOUS UNDERNEATH THE SKINS...
On Anti-homosexual Violence: Its Nature and the Needs of the Victims

Henk van den Boogaard

Men who come up against anti-homosexual violence are cruelly confronted with the fact that homosexuality is anything but accepted in Dutch society. They discover that there are other men, youths in their twenties, who express the way they relate to homosexuality by using their fists to add force to their feelings and opinions.

Moreover, victims of this kind of violence continue to meet with deeply ingrained negative opinions about homosexuality and homosexuals in wider society. This hinders them further in dealing with the effects of the violence they underwent.

SCHORER FOUNDATION

Though aggression and violence against homosexuality is no recent innovation, the interest this phenomenon arouses *is*. This is undoubtedly due to the existence in the eighties of a reasonably well-organized gay and lesbian movement, as well as to increased attention to crime victims. Events in the Dutch city of Amersfoort in 1982 accelerated this process. During the annual national gay demonstration the male and female participants were confronted with aggressive youths who obviously enjoyed the support of adults looking on from the background. The gay and lesbian movement was appalled, but this also gave them cause for increased vigilance. Steps were taken in various places to counteract the violence, or at any rate to expose it to public attention. While these efforts seem to have had practically no impact on the general public, they *have* led to increased action on the part of the police.

The Schorer Foundation has concerned itself with this problem since the early eighties. Incidental help is offered to assault victims, and the Foundation has made a financial contribution towards setting up a national help line.

Even with all these activities there still seemed to be a lack of insight into the nature of the violence and the needs of the victims. It is for this reason that the Schorer Foundation took the initiative in 1985 to start the first systematic investigation in the Netherlands into the experiences of victims of anti-homosexual violence, or as it was then called 'An investigation into homosexual men who were the victims of gay-bashing'.[1]

The purpose of the study was to systematically gather information about the nature and location of the violence and its consequences for the victims. The study showed that there were many prejudices and myths: That anti-homosexual violence was only a matter of isolated incidents – an image which was reinforced by the anecdotal and sometimes even sensational nature of media reporting. That it mainly occurred in the larger cities and, within them, mainly in cruising areas (the circuit of meeting places like parks or parking lots where men meet for sexual contact). That these places are frequented mainly by closet gays – men leading double lives, having homosexual contacts on the sly while publicly leading an upright heterosexual life. That those who did not look 'manly' were more at risk. That they never fought back. That they showed no solidarity towards each other. That they rarely reported the attack to the police.

As for the perpetrators, it was presumed that they victimized this group of men in particular because they were themselves homosexuals and could stamp out the fire within them by the use of violence against 'obvious' gays.

THE STUDY

This investigation does not cover the wider area of negative discrimination and aggression but is restricted to physical violence: assault and battery and threatened assault.

It seems obvious to talk about 'violence against gay men'. But it isn't, because any male can, in theory, fall victim to anti-homosexual violence. The point is that the perpetrators *assume they are dealing with men who are sexually interested in other men. In their eyes these men are probably homosexuals. In fact they could be men who do have homosexual contacts but do not call themselves gay, or men that lead a homosexual lifestyle. Or they could be men who neither have nor show interest in homosexuality. The violence is intended* to be directed towards homosexuality, and the victim is a fairly arbitrary choice, which is why some people speak of sexual violence. Certain kinds of sexual experience and lifestyle are not considered acceptable; there is an enforced restriction of sexual self-determination.

The actual study was preceded by a review of the literature on anti-homosexual violence and on violence in general. I will return to the differences and similarities between these two kinds of violence later.

It is striking that most studies about 'the homosexual' pay almost no attention to experiences of homosexuals with violence, and this is why most information must come from men who have been associated with violence in one way or another. That is, men working for the police, the social services and the gay movement. And, of course, the victims themselves: in-depth interviews were done with 25 victims.

Because it is unlikely that anti-homosexual violence remains restricted to men of one particular social level, age group, or social scene, I tried to achieve as wide a distribution as possible. Representativity cannot be attained by research into homosexuality; it can only be approximated by using the largest possible distribution with as many variables as possible. Almost all respondents in this investigation identified themselves as gay. They were all white, between the ages of 20 and 40, and they all lived on their own. As far as social backgrounds and education were concerned, the majority fell in the higher levels of the social scale. This kind of sample is quite common in gay studies research, and this should be taken into account in interpreting the data. The results of this kind of study do not give a picture of homosexuality as a whole, but of homosexuality within a certain section of society – usually the middle class.

The interviews were carried out at the respondents' own homes and consisted of a non-directive phase and a more confronting phase. In the non-directive phase the interviewee was given full opportunity to tell, in his own words and at his own tempo, what actually had happened. The second phase was more in-depth recall-oriented, sometimes using confrontation techniques.

Each respondent was questioned about the onset and the progression of the assault; his own reactions and those of the perpetrators during the assault; the reactions after the assault from family, friends and colleagues; and the contact with police, judicial authorities, social services, and also with the gay movement. I was surprised to discover that the majority of the interviewees were able and willing to talk not only about the facts of the assault, but also about their feelings regarding the attack. It seemed that for the majority of them it was their first opportunity to tell the entire story to someone who showed unbiased interest.

RESULTS OF THE INVESTIGATION

Location

It is clear that men can be confronted with violence at many different places – in front of a bar, on the beach, on cruising grounds or even walking down the street. My investigation could not determine any location-related pattern for the assaults.

It is taken for granted that public meeting places play an important role in anti-homosexual violence. Because this assumption is made too readily and because there are prejudices and misunderstandings about cruising, I would like to examine this point further. Cruising grounds seem to form not only an arena for sex contacts, but also a locus where different homosexualities can come into contact. This is, perhaps, unique within the gay infrastructure. The differences in lifestyle among those who frequent cruising grounds are very great indeed.

One misconception is that it is cruisers in particular who are unwilling to report an assault to the police, the reason being that they are closet gays leading a double life and are therefore afraid of being publicly 'exposed'. A related assumption is that they suffer from feelings of shame and guilt about satisfying their homosexual feelings and needs.

It seems to me that it is too simple to equate a desire for anonymity with feelings of guilt and shame. Guilt and shame, if present at all, have more to do with acceptance by others of this way of making contacts than with homosexuality itself. Bar pickups are much more socially acceptable. Moreover, although mutual affection is nowadays accepted as a basis for a sexual relationship, sexual gratification as an end in itself is not. The presence or absence of anonymity in sexual contact reveals, of course, nothing about the degree of intimacy experienced in that contact. Besides, why is it so important for gay men to be open about their homosexuality and about their sexual contacts with other men? Behind all this lies, in fact, a struggle as to which kind of homosexuality is proper or decent and which is not.

The results of my investigation show that some of the men who go cruising are reticent about their activities because they wish to protect their male subculture from biased judgements and condemnations from outsiders. The men I interviewed reported experiencing a pleasant excitement when partaking of these contact opportunities, while at the same time being fully aware of the higher risks involved. They however felt protected by their ability to judge other men's intentions, using what they called their 'intuition', 'third eye', 'special antenna' or, more modern, 'a feeling'.

The probability of encountering violence

In principle, anyone could come into contact with violence – but not everybody does. Some investigators have looked for a possible correlation between being a victim and social characteristics. From research carried out in Chicago in 1982 it seems, for example, that effeminate gays, men that live in gay ghettos, and men that regularly frequent cruising grounds are more often victims of violence than others.[2] It should be borne in mind here that the issue at question is not that these characteristics make them responsible for the violence.

Statistics regarding the frequency of anti-homosexual violence in the Netherlands are a matter of speculation; according to the police at least 90% of the cases remain unreported.[3]

How do the perpetrators of the violence connect their victim to homosexuality or come to see him as homosexual? Sometimes, probably, because of the nature of the location – on cruising grounds at night or outside a gay bar. The results from the Schorer Foundation research, which investigated the victims and not the attackers, show no definite answers regarding this point. What did come out of the investigation was that the victims were *taken off guard* at the time of the violent confrontation, not knowing they were being labelled as homosexuals by strangers.

The questions 'why?' and 'why me?' are for them both crucial and pressing.

The interviews show that they first sought an answer in the areas of 'provocation' and 'effeminacy'. None of the interviewees thought their own behaviour or mannerisms had been provocative, although they did realize that almost any behaviour could be regarded as provocative by others. 'Effeminacy' was for them closely connected with outward appearance, clothing, jewelry, way of walking. It seems to me better to talk about behaviour or appearance not corresponding to accepted norms for maleness, rather than about 'effeminacy'.

It is striking that victims overlook what I consider to be a more important cause for the violence, namely, that most of them had been seen in the company of *other men* prior to the assault. Is this an indication that the attackers, mainly boys of 20 years of age and younger, are sensitive to inter-male behaviour? Do they draw a sharp line between acceptable and non-acceptable male behaviour? Does this mean that anti-homosexuality and anti-homosexual violence should be seen as part of the coming-of-age rites for males in our culture? Causes for anti-homosexual violence are usually presented in general terms like anti-homosexuality or homophobia, or they are ascribed to economic factors such as robbery and blackmail. However, if it is true that the perpetrators of violence surmise homosexuality after observing inter-male behaviour, then this could be an indication of their own uptightness in their contacts with men. I do not mean to imply that the perpetrators are themselves gay, but that their behaviour betrays a strong involvement with homosexuality. What does this involvement mean? Finding an answer to this question requires an investigation into the rituals between men and the significance of these in our culture. This is a question gay studies neglects when it limits itself to the study of homosexuality and the homosexual. The Schorer Foundation and the Gay Studies Section at the Catholic University of Nijmegen are planning further research into this area.

During the attack

The initiative to carry out a violent attack comes from the perpetrators, with the victim being taken unawares. It is not the duration of the assault, which averages about five minutes, but the viciousness and hatred shown that throws the victim off balance. The intensity of the violence and the hatred in the attackers' eyes will stay with him for a long time afterwards.

All interviewees were to a greater or lesser extent seriously injured. All suffered some material damage – more, of course, in those cases where robbery was also a factor. The combination of these two factors, by the way, is not always present in cases of anti-homosexual violence in the Netherlands.

Reactions

Because of the unexpectedness of the attack the victims are not, as a rule, able to react immediately in an effective manner. This perfectly understandable response is seen by the police, and even by the gay movement, as passive acceptance. 'They don't fight back,' and this feeds the prejudice that they are just defenceless victims – not 'real' men. In fact, it is the situation itself that makes them defenceless.

The most obvious reaction to a sudden, unexpected violation of one's person appears to be to cut oneself off physically and psychologically. As soon as the victim regains his senses, he tries to escape from the violence and from the superior strength and numbers of the attackers.

Violence in general

I want to go on now to make a comparison between anti-homosexual violence and violence in general. In the former case the attack is sudden and unexpected, generally perpetrated by a group of youths unknown to the victim. It has not been preceded by any personal conflict between the two parties. The presumption that someone is homosexual seems sufficient cause to touch off a violent attack. Assault in general, on the other hand, is most often precipitated by a personal conflict, which means that victim and perpetrator are not complete strangers. Usually it takes place in a one-to-one situation.

Assistance

These factors must be taken into account when the victims are offered help after the attack. They will have to deal with the effects of the assault themselves, but help and support will speed up this process considerably.

Trust in one's own capabilities and in one's surroundings is fully put to the test. The victim feels vulnerable, helpless and deserted. Besides grief and fear, the victim's anger about the attack and misgivings as to his own behaviour during the attack play a role in the process of recovery.

It is important to be able to talk openly about the incident. The Schorer Foundation study shows once again that few people one encounters are able to talk about homosexuality without revealing prejudices, taboos, or ignorance. The victim often hears comments like 'you gays' from people in his surroundings. He takes offence at having all the so-called characteristics of the 'group' being attributed to himself.

Victims expect and receive little support from their family. If they do talk about the incident this tends to threaten the balance of acceptance of their homosexuality which had been built up with difficulty. The possibility of talking about the incident to colleagues and friends is seen by many as a gauge of the quality of these contacts. Noteworthy here is that gay friends respond either very strongly or remain rather reserved. Perhaps they realize that they too could fall victim to this sort of violence.

The study revealed that in the Netherlands an appeal is seldom made to the national gay and lesbian organization, the COC, except in those cases where protest actions need to be organized, where contact with the police is not proceeding smoothly, or where one wants to give more publicity to the incident. In such situations, a very real danger exists that the movement will try to turn the victim into a martyr.

Moreover, the gay movement does not in all cases show equal solidarity. It appears that in these circles one often adopts the line that the victims are vulnerable because they are in the closet, implying that 'emancipated homosexuals' should be less vulnerable. In fact, the question of guilt is being asked and answered here – at the expense of the victim.

It should not be left unsaid that in the long run there can also be positive sides to the effects of an assault. The attack forces the victim to reflect anew on homosexuality and society's awareness of it, but also on his own personal recognition. Several of the interviewees stated that since the incident they have been more inclined to put things into perspective and enjoy life more consciously. A few seem to have distanced themselves from 'being' a homosexual, replacing this with friendship and pleasure.

Police

The results of recent research into the police and homosexuality has provided insight into why communication is so poor between police officials and men who want to report anti-homosexual violence.[4] This study showed that the police subculture is typified by conservatism and macho behaviour. Police officers have the tendency to moralize and to regard all or certain expressions of homosexuality as improper or disorderly.

This evokes comparisons to what we know about the perpetrators, for the rigid opinions about masculinity which both groups harbour sustain existing prejudices and stereotypes that equate male homosexuality with 'effeminacy' (and thus with reprehensible conduct).

Also, homosexual policemen and -women will often either be completely closeted within police circles, or extremely selective in their openness towards colleagues. We can assume that this image of the police is well-known to victims, who would have to personally file the complaint and as a result often do not bother. But the police tend to attribute the low incidence of reporting assaults to shame about one's homosexuality.

This touches upon an interesting and dubious change in police attitudes during the past ten years. Previously, not even so long ago, they did their best to force homosexuality into the darker corners on the fringe of society, while today those gay men who do not wish to be openly associated with homosexuality are regarded as obscure and disreputable. What progress! The gay

movement itself has contributed to this image of 'normal' homosexuality. For example, in one town the COC and the police
worked closely together spreading pamphlets door-to-door containing comments like 'How long can you go on thinking secrecy
is easier than being out of the closet?' In this way the struggle
against anti-homosexual violence is in fact turned into a battle
about homosexuality in which the 'emancipated' homosexual
towers high above the 'closet queen'.

Another problem with the police is that they are not willing
to classify this kind of violence as anti-homosexual violence. The
reason they give is that they are no longer allowed to register an
individual as homosexual, as if there is no distinction between the
criminal offence and the party involved. After all, they also
record a mugging according to the nature of the *crime* ('mugging'), not according to that of those involved ('mugger' or 'mugging victim'.)

For a short time now in the Netherlands there has been a
noteworthy increase in the willingness of the police to take action
against anti-homosexual violence. Unfortunately there is far less
increase in their knowledge about homosexuality, and one
should not be reluctant to seek the cause of this ignorance in
circles of the gay movement and the gay social scientists from
whom the police receive their guidance. They take the police by
the hand with their views about the subject and expect wonders
from concepts as 'nature', 'minority group', 'oppression', and
'emancipation'.

Psychosocial assistance

A few words about psychosocial assistance. Various studies show
that all victims of violent crimes suffer psychosocial damage to
a greater or lesser degree: shock reactions, fear of repetition, and
feelings of guilt and shame.

In the Netherlands a limited amount of experience has been
acquired by the Schorer Foundation in providing aid to victims
of anti-homosexual violence. Initially, help was extended in the
form of an ongoing therapy group which made use of role playing,
fitness training, fighting techniques, group sessions and nonver-
bal exercises. This approach, as shown by my research, was based

on a faulty assessment of the nature of the violence and the needs of the victims. Becoming a victim of violence was mistakenly confused with behaving like a victim. It was erroneously assumed that those with a 'fighting spirit' would not come up against violence. Concern for the individual lost out to concern for the emancipation of homosexuality.

The Schorer Foundation now offers individual assistance to victims and also provides a training course for men who want to examine their own attitudes towards aggression.

IN CONCLUSION

From the literature we can see that some authors try to suggest that men who have been victims of anti-homosexual violence, are less able to enjoy sex with other men following an assault.[5] It seems to me more likely that the outrage is such an invasion of their physical integrity that for a long time they may have difficulty in expressing their feelings or allowing others to get close to them or their bodies.

My investigation into anti-homosexual violence was strongly motivated by my indignation about violence against gay men. The indignation has remained, but my research has become more and more a study of *men*. How do men deal with homosexuality? How do they put these thoughts and feelings into practice? What words do they use to either come out or stay in the closet?

This investigation confirms my suspicion that gay studies will reach a dead end if it continues to believe in the existence of a homosexual nature and continues to see gays as belonging to an oppressed minority that has to be emancipated. All of this is true, but not true as well. The written story of homosexuality is not a story about truth, about the real day-to-day world. In my view it should be about studying the rituals between men, including those rituals around sexual interest. Rituals that we trace and recognize as such in other cultures, but fail to do so when it comes to ourselves and our own culture. Identifying oneself as homosexual is only one factor.

Life is faster than knowledge. The truth, also about homosexuality, has already slipped away just when you think you've found it. All that thinking about 'the truth' about homosexuality presses us into a preformed *mould* 'the homosexual', but anyone that looks around can see that life is richer and more varied in form. There is more homosexuality than there are homosexuals.

The force of life, or as some prefer, of blood, is greater than the force of order. Or, to use the words of someone who loved men and not homosexuals, the Andalusian master in the art of living Federico García Lorca, *'Sangre furiosa por debajo de las pieles...'*[6] – Blood furious underneath their skins....

NOTES

This article was translated from Dutch to English by Pat Raf.

1   The results were presented in a report entitled Henk van den Boogaard, *Een onderzoek naar anti-homosexueel geweld en de gevolgen daarvan voor slachtoffers.* Amsterdam: Schorer Foundation, 1986. They were adapted for a more general public in *Flikkers moeten we niet. Mannen als doelwit van anti-homoseksueel geweld.* Amsterdam: SUA, 1987.

2   J. Harry, 'Derivative Deviance. The Cases of Extortion, Fagbashing, and Shakedown of Gay Men'. *Criminology* 9 (February 1982).

3   COC Groningen, *Geweld en homoseksualiteit. Zwijgen kost een bult.* Groningen: Nederlandse Vereniging tot Integratie van Homoseksualiteit COC, 1985.

4   J. Aandewiel, Th. van Soerland, and P. van Weert, *Politie en homoseksualiteit.* Utrecht: University of Utrecht, Department of Gay Studies, 1986.

5   C. Anderson, 'Males as Sexual Assault Victims: Multiple Levels of Trauma'. *Journal of Homosexuality* 7 (1982).

6   Frederico García Lorca, *Obras completas.* Madrid, 1973.

BETWEEN ESSENCE AND PRESENCE
Politics, Self, and Symbols in Contemporary American Lesbian Poetry

Liana Borghi

MYTHS

This paper deals largely with the tensions between history and myth[1] which can be found in that not so narrow band of poetry written by American lesbians who have been actively connected with the Movement during the past ten years or so.

As I write, I am quite aware of the irony of discussing 'essentialist' traits in lesbian discourse by referring to a mythical persona called the 'lesbian poet'. In real life, I know quite a few individuals who are both lesbians and poets, but I know no archetypal lesbian poet – except Sappho 'of the triple blackness'[2] – who meets the specifications of being nebulous, fabulous, and encrusted in tradition. Paula Gunn Allen, Olga Broumas, Judy Grahn, Adrienne Rich, Audre Lorde, Joan Larkin, Jacqueline Lapidus, Irena Klepfisz, Marilyn Hacker, among many others, are very different poets, each with her own distinctive voice, life experience, racial affiliations, political priorities. But still, it seems to me that during the seventies, as the women's movement took shape (creating a community of readers) and these poets came to choose women as their primary referent, both as source of inspiration and privileged audience, their poetry took on a quality of shared cultural identity expressed in recognizable symbolic language. For this reason I feel justified in collapsing their individualities into the persona of the Lesbian Poet.

A similar kind of inconsistency marks my discussion on the Community. My daily experience leads me to view lesbians as women strongly differentiated by provenance, language, class, race and politics, whereas the necessity of theorizing on my topic leads me not only to collapse individual differences but also to map consequential connections for situations which should be viewed as space- and time-bound. However, during the years I have given close and passionate attention to all things lesbian, far and near, I experienced the Community (not just the vast American network, but the other national networks in Europe as well) as a strong presence in state of flux, as a sort of collective murmur in the background, out of which stronger voices emerged, posing issues that spread and reverberated far and wide, leading to theoretical and political trends. These meshed with other themes to affect in different measure the way we thought about our own lives. Certainly, individual communities had their own specific problems and interests, but because of the 'grapevine' and the capillary diffusion of small and larger presses, it was possible to map and follow generalized trends. Similarly, rereading American lesbian poetry of the seventies and early eighties, I can sense periods of synchrony and assonance, and then a creeping dissonance as diversification increased, indicating, no doubt, healthy growth.

These are the premises from which I begin, assuming that there is and has been among us, both within and beyond national and local boundaries, a Community with a sense of shared cultural identity both expressed through and created by a shared symbolic language. Language and symbols can be employed, and are, as political tools in order to organize and act for specific ends, to increase power and impose ideology. It is this particular use of language and symbols which I shall discuss both in relation to lesbian poetry and to our community. I feel that our political ideology, while aiming at the political construction of a collective (female) consciousness, tends at times to level and discourage varieties of interpretation and endeavour, and even to encourage self-censorship.

Certainly, we need a 'common language' to provoke fundamental changes in thought and social practices; we need to develop our own culture; we need, in other words, powerful myths to propel us. The past is a construct of the symbolic activity of the mind. Thus, all cultures are mythical, all traditions are invented out of the need to impose meaning, order, patterns. We lesbians have such a need too.

In the same way, we seem to have the universal compulsion to repeat patterns. How else can we explain why in the United States, the most powerful country of the world, the city-based lesbian subculture, with a small minority of significant exceptions, felt the need to rethink itself in terms of a past of radical innocence, a sort of Lesbian American Dream? To revert to agrarianism, to strict separatism, even to menstrual sponges. Still, myths often 'both state and enforce culture's sentences' most accurately.[3] In this case, the Dream accurately expresses the desperate wish to revert to the initial premise and promise of a society gone, it appears, irrevocably wrong; the refusal of an imperfect reality, the aspiration to identify with a perfect model, the utopian attempt to refound a society expressive of the repressed: in our terms, of women and lesbians. Moreover, myth has a strong link with human subjective awareness. It enables us to escape hierarchies and tradition, to gain access to the power of definition.[4]

I do not speak as one who did not join in myth-making, quite the reverse. Now, however, I wish to understand why we made certain choices and how experience and ideology, myth and reality became part of the tradition we live by and of my own history. As lesbians, we cultivate our critical faculties. Yet we are both creators and victims of a 're-visionary' mythology intended to open up 'the possibility of a woman-centred discourse'.[5]

We have deconstructed the universe and mapped a grid of differences, starting from the archetypal Difference (in the sense of opposition) between male and female, and followed this with the other archetypal split between heterosexual and homosexual. Along these coordinates we have rebuilt our world. And we have made it revolve around two myths that shape our imagination and our language: the Lesbian continuum and the female-coded Symbolic.

I find it significant that the spreading influence of the second, after the first was already established, has produced an ideological rift in the Community dividing it into two camps which hardly communicate with one another. The fact that in the United States the second is still mostly entrenched in the academic world because of its (especially literary) cultural requirements, should not blind us to political implications: the widening gap between theory and practice, ideologues and the movement, those who think and those who do.

This gap has long and intricate roots in patriarchal soil as well as in the women's movement. Mind/body, thought/action, intellectual/manual or political, are dichotomies which have been investigated, deconstructed, resolved, or left unresolved over and over again by feminist analyses, and not just during the first wave. The dream of a common language rests on our ability to avoid those juxtapositions which inevitably translate into political divisions and colonizations among women. Language levels (high, low, common, scientific) are never innocent of social privilege and power politics. Theory has its own unquestionable freedoms, it has been said; but philosophical speculation needs to be linked to political necessity. At the same time, action has little direction and meaning unless based on some form of existential and political lesbian theory.

Lately, I think, the problem has become not how to reconcile theory and practice, but how to make people act according to some theoretical construction justifiable under the heading of political necessity. In Italy I have witnessed, I am witnessing, the attempt to apply the theory of sexual difference to politics.[6] The give-and-take between grassroots feminists and 'thinkers', both traditionally opposed to hierarchies and therefore resistant to organization, has been revolutionized through the very accessible simile of the 'teacher-pupil' relationship. The necessary 'trust' required with much simplicity from the pupil has become the vehicle to ensure that the 'teacher-ideologue' receives the consensus and support of the women's community at large. Through one very innocent-looking operation, involving the recognition of the 'teacher's' value (or superiority), the individual woman has abdicated the authority and sovereignty which the first wave of feminism had won for us all.

One may say, of course, that the American theory of 'empowerment' has also been, for some years and in all Communities, a powerful and necessary strategy to gain consensus. But it was devised and used to support efforts, individual and collective, of general and tangible benefit, and it recommended the scrupulous, ethical recognition of all kinds of differences, of a multitude of centres of value.

The *political* application of the theory of Sexual Difference, instead, has reintroduced linear hierarchies, and issues of authority and power among women. The American theory deconstructed the patriarchal power structure. The French theory applies deconstructive methodologies in order to reconstruct its female mirror image. But we must not forget that it is proving itself, as claimed, functional to the self-assertive woman of the 'third wave' who wants to live at ease and with ease in a society also hers by right, a woman who has outgrown the need for the hothouse of separatist space.

In moments of detachment, I view the juxtaposition of the two as typical of the mother-daughter generation gap. One seems to me the mother of the other, and not necessarily incompatible – because they are both essentialist myths expressive of different historical necessities. The one feminist, the other post-feminist, they are still myths of power. They try to reconcile visions which political practice had unavoidably fragmented; they aim at reconstituting whole pictures from those individual segments, from those differences within, between, among women which we have so painfully learnt to consider and of which this rift is yet another example. By glossing over clefts, leaps, discontinuities, both theories postulate a community aware of a line of continuity with the past, ready to unite in the formulation of a present-future where women inscribe their authorial I.

Although the rift barely masks the understandable power struggle aimed at winning over a wider audience and a larger territory, both theories reflect a dream of wholeness: the dream of a common language, whose aim is the ethical construction of a new symbolic and social order. The original formulation of the lesbian continuum encompassed all women, not just lesbians. The theory of sexual difference makes no distinction between lesbian and straight, white and black, rich and poor, so as to avoid the pitfall of categorizing oppressions.

The combination of these factors led me to change the terms 'essentialism' and 'constructionism' proposed for discussion into the different but not unrelated categories of 'essence' and 'presence', as I was considering lesbian poets. I have often wondered about the tensions between an original, intrinsically feminine poetic self (if such a thing exists), and the construction of a lesbian-feminist poetic persona which, in Adrienne Rich's terms, is that poet's *presence* to the world.

There are points which I consider relevant here: that this presence is inextricably linked to both the myths and the realities of community life; that lesbian ethics find a political arena in textual politics; that lesbian myths become the symbolic projection which enables the poet to give 'universal' signficance to inner experience; and finally, that for a lesbian, the lesbian community is the third person necessary to achieve the transition from the imaginary dyad (I-thou) to the symbolic order. This complex network is difficult to negotiate, as I will show while I move through my discussion.

SYMBOLIC MOTHERS: TRADITION AND COMMUNITY

In *Lesbian Poetry* (1981), Elly Bulkin and Joan Larkin reprinted as a preface the introduction to their *Amazon Poetry*, an anthology they had edited in 1975, where the 38 poets included identified themselves as lesbians.[7] Their poems, it was announced, belied 'a simple sexual definition of lesbianism; they expressed, rather, the many sides of their lives, marred by the patriarchal oppression which is especially hard on those who do not meet society's standards. The preface ended by quoting Susan Griffin, who acknowledged:

> The risks other women take in their writings, casting off the academic shroud over their feelings, naming the unspeakable, moving with courage into new forms and new perceptions, make me able to write what before could not be written. In every sense we do not work alone.

Lesbian Poetry included 64 poets. In the introduction, the editors expressed their relief that the long drought was over. After surviving for centuries without 'knowledge of a tradition, a continuity, a social underpinning', ... the work has already begun that gives historical shape to our lives and our literature. Hopefully it will continue in directions that encompass the diversity of past and present lesbian poetry and lesbian existence.[8]

In 1985, Judy Grahn published *The Highest Apple: Sappho and the Lesbian Poetic Tradition*.[9] In the chapter called 'The Ideal Place of Wholeness Appears in All Our Work', she speaks of the myth of wholeness connecting 'the commonality' (i.e. the number of overlapping groups that constitute the American Lesbian Community) in 'a House of Women, a House of Muses'. Mythical realism, as she calls it, appears in the imagery of most lesbian poetry and signifies both the recovery of a (sapphic) tradition and the creation of a new paradigm.

In ten years, the lesbian poets had progressed from the celebration of a first collective coming out to the celebration of an established mythology that compensated for alienation, oppression, and the 'culture trance' that had so far blinded society to the lesbian tradition.

Having established these landmarks, I will, at this point, recall some definitions given, by women critics and poets, of poetry by women and lesbians and of poetic tradition:
- Poetry is a privileged access to the poet's own experience;
- Poetry is a highly charged collective repository of female experience;
- Poetry is the concentration of the power of language which is the power of our ultimate relationship to everything in the universe;
- It is a means to transform the symbolic order;
- Tradition is the context where poems are not haunted by patriarchal suggestions and symbols;[10]
- It is a field of precedents which determines the referential and symbolic context of the poem;
- It is an area of perpetual struggle, both political and intellectual.[11]

As Jan Montefiore has said, some of these definitions rest on, and promote, often (as I have said) for strategic reasons, romantic myths of universality which idealize poetry as universal consciousness, and see women's tradition as autonomous, discounting the fact that the mode itself, the 'material formalities' of making a poem, keep it anchored to (male) poetic tradition.

However, I do not agree with Montefiore that women's and men's traditions should be seen in *opposition*, for this would imply that the submerged text is always male, whereas in fact all writing could be considered a palimpsest containing male, female, and also lesbian texts.[12] Thus, I prefer to see the male tradition as the foreign tongue one must perforce use to express oneself, but one which the woman poet reconstructs and genders through equivocations, gaps, spillages, quotations – the techniques of indirection illustrated by Luce Irigaray which, by preventing dual

oppositions, allow new possibilities to take shape. But Montefiore, when speaking of language, will also conclude (as we shall see)
that the male text is always present and that therefore we cannot
speak of a wholly feminine language.

I am particulary interested in the last definition of poetry given
above and quoted from Montefiore, which sees tradition as an
area of perpetual struggle. A feminist line of interpretation re-
verses Harold Bloom's theory of the 'anxiety of influence' in the
case of women poets, stressing instead the symbolic mother-
daughter link between and among them, which leads to cooperation and authorial empowerment.[13]

In *The Highest Apple*, Judy Grahn expands this relationship to
include the Lesbian Community both as audience and as a reservoir of positive consciousness made available to the lesbian poet.
Similarly, Rachel Blau du Plessis, quoting Myra Jehlen, speaks
of the poet's need to situate 'the self in relation to conventions of
representation, and of constructing "enabling relationships"',
and also of how women create and recreate for themselves and
others the possibility of creativity.

The pattern seems to be that moments of connection lead to
expansion and then on to moments of detachment which are
essential for self-preservation. Following through this pattern, at
one point, Du Plessis (re-reading Virginia Woolf) comments on
the repetitive struggle of the woman writer for the authority to
write, that is to transcend (and to mend the damage of) the
feminine. One part of this struggle involves 'killing the angel in
the house', a provocatively blasphemous conjuncture. The
angel's maternal conservatism restricts boldness, judgement,
and outspokenness.[14]

Extending this argument to lesbian poets, one could assert,
therefore, that the lesbian who has re-viewed her own female
identity by recasting it in patterns that do not accept traditional
male/female demarcation lines is more likely to express herself
with authority. The lesbian who can rely on a strong community
is even more likely to do so. The example of Adrienne Rich and
Audre Lorde, with their careers as poets, speakers, theoreticians
and charismatic leaders of the lesbian Community, might seem
enough to prove the issue.

But what if the Community, besides acting as a reservoir of

consciousness, also acts as an overbearing symbolic mother restricting 'boldness, judgement, outspokenness' in the name of the symbolic and political significance the poem must have in order to be representative and inspirational? What if, as in the case of the 19th-century authors described by Nina Baym and Joan Kelley, the community does not view the poem as detached from the poet and insists rather on the (political) coherence of life and art?[15] Under these conditions, does lesbian ideology act as a repressing factor?

At first sight one would think that it doesn't. In their introduction to *Lesbian Poetry*, Elly Bulkin and Joan Larkin stated that the poets included in the collection 'sought to create a tradition that was anti-literary, anti-traditional, anti-hierarchical'. Indeed, lesbian poetry seemed born to express the unspeakable, the off-limits. It was, and still is, daring, dashing, iconoclastic, innovative. Sometimes.

Yet I would suggest that the myth of nurturance and sisterhood that to a great extent cements our community has tended to encourage a new orthodoxy which lesbian poets have had to outgrow in order to speak with their own voice. Virginia Woolf's angel in the house had to be killed for the writer to achieve authority, but the 'angel in the community' may plead successfully for her life because she has taken the shape not only of necessity but also of creativity.

The need to connect with the Community on the one hand, and the need to disconnect from it on the other often place the lesbian poet in a difficult bind. The lesbian author as a rule agrees with and accepts communitarian principles which set cooperation, harmony and nurturance above and beyond power and authority. Therefore it is in the name of lesbian ethics that the poet strives to establish a non-threatening identity that rides the narrow boundary between authorship and authority.

The outcome often takes the shape of safe explorations of feeling and behaviour according to lesbian-feminist ethics. The cost of trespassing could be a community mirror cracked from side to side. All the same, the ethical code pointing to selflessness is matched, in all of us, by an opposing and necessary drive toward self-expression and self-affirmation. To be accepted as representative, the poet must balance one with the other by using ploys to justify the need for self-possession, self-ownership and self-esteem in the light of prevalent lesbian-feminist tenets.

I am not saying that this balance is required only by our community. The mainstream poet has also always walked the tightrope between the world's dictum and private conscience. But although we recognize that poetry interprets and attains to the common reservoir of images and dreams, we usually praise the poet for being out of phase with the world while yet being in synchrony with some private vision of her/his own, we praise the poet for her/his unique voice above and beyond the background noise of current ideas. Still, in the case of lesbian poetry we seem to apply a double standard, for we expect it to be attuned to a set of beliefs which, no matter how at variance with the heterosexual and patriarchal establishment, are orthodox in the community of origin. We may therefore speak of functional poetry, one that serves the interests of the community. Could this be, I ask myself, Lesbo's highest apple?

Lesbian poets, however, at least those who are part of the community and have themselves codified some of its principles, believe that lesbian poetry should speak from the margin. Grahn states: 'In all our work it is clear we understand our role as that of the outsider.'[16] Indeed, Lorde and Rich among others have stated, demonstrated, embedded in their texts the necessity for 'a decentering polylogue', as Elizabeth Meese points out. Multivocality is essential to permit the expression of all women. 'The dynamics of becoming', and the 'freedom of process' are more important than 'the permanence of product'.[17] But what if the margin has since become a hard centre?

Originating in radical grassroots politics, American lesbian-feminism has grown by carefully balancing the needs of many minorities and allowing each and all the legitimacy of self-expression. *Provided* the liberal view of an integrated, multiracial and multicultural community remained finalized to the myth of a whole and wholesome lesbian culture. If individual interests prevailed and/or failed to meet this standard, community approval has been slow in coming.

When Irena Klepfisz wrote her first book, *Periods of Stress* (1978)[18], she spoke 'from the margin' of two separate but equally powerful centres of consciousness: her Jewishness and her lesbiansm. When the poems were published, she was shocked to find that her Jewish friends could not relate to the lesbian themes, and, worse perhaps, her lesbian friends could not relate to the Jewish themes. As Rich did later, she persevered further into marginality; her next book was that small masterpiece *Keeper of Accounts* (1983)[19] where the two themes join and proliferate.

On the other hand, the special interests of community leaders often point the way to new trends and developments. Audre Lorde's *Cancer Journals*[20], for instance. Or Rich's *Sources*[21], where, coming out as a Jew, she theorized an 'identity of the diaspora' which was lesbian but not only lesbian, and which at the time served the purpose of hushing the ugly politics of pain dividing black and Jewish women. This book, I think, marked yet another turning point for Rich. For the first time in years she made lesbianism the submerged, and not the overt text in her poetry. Many in the community found that 'the powerful womanly lens' she used to analyze the patriarchal and Jewish world was not explicit enough. Immediately afterwards, Rich wrote one of her great poems, 'North American Time', which begins:

'When my dreams showed signs
of becoming
politically correct....'[22]

It marks the phase when Rich realized she had become her own bearer of lesbian-feminist orthodoxy. It was time for her to fall silent and lie fallow, in order to begin speaking again. In Du Plessis's pattern, this was the time for detachment. But Rich was lucky, for she was largely her own victim, trapped by her own power.

Audre Lorde, however, seems as yet to have no qualms about her leader's role. She has relentlessly continued to follow her stern, even grim, path of political indictment of racism and class oppression outside and within the women's community. In her poetry integrity, freedom, and orthodoxy seem to overlap via the acknowledgment of her roots and the absolute needs of her black community.

The strength of these ethical choices – which are also textual choices – rests on a set of beliefs shared by most contemporary lesbian poets active in our community, once all due differences are taken into account: a belief in a sapphic tradition; in the poetry of the common life of women – a poetic matter culled from details and small signs invested with symbolic value; in the transforming power of language; in a lesbian consciousness that crosses the boundaries of time and space; in a women-identified culture investing every existential component with political significance; in love, because it is 'dually' that we test the knowledge gathered alone, in groups, or community; in a poetry of awareness coded in a language 'common' to the community, directed to an audience of the like-minded, an audience of potential lovers.

For all our poets, lesbian feminism has come fairly late in life. When it came, it shaped their existence and imagination, and shook them with a passion of re-vision and awareness. However, they were not born to the feminist mode, even if they were re-born of it; they embraced, developed, nurtured it. Whereas their poetry was born earlier on, and took root in dark places. Isn't it a truism that the poet will have to tear through the layers of present consciousness in order to articulate the child that cries out deep down and the dark side of adult dreams impermeable to reason? Can lesbian-feminism reach that deep? Or is it not rather, that even in the midst of a rich community, loneliness and angst cry out, defying our common world and defying any hope of perfect communication? Is it not that angst and hope are the matter of poetry? and that no matter how deeply social responsibility is felt, the poet's ultimate commitment is to the inner voice and to the form that best expresses that voice?

Let us look again at the situation of the lesbian-feminist poet. She feels part of the community, considers it her privileged audience and acknowledges its influence and importance in her life as her reservoir of ideas and inspiration. The community, in turn, has a great investment in her vatic value, in the gift of tongues of this sister-daughter, and consequently exacts a price: that she speak for them.

The request is subtle and almost inescapable, because the poet is, in a sense, the product of the community. It is the community's greatest homage to finalize, almost, her existence to reflecting the community back to itself. It is also a reasonable request. Lesbian feminist ideology is all-encompassing and pervasive to the point, it seems, that it is not only a way of life but almost a second nature. Besides, according to the principle of Visibility, experience does not exist until it can be named and articulated. Hence, lesbian lifestyles do not exist until they are witnessed and spoken for. By her act of witnessing, the poet not only confirms the community's existence, but also her own as a lesbian. This give-and-take makes the request by the community both ethical and understandable.

One can expect lesbian poets to be witnesses and bards, those who have crossed this ideological terrain, investigating the nature of the feminine, of sexuality, of woman-to-woman relationships; those who have made a critique of existing conditions and investigated political changes. Those, like the poets, for whom lesbian-feminism, in its meta-linguistic aspects, involved investigating the art of poetry. In this lesbian universe a poem is a symbolic act, an act of representation and acknowledgment of the political connection – charged in and by itself with political significance.

The poem is also a symbolic act of love, because of the primary, sexual, emotional, social involvement of the poet with other women. This crucial element in the interaction between lesbian author, text and reader may be one of the reasons why lesbian poetry so often addresses the audience directly, or uses strategies of involvement, like Rich's sophisticated extension of the I to the many or even, at times, to the Cosmos.

However, this game of demand and accession to the request can also be explained through the observation that the (feminine) self is often experienced as both dual and multiple by lesbians. In the game of mirrors which we play in life, the self reflects other selves, forever changing and being changed. Essence and presence are indistinguishable. Relationships become maps of mutations. For a lesbian, lesbian identity is inextricably connected with a lover. I am a lesbian because I love women/make love to them.

Predictably, in lesbian love poetry the beloved becomes a signpost in the poet's process of becoming; at worst she exists to establish the poet's own identity, at best she enjoys a primary presence, 'the crucible of a new language'.[23] She tells the lover where she is; she is the measure of sameness and of difference. She marks the territory in between. Because fusion cannot, even in poetry, be sustained, the beloved sooner or later becomes the Other. Her individuality, by the very matter of poetry, becomes objectified into the landmark, into the body one crosses, into the experience shared but used for the poet's own purposes.

Such is the stuff of desire, that from the desire of desire per se, we fix our attention upon a subject, and make it into an object for our gratification. Yet, in the semiotics of passion all excess escapes this economy by seeking re-presentation and transcendence.

If we transpose this pattern to the relationship of the poet with her audience, the poem is finally greater than the poet, greater than the beloved, greater than the audience. The poem is the presence of the poet to the world. Her access to the symbolic universe. Her badge of authority.

THE DOUBLE-CROSSING POINT: WHERE LOVERS MEET

I would like, at this point, to postulate a pattern to be found in some textual strategies used by poets, particularly in the seventies, in order to connect their love poetry to the sapphic tradition, especially by way of imagery, echoes and quotations, general style.

It seems to me that the poets try to establish a complicity with the reader through two parallel moves. The first tends, by the very simplicity of the occasion described, to posit the relationship as common, recognizable and shareable beyond a possibly exotic setting – this I would associate with 'presence' in actual time and space. The second connects the commonality of feeling and experience through metaphor and simile to the ennobling tradition of sapphic love, myth and epiphanies experienced in and through nature. This I would associate with 'essence' and the use of 'symbols'. The pattern appears to fit the mythical realism praised by Judy Grahn; the poetry meets community approval because it is both expressive of the poet's subjectivity and accessible to a wider audience; it can be labelled essentialist because the lover and the beloved both acquire mythical status; and the whole operation is ultimately 'politically correct' because the lover cannot be faulted with casting the beloved subject as an object if the lover herself has been turned into myth. There remains the suspicion of a taint arising from the fact that in real life the poet acquires status through her poetry by using the beloved as muse – which is, hélas, unavoidable. This suspicion is well grounded, because it demonstrates once again that the poet's ultimate commitment is to the poem, hence, if you will, to the poet who writes the poem. It is the poet who ultimately double-crosses both the beloved and the community.

If this pattern can indeed be found, it is not, however, as interesting as more sophisticated ones. It is too acquiescent, too innocent, a little too essentialist. A poet's poetry evolves as her life evolves, poem after poem, situation after situation. The innocence of early lesbian love poetry, prone to myth, evolves into more complicated forms, no matter what returns and repetitions we may find. The early joyful acceptance of the Community after a while turns into qualified participation. It is in this maturer and more recent poetry that I prefer to look for the way one poet at least cuts across a love relationship where lesbian ethics, community pressures, and the commitment to poetry overlap.

The poets so far under consideration have been in the community a long time. Among them, one is a little (more) different from the rest, less of an insider as far as politics are concerned, but certainly an insider as the former editor of the poetry magazine *Thirteenth Moon*. I would like now to consider Marilyn Hacker, author of five major poetry collections, and in particular her recent sequence of love sonnets called *Love, Death, and the Changing of the Seasons*.[24]

The book tells the story of a love affair with another, younger poet: its non-consummation, consummation, difficulties, resolutions, arrangements, its ending. Hacker is a poet who believes in the craft of poetry. When I asked her why she is so insistent on the use of meter and other traditional forms in poetry, she said, rather evasively, that after all women have been writing free verse since the beginning of the century, and free verse is also form.[25] But it seems to me that Hacker, who nurses no illusion as to the transparency of language, has been attempting to challenge the medium itself and to tell women they ought to do the same.

The insistence on high forms alone would set Hacker up as a disturbing factor in a community which upholds the right of every woman to express herself creatively. If craft distinguishes the real poet from the 'natural', the first line of authority is drawn, the first boundary set. Professional know-how becomes a filter, a parameter for discrimination. This kind of argument would probably seem demagogical to Hacker. Language is not a transparent medium for one's feelings; it is a tough, resilient dimension with its own consistency which we must learn to fashion for our own purposes. It is the prehensile thumb needed to express what we perceive.

Certainly, the use of poetic forms can be seen as a pass-key to the precinct of male poetic tradition. A way to show we can do it just as well and better. But in Hacker's case we soon discover that form means essence, presence and symbol all at once. We watch Hacker challenge the reader with sonnets, rondeaux, and villanelles, challenge her lover to yet another sonnet, her students to tighter forms. Tight forms, she says, 'only make them funkier, slang their diction down' (p. 86). Mixing high structures with low form is a deconstructive strategy. It is not just that, sonnet after sonnet, writing, food, and lovemaking interweave. But that orality and semiosis (in the shape of puns, irony, nonsense) signify the presence of the body together and beyond the subject matter. They break through the abstract pattern of form, make fun of it, debunk it, control it, enjoy it. They point past words and through sounds to the underlying semiotic patterns. Her manipulation of language into new semantic combinations expressive of the body feels voluptuous, somewhat perverse, definitely naughty. But if this strategy can be labelled a high transgression in the domain of signification[26], it is nonetheless constantly redressed by the hard boundaries of the poetic symbolic structure.

There is another reason why I find this book relevant to my argument. It deals with the love of two poets with strong egos tempted by passion and commitment to a relationship endangered from the start by age difference and unequal professional experience. One, an established and very knowledgeable poet very much in love; the other a young, untried poet still learning her craft, hungry for experience and freedom.

Such difficult premises can only be met if individual autonomy is never in jeopardy. The question of community pressure seems to be ruled out from the start: 'The uniform of the politically correct, dear, would be grounds for a divorce,' one lover tells the other (p. 101). Community authority is here challenged, by-passed, dismissed. One may live by and for the book, but not by and for community rule(s). The poet is first of all an individual.

Although the ethical plane is not entrusted to an outside code, it does exist as an inner dimension inextricable, at least for the speaker, from poetic identity. Whether they make love or not, whether they look like lesbians or not, they are lesbians. But they are also poets. Their ultimate allegiance is to poetry. The relationship must be functional to it. Bliss is talking in some bar 'about us, and poetry' (p. 42). Completion is being together, 'in love with our work' (p. 69). Just as in poetry the 'anarchistic libido' is always in conflict with the repressive ordering of form, in life self-possession is essential; and this love relationship takes shape according to a pattern of temptation, abandon, fear, resistance, refusal of symbiosis.

Whereas merging with the beloved is both longed for and feared, there is no ambiguity about the longing to marry art and life. In fact, these love sonnets look more often like a courtship of poetry than of the beloved. Text and body continuously merge; one reflects on the other. Rachel's body 'is a text I need the art to be constructed by'; the speaker's body is 'a book made for your hands to read'. The lover's permanent address is the cardboard covers of the notebook 'between which I live with you' (p. 38). A clean page is where Rachel can be found again.

Such commitment to art clearly cannot be separated from the search for control and order in one's life. 'I will not go to bed with you because I want to very much,' states the first poem, thus expressing a perverse yet ethical principe. It is not that sleeping with someone else's lover is bad because the Community says that to do so is immoral. It's bad *'for one'* because it's messy; it endangers the clean lines of one's life; it leaves a bad taste. This much becomes obvious, by implication, in a later poem ('Lacoste V', p. 25), one of those where writing, cooking, and longing inter-weave. The grit and patience needed to keep the long vow of silence in order to write a set of Welsh quatrains will be rewarded with a cassoulet of goose simmering in the meantime on the burn-er. That kind of stamina is no different from the self-control needed to wait for Rachel to leave her present 'wife' so that the new relationship, when it really starts, can be well-lived.

However, this is a book about a relationship that will not last, except on paper, as a sequence of sonnets. Perhaps Jan Montefiore is right when she calls the sonnet the narrative donnée of deprivation.[27] These sonnets are best when they cast the other's absence as a presence in the lover's body, in her mind – even if this can be said of all writing, which is perforce a substitute. But here, the sonnet is the real and most privileged space in between lover and beloved – the place of interaction of two lovers where the highest hopes are placed. Writing can only come from the gap between I and thou, as we look at us together, there where the others also are.

The existence of a Community is never questioned but is perceived as a loose network of individuals on the move, interrelating, supporting, listening, loving, turning up at expected or unexpected places. The Community is also perceived as ancestry. Hacker's many returns to Paris in the guise of yet another Jewish dyke (expatriate) in France claim kinship with Stein & Co. If this is yet another myth – one that passes through food, language and hard sex, one that associates sapphic love with laxatives and tummy-aches in the attempt to bring a tangible, concrete lesbian body to a father-form where the daughters have been erased – then it is welcome. For this is not an act of seduction, but a raid, whose aim is not to deface with graffiti the walls of a male bastion, but to claim the structure itself. We need this mythology too, the way we need all new formulations that show our communities to be fluid, heterogeneous, multivocal and authoritative.

NOTES

1   My definition of 'myth' is eclectic and my use of the term does not necessarily carry negative connotations. I see myth as the extrapolation of symbolic forms from experiential data; as related to fabulation and juxtaposes to *logos*, the language of reason; as related to *agon* in the complex pattern explored by John Barth in *Chimera*, where *mythos* acts as the heroic and symbolic representation of *agon*. Furthermore, I owe the concept of myth as de-politicized language, suppres-

sive of dialectics and complexities, and elusive of social realities to the last chapter of Roland Barthe's *Mythologies*. In this sense, this very text may be considered mythical, but I hope also expressive of a heterogeneous subjectivity and multiple identity (quoting Teresa de Lauretis) networking with other textual mythologies by women.

2   Rachel Blau du Plessis, *Writing Beyond the Ending. Narrative Strategies of Twentieth-Century Women Writers*. Bloomington: Indiana University Press, 1985, p. 23.

3   Sandra M. Gilbert and Susan Gubar, *The Madwoman in the Attic. The Woman Writer and the Nineteenth-Century Imagination*. Bloomington: Indiana University Press, 1979, p. 36.

4   Jan Montefiore, *Feminism and Poetry. Language, Experience, Identity in Women's Writing*. London: Pandora, 1987, p. 56. I substantially altered an early draft on this paper after reading Montefiore's text. I wish to thank the author, whom I have never met, for a book that filled so many needs.

5   Montefiore, *op.cit.*, pp. 84-85.

6   Luisa Muraro, a respected philosopher who has worked for years with the group of the Libreria delle Donne in Milan, is considered the symbolic mother of the 'Affidamento' (here translated, somewhat improperly, as 'trust': the Italian formulation of the theory of Sexual Difference). For her viewpoint on the history of feminism in Milan, see Libreria delle Donne di Milano, *Non credere di avere dei diritti* (Turin: Rosenberg & Sellier, 1987); and for the theory developed by her philosophy group 'Diotima', see Adriana Cavarero *et al.*, *Diotima. Il pensiero della differenza sessuale* (Milan: La Tartaruga, 1987). For a view of the debate as it intersects Italian lesbian-feminism, see Liana Borghi, Gloria Corsi, Allessandra de Perini and Simonetta Spinelli, 'Italian Lesbians: Maps and Signs'. In *Homosexuality, Which Homosexuality? Conference Papers*, Social Sciences, Vol. 2. Amsterdam: Free University and Schorer Foundation, 1987, pp. 112-125.

7   Elly Bulkin and Joan Larkin (eds.), *Lesbian Poetry: An Anthology*. Watertown, Mass.: Persephone Press, 1981; and *Amazon Poetry: An Anthology*. New York: Out and Out Books, 1975.

8   Bulkin and Larkin, *Lesbian Poetry, op.cit.*

9   Judy Grahn, *The Highest Apple: Sappho and the Lesbian Poetic Tradition*. San Francisco: Spinsters Ink, 1985.

10   Montefiore, *op.cit.*, p. 57.

11   Montefiore, *op.cit.*, p. 20.

12   The best formulation of textual strategies related to lesbian-feminist poetry is to be found in the work of Myriam Díaz-Diocaretz. See among other essays: *The Transforming Power of Language: the Poetry of Adrienne Rich*. Utrecht: Hes Publishers, 1984; and *Translating Poetic Discourse. Questions on Feminist Strategies in Adrienne Rich*. Amsterdam/Philadelphia: John Benjamins, 1985.

13   For a summary of the debate, see Betsy Erkkila, 'Dickinson and Rich: Toward a Theory of Female Poetic Influence'. *American Literature* 56:4 (1984) pp. 540-60.

14   Du Plessis, *op.cit.*, p. 102.

15   Nina Baym, *Novels, Readers, and Reviewers. Responses to Fiction in Antebellum America*. Ithaca: Cornell University Press, 1984; and
     Mary Kelley, *Private Woman, Public Stage. Literary Domesticity in Nineteenth-Century America*. New York: Oxford University Press, 1984.

16   Grahn, *op.cit.*, p. 82.

17   Elizabeth Meese, *Crossing the Double-Cross: The Practice of Feminist Criticism*. Chapel Hill: University of North Carolina Press, p. 148.

18   Irena Klepfisz, *Periods of Stress*. Brooklyn: Out & Out Books, 1975, 1977.

19   Irena Klepfisz, *Keeper of Accounts*. Watertown, Mass.: Persephone Press, 1982.

20   Audre Lorde, *Cancer Journals*. Argyle, New York: Spinsters Ink, 1981.

21   Adrienne Rich, *Sources*. Woodside: Heyeck Press, 1983.

22   Adrienne Rich, *The Fact of a Door Frame: Poems Selected and New 1950-1984*. New York: W.W. Norton, 1984, p. 324.

23   Adrienne Rich, 'Power and Danger: Works of a Common Woman'. In *On Lies, Secrets, and Silence. Selected Prose 1966-1978*. New York: W.W. Norton, 1979, pp. 250-51. In the original sentence, Rich includes a reference to Mary Daly. Discussing Grahn's poetry in this essay, she also speaks of

what the word 'lover' might mean 'in a world where each person held both power and responsiblity' and, further on, adds the following: 'love-sustaining love-poetry is not "about" the lover, but about the poet's attempt to live with her experience of love.... For the lesbian poet it means rejecting the entire convention of love poetry and undertaking to create a new tradition'.

24 Marilyn Hacker, *Love, Death and the Changing of the Seasons.* New York: Arbor House, 1986. Page references are given after each quotation.

25 This conversation took place in New York on 19 September 1987.

26 Andrea Nye, 'Woman Clothed with the Sun: Julia Kristeva and the Escape from/to Language'. *Signs* 12:4 (Summer 1987) p. 680.

27 Jan Montefiore, *op.cit.*

A RITUAL A DAY KEEPS THE THERAPIST AWAY
The merger process in a new perspective

Ingrid Foeken

Most of you know the expression: An apple a day keeps the doctor away. Or: An orgasm a day keeps the doctor away. My association is: A ritual a day keeps the therapist away.

Rituals are important to lesbian women. We have few lesbian rituals, or we don't recognize them. Only a few lesbians in Holland celebrate their process of change toward becoming a lesbian, or remember every year the moment they met their lovers. Our gay pride parade takes place every year, just as in some other Western countries. Visible and clearly recognizable, we walk through some town or other. In the seventies the gay demonstration started as a protest against discrimination, nowadays it is also a fantastic festivity. A lesbian-gay congress can also be a type of ritual for lesbian and homosexual activities: meeting your type of people like in a reunion, talking and writing about issues of changing realities and political themes important to us.

When I speak about rituals, I mean special organized events to remember or celebrate an important moment from the past or affirm a transition from one stage of life to another. Most progressive Western feminists start to giggle or shiver if we talk about rituals, and for good reasons. Rituals are not fashionable. Later on I shall discuss a popular theme among lesbian women and lesbian therapists: the so-called merger or fusion process in some lesbian relationships. I shall review various explanatory models from past decades, and I shall finish by giving my ideas about the use of rituals to influence merging processes in a positive way.

My thesis is that rituals can contribute to clarifying emotions and differences in positions between people. Aspects of a balance of power within relationships can be exposed, and this enables better monitoring by both partners, at least in cases, as in many lesbian relationships, where non-material aspects are more or less equal. Rituals and the symbols used indicate non-visible realities.

They penetrate into the deeper layers of the consciousness. Symbols mostly have at least two meanings which are complementary. The symbolism has to dovetail into the reference framework of the participants. Every culture has its own rituals, which have a specific function at a specific period of time.

WHAT IS LESBIANISM?

To elaborate on the theoretical theme of this congress, namely essentialism and constructionism, I will begin at once with the visions of the late sixties. As a protest against the fixed ideas in science, in particular sexology, biology, and psychology, the social sciences emphasized that there are many different types of same-sex activities, different lifestyles, and various identities. A homosexual or lesbian identity is called a historical Western construction of the last century.[1]

The feminist movement has influenced many women. Choosing for a lesbian lifestyle was propagated. 'I'D RATHER BE LESBIAN', the slogan of the seventies in Holland shows clearly the character of preference for a lifestyle and says nothing about anyone's sexual identity.

An example to illustrate:

In 1976 I was travelling in Benin, formerly Dahomey, a West African state. In the bus I met a friendly woman who invited me to stay with her large family. That night I slept together with her in one bed. We talked a little, and then she grasped my hand and laid it on her breasts. I was rather surprised, but didn't object. A moment later she led my hand daringly further, and I understood what she meant. The next day I asked her whether she petted with women more often and what she thought about being lesbian. Astonished, she answered that it was normal for her to let a friend comfort her in this way. Surely I had understood how difficult life with her family was? For her, the incident had nothing to do with homosexuality. She asked me how my friends and I offered each other comfort, which was when I realized how painfully our Western habits contrasted with hers. What she had experienced as comfort had seemed to me at that time to be lesbian lovemaking.

IDEAS ABOUT LESBIAN IDENTITIES IN DUTCH SOCIETY

a. A friend in her sixties does not want herself to be labelled a lesbian. I understand that her most intimate relationships have been with women. She feels that if men had been better able to conduct relationships with women on equal terms, her life would perhaps have turned out different. This seems to show a great freedom of choice, according to a constructionist vision. But according to essentialists this may also be an illustration of the second phase of coming out: knowing, but not really accepting lesbianism in herself, for fear of discrimination.

b. Those of my generation have fought many battles to be able to experience lesbian feelings positively. The woman's movement offered the framework which enabled us to square things with self-discrimination and personal oppression. This also included taking a public stand whenever lesbianism was discriminated against.

c. My niece of 22, active in the Dutch homosexual and lesbian organization, the COC, is going through her second stable lesbian relationship but nevertheless does not want to be labelled a lesbian. She doesn't want to be categorized, and she doesn't want to tie herself down for the future. She is keeping an open mind about changing again later. At the same time she told me that she kissed a girl for the first time when she was seventeen and finally understood what she had been missing in boyfriends all those years!

d. I have another niece, 15 years old. She had been very worried about becoming lesbian, for, as you have probably already understood, there's quite a bit of homosexuality in my family. For some reason, although she was unable to say why, she wanted to study genetics.... These four examples illustrate that essentialist and constructionist views exist side by side in the ideas of contemporary lesbian women in Holland.

RITUALS

Rituals not only influence the nature of social reality, but, in another way, they also reflect and form the social context in which rituals are performed. Every ritual consists of a series of symbolic acts. Rituals are carried out at a specific place and at a specific time, with carefully selected people witnessing. The goal of a ritual is to pay specific attention to a development phase or a transitional situation. The use of symbols increases the concentration on the specific meanings of the situation. Initiation rites and cleansing rituals are well-known from long ago. Farewell and mourning rituals are now known only on a very small scale in Holland. Every symbol has specific emotional meanings that are used consciously. A friendship ring, for example, is something well-known to us all. Some rituals take place daily, for example a goodbye kiss, or a nighttime phone conversation, in a living-apart-together-relation, before going to sleep. Others are used in therapeutic relationships, mostly to help when people become stuck in transitional situations.[2]

There is no ritual for the transition from heterosexuality to lesbianism. The transition can sometimes be laborious. A consciously chosen ritual can be a useful guide in the emotional chaos which then arises. I will give two examples:

1 The use of rituals when coming out

A lesbian woman consciously creates a transitional situation for herself and her family. She wants to profile herself clearly and make the change visible. She wants to provoke reaction precisely in order to be able to influence it. This woman prepares herself with her lesbian friends to be able to tell her mother. In this way she learns to understand her own emotions better. She will realize that what she fears most is rejection. Only when she feels able to bear even negative reactions does she decide to visit her mother. She will choose a special weekend for this. Her account will be tailored to meet her mother's emotions. For this conversation a notebook lies in her lap, filled with lesbian poems, as a symbol of loving friendships. The notebook is comparable to the object of comfort small children have, or the so-called transitional object like a teddy bear, a doll, or a blanket. The presence of a positive love object functions as a symbol for what comfort can offer during the absence of that love object. Her friends were, as it were, present during the conversation. In this way she did not lose control and was able to cope with the rejection and the attack that was indeed made on her choice. She is able to tell her mother that she is very disappointed in her reaction. She experiences the change in their relationship strongly: she came as an unmarried, single daughter, and leaves as an adult lesbian woman.

Sometimes the hope that lesbian life is only of a temporary nature lingers for a long time. A friend of mine who finished with her girlfriend received a tremendous number of presents from her parents. What she didn't tell them was that she had ended the relationship because she had another lover: a woman.

2 Bereavement, of which I shall name only one type: funeral cards

The father of a lesbian woman dies. Nothing has ever been said about her lesbian life at home. That's why she didn't know exactly what they thought about it. She asks her mother whether her girlfriend's name can be printed next to hers on the bereavement card. Her mother agrees directly, automatically in fact. She sees both their names on the card as a sign or symbol that her mother and her family feel that her lesbian relationship is more important than the possibility of negative reactions from those around her. Her lesbian relationship is clearly acknowledged within her family in this way.

THE INTERWOVEN IDENTITY OR THE SO-CALLED MERGER

There is a great difference between large-scale research on lesbians and the type-casting of lesbian clients in therapeutic literature. In most sociological studies it has been established that lesbians are more often autonomous and economically independent of their partners in comparison to heterosexual women. Away-from-home activities like work usually determine her identity more strongly than her private relationship. Equality is aimed at in love relationships and is often achieved. So lesbians in general come across as non-problematic, very autonomous, and so on. However, in lesbian and feminist therapeutic articles a relatively large amount of attention has been paid to symbiosis, fusion, and merger. So, lesbian clients in our white Western therapies in fact do seem to complain quite often about losing their independence in a relationship. Does this problem really exist on a large scale or has it been constructed by therapists? I think we have to be aware of the select group of lesbians that come to therapy when making generalizations about lesbian relationships.

The phenomenon called 'merger' appears as follows: One of the two women notices that she is completely losing herself in her girlfriend, she no longer knows who she is. The feeling of engulfment is wonderful at first, but if it doesn't develop back to reasonable proportions she begins to panic. For some unexplainable reason she feels completely abandoned, unnoticed, afraid, and filled with self-doubt. It seems as though she is losing her independence, whereas it is far more threatening than this: this woman is experiencing the process of limitless merger, in which she herself disappears. She experiences conflicting emotions that are related to the struggle to be herself as an individual. She wants to become free from the interwoven identity with her lover, without having to lose her. Anger or pure rage can be directed at a partner whom she has no control over. Desperately, she looks for 'something' to release her from her painful struggle. Unsolvable arguments and never-ending squabbles occur, or tension without a means of discharge.

The right combination of distance and closeness is a balance which every couple is searching for, whether hetero or homo. For two women this seems to be extra difficult. Clear differences due to race, class, or education and problems connected with enmeshment also play a large part in a number of relationships.

The explanation for this has often changed during the past decades. Classical psychoanalysts, like Joyce McDougall in 1970[3], point towards hate or contempt of one's own mother, who is then defended by sham love. Or fury, because a woman is unable to detach herself from her mother. This is most strongly re-experienced in the relationship with a female partner. For example, concern about someone is thought in this concept to be a wish that the other person should die. Similar conclusions are drawn on the basis of less than five treated lesbians, just to mention a few prejudices.

In the *Journal of Homosexuality*, a leading magazine for homosexual therapists, particular attention is paid to social factors that influence lesbian relationships, e.g. discrimination and homophobia, stigmatization, and discomfort about the division of tasks. The social isolation surrounding a number of lesbian couples might increase the mutual merger. This looks like an attempt at collective strength against a hostile outside world.

The standard work by Nancy Chodorow[4], offered a welcome theoretical framework to enable feminists to understand women's problems. Chodorow analyzed the specific socialization directed at boys and girls and was able to link intrapsychological explanation to sociological interpretations. In her concept, women have much more flexible ego boundaries than most men. Chodorow is not talking about lesbian women, but many lesbian therapist writers after her do feel that the little-differentiated mother-daughter relationship together with social factors promotes merger in lesbian relationships. My experience is that many lesbian women do not or only partly recognize themselves in Chodorow's description. Although her theories are of great value, they have their limitations. At present we need to write about our lesbian experiences in order to differentiate theories like Chodorow's. Lesbian women differ greatly, and in many ways, from their mothers. They do not want a husband; they occupy vulnerable social minority positions; and mostly their work determines their identity more than things like motherhood. In other words, all differences between mothers and daughters can often have led to real breaks between them. In 1983 I wrote about this but did not, at the time, have better explanations. I pointed out the dangers of various feminists using terms such as symbiosis, for the process of merger, when discussing lesbian women. Once again, it suggests pathology, and that is not something we want to re-introduce. Now, four years later, I think that the phenomenon of a faltering interweaving process in a number of lesbian relationships is true and is not really as negative as I had originally thought. What is necessary is an analysis that treatment of this phenomenon in therapies will be determined by the framework and point of reference of the therapist and the explanation used by the therapist. Roth[5] showed how classic relationship therapy with lesbian couples often strands because insufficient account has been taken of the specific point that two *women* are involved. Also individual support for both women only appeared to give limited results, because *relational* aspects had not been taken into account.

It is no doubt logical that because many feminist writers reach back to Chodorow's theoretical concepts they propose solutions which boil down to a reinforcement of ego boundaries. This is, for example, why the importance of learning to distance oneself was described to enable the development of stronger ego boundaries.[6] Others argue for the permissibility of more aggression in lesbian relationships and on learning to express this aggression towards each other.[7]

Lindenbaum sees the development of mutually positive rivalry as a method of converting or changing jealousy and anger into creativity and productivity. Self-confidence then increases. The perception that one is well able to survive away from the other person is growing.[8] Generally speaking, the objections to fusion and its consequences were pointed out. For example, being non-monogamous was presumed to be a choice for escaping from the closeness of too strong a relationship. Implicitly, being non-monogamous was condemned. Kassoff points out that promiscuity can in fact reinforce one's self-awareness and the perception of being the sole owner of one's owns body.[9] This can reinforce the feeling of being someone, particularly for those women who have experienced sexual abuse, according to Kassoff. This can have a positive effect on the primary relationship, and therefore non-monogamousness can be useful.

MERGER, IT CAN ALSO BE EXPERIENCED AS GROWTH!

It will not have escaped your attention that I have emphasized the historical moments of the explanatory model. Together we all make new constructions to explain certain facets of lesbian relationships. The most recent articles I have read on the theme of merger point to the positive sides of this merger process.

In the Dutch bimonthly magazine for feminist therapy *VIAVIA*, the positive sides have also repeatedly been emphasized such as two women receiving love and positive attention that was previously lacking.[10] Acceptance on a fundamental level is so intensely experienced that it may certainly give rise to satisfaction, but it can also give rise to anxiety, especially if a partner has never experienced such deep unconditional love. And in particular, it seems important to me to learn to recognize merger or interweaving processes as fairly natural processes belonging to and reappearing in certain phases of the relationship.

THE SYMBOLISM OF THE UMBILICAL CORD

A lesbian friend of mine who was pregnant was very conscious of the risk that she might bind her baby too closely to her. Therefore, when her girlchild was born she asked for the scissors and cut the umbilical cord herself, surrounded by her close friends. She chose this act to symbolize her acceptance of her daughter as a human being growing towards independence, guided by her, as mother, and her close friends. The image of this situation shall serve as a vivid reminder of her decision and shall underline the combination of giving love and accepting her daughter's freedom and individuality.

Another example: I suggested to a couple in therapy for interweaving difficulties, that each of them separately make a list. Each was to consider on one sheet of paper how she idealized her partner and what she herself needed most from the other. Then each was to write down the reality of what her partner was giving to her. Afterwards they were asked to read these two papers to each other and make comments. This turned out to be insufficient to distinguish fantasy and unrealistic images from reality. I then proposed that one woman act for one day exactly as though she were her ideal partner. The next day the partner was to behave exactly according to the wishes *she* had of the other. The third day *both* had to behave exactly according to the wishes they had of the other in the relationship.

Both sustained this with difficulty and found it extremely claustrophobic. The next session I suggested they put the papers with the ideal description of the other into an envelope. Then they had to choose a special moment for the two of them and bury these pages together. As it happened, they had decided at home to burn the notes. This symbolized for them letting the too highly strung expectations go up in smoke, in favour of the reality of their relationship.

Finally, I would like to say something about the use of rituals in a women's collective where merger problems had occurred at all levels:

Every woman began by enjoying the creation of her own women's collective. After a while they each wanted more recognition and appreciation for what they as an individual had done for the collective. Each wanted her own special qualities to be seen. Criticism of one another's work was felt as personal rejection. They accused one another of arrogance, even when sincere compliments had been made. One woman was told she had run away with someone else's honour when she dared to write an article based on collective ideas. Jealousy arose if one of the women received a lot of appreciation. Mutual irritations were swallowed for some time. Some felt married to their project. The self-confidence of each of them individually seemed to be deteriorating. Confusion became greater, indirect forms of aggression increased, and you could cut the air with a knife.

This is not unique to women's collectives. Every group that works together closely is subject to similar risks. Just think of drama groups, study groups, small businesses, etc. It is almost as if work or the collective has to replace the 'ideal mother'. The collective has to ensure appreciation, recognition, emotional involvement. The 'mother' as metaphor for warmth, security, love, inspiration, support, care, stimulation, snugness, and equality.

What I have just said is almost identical to phases of faltering merger in lesbian relationships. What I am aiming at in my proposed solution is therefore only one practical possibility, next to the many others already mentioned in the various studies.

The first ritual consisted of all of the women allocating themselves places in an orchestra: Who would be the conductor, the soloists, and the orchestra? How did they look at one another's power, influence, and dependency?

The second ritual consisted of breaking unspoken team secrets, and then expressing what everyone had felt to be the worst event in previous years. This had to be put into words. Anger and sadness were shared without discussing complete details or what was true or not for different members.

The third ritual involved everyone depicting, by means of

tableaux vivants (live images), what their position and personal involvement had been at particular moments during the previous years. This sculpturing illustrated the emotional ties and their changes.

During the fourth ritual, everyone had to select two small symbolic gifts for each member of the collective. In this way each had to show her relationship to that member of the collective at that moment: one to express what she found annoying and one to show what she appreciated in the other. This led to an exchange of postcards, small stones, carefully chosen books, and a series of small objects. An explanation was given with each symbol.

The balance of power and influence and how this continually changed became clear to everyone. Personal relationships were redefined throughout the different periods of time. This took away much tension. This ritual helped the participants bridge the gap between the present and the future situation. It looked as though a number of unsolvable problems from the past had been said farewell to. Everyone seemed to have become a little more free. A certain peace took over, and there was a foundation to build on.

CONCLUSIONS

Merger often occurs in relationships; it is not a general characteristic of lesbian relationships. Mergers can stimulate women to develop further as long as they can cope with the merger. Complete involvement in the relationship and temporary fusion can contribute to growing maturity. The feeling of lost identity can re-occur somewhat differently in various phases of life. Panic, sometimes inherent to this period, does not have to be a sign that something is completely wrong or that pathology is dominating the relationship. It can also be the beginning of exciting and favourable changes, as long as both partners do not get stuck in these processes. The use of symbols to indicate certain emotional stages or series of feelings can heighten awareness. Working with these symbols, carefully chosen and usually unique to one or two clients, can regulate overwhelming emotions and guide lesbians towards making smooth transitions.

A couple stuck in a complicated dyadic process can pacify their situation by inviting a therapist, or using a ritual. Both structure the confused situation into proportions people can handle, or the third 'part' can help diminish high tensions.

This is, at this moment at the end of 1987, my new construction: *A ritual a day keeps the therapist away*.

NOTES

This article was translated from Dutch to English by Paul Barnett.

1   See the Introduction to this volume.
2   O. van der Hart, *Overgang en bestendiging. Over het ontwerpen van rituelen in psychotherapie*. Deventer: Van Loghum Slaterus, 1978.
3   J. McDougall, 'Homosexuality in Women'. In J. Chasseguet, *et al. Female Sexuality*. Ann Arbor: Michigan University Press, 1970, pp. 171-213.
    O. van der Hart, *Rituals in Psychotherapy: Transition and Continuity*. New York: Irvington, 1983.
4   N. Chodorow, *The Reproduction of Mothering. Psychoanalysis and the Sociology of Gender*. University of California Press, 1978.
5   S. Roth, 'Psychotherapy with Lesbian Couples: Individual Issues, Female socialization and the Social Context, *Journal of Marital and Family Therapy* 11: 3 (1985) pp. 273-86.
6   P.A. Kaufman, E. Harrison and M.L. Hyde, 'Distancing for Intimacy in Lesbian Relationships, *Journal of American Psychiatry* 141 (1984) pp. 530-533.
7   For typical examples of this approach see: J.A. Krestan and C.S. Bepho, 'The Problem of Fusion in the lesbian Relationship. *Family Process* 19 (1980), pp. 277-290. M. Nicols: The treatment of Inhibited Sexual Desire (I.S.D.) in lesbian couples. *Women and Therapy*. No. 1, 1982, pp. 49-66. M. Nicols: Lesbian Sexuality: Issues and Developing Theory. *Lesbian Psychologies*. 1987, pp. 97-216. B. Burch: Psychological Merger in Lesbian Couples. A joint ego psychological

system approach. *Family Therapy*. No. 201, 1980. B. Burch: Another perspective on merger in lesbian relationships. In: L.B. Rosewater and L. Walker: *Handbook of feminist Therapy*. New York, Springer, 1985. B. Burch: Barriers to Intimacy: Conflicts over Power, Dependency and Nurturance in Lesbian Relations. (Unpubl. paper)

8   J.P. Lindenbaum: The shattering of illusion. In: V. Mirer and H.E. Longino: *Competetion a feminist tatoo?*, 1987.

9   B. Kassoff: Seperation/Individuation in Lesbian Relationships. Lesbians Non Monogamy. Presentation for the Association of Women in Psychology. Oakland, Ca. 1986.

10   C. van Nieuwkerk: Seksuele problemen bij lesbische paren. *VIA VIA, Nieuwsbrief voor vrouwenhulpverlening*. 1985.

ON RELIGIOUS LESBIANS: CONTRADICTIONS AND CHALLENGES

Mary E. Hunt

INTRODUCTION

I am grateful to the organizers of the conference *Homosexuality, Which Homosexuality?* for the opportunity to share information and insights on issues of lesbians and religion.

This essay is an effort to present an overview of the field, with special emphasis on developments among Christian feminists on lesbian issues. I include a brief look at the question of lesbian identity as well as a mention of the impact (or lack thereof) of the essentialist versus the social constructionist argument. I conclude with some future directions that I see for lesbian feminist work in theology, in its impact both on the larger theological project and on lesbian/gay theory in general.

It is important to point out that my personal starting point for this work is as a theologian who is a white, lesbian feminist coming from the Catholic tradition in the United States. This accounts for my stress on the Christian literature, even though I am influenced by the work of Evelyn Torton Beck and other Jewish writers who are making significant contributions to the field of feminist spirituality.[1]

Further, my effort is to limit my claims to those which emerge from the particularity of my experience, rather than trying to universalize such claims as if all lesbians everywhere would see things in the same way. Such a starting point is particularly crucial in distinguishing between a feminist and a womanist stance. That is, racial, ethnic and religious roots radically shape perspective, an insight that white feminists in the U.S. continue to learn from women of color. Thus my claims are all partial, limited and contextual, as I presume all good theology is today.

Note that I have limited myself to the work being done in the United States, even though I realize that there are similar efforts in Holland, England and West Germany, among other countries. It is, in my judgement, too early to make useful comparisons. The first job, which this essay is about, is to get the data on the table.

FEMINIST STARTING POINT AND CONTRADICTIONS

Theological investigations usually start with or at least include church teachings and commentaries. But in the case of lesbians and the church there is virtually nothing with which to begin. Female homosexual experience is subsumed under the false generic of male homosexuality in Christian documents. Everything from promiscuity to celibacy is refracted through a male prism with little bearing on women's real experiences. Thus lesbian women do not find, any more than gay men do, many hints or glimpses of an appropiate sexual ethic in Christian moral theology.

Moreover, for most feminists who are lesbian the primary contradiction in a patriarchal church is being a woman. A secondary contradiction is being a lesbian. This is quite different for gay men because for them the primary contradiction is being gay, while being a man is a source of sameness in the institutional church. This is an important factor in the development of lesbian/gay organizations in most mainline denominations in the United States, for example, Dignity for the Catholics, Integrity for the Episcopalians, Affirmation for the Methodists and so forth. All of these are made up predominantly of male members, reflecting the larger patriarchal nature of the churches which has already alienated many women regardless of sexual preference.

For lesbian feminists there is a fundamental contradiction at the level of gender. It is not possible simply to tinker with one or another aspect of the church's teaching about homosexuality as some gay men do. A lesbian feminist critique begins with the same feminist critique which has been leveled by feminist theologians and activists for the past twenty years. But it adds to that critique another dimension, namely the impact of sexual preference on what it means to be a faithful woman.[2]

Many religious lesbians have long since left their churches. Some are part of women's spirituality groups. Others are active in women's base communities, especially as part of the women-church movement which was started by Catholic feminists (including lesbians) and is now an exciting way to challenge patriarchal Christianity by 'claiming the center', as Elisabeth Schüssler Fiorenza has argued.[3]

The further complication comes in the challenge that religious lesbians provide for both the churches and for the lesbian/gay communities. Whether Roman Catholic, Dutch Reformed, Methodist or whatever, sexually active, self-affirming lesbians run counter to the marriage norm. Even the most monogamously committed among us defy the teachings of our churches by our very being and loving.

But what is even more difficult is the extent to which we are also a sign of contradiction within our own communities of choice. Lesbian and gay people who are religious, even those who profess an interest in religion, are seen as suspect. It is considered antithetical to the 'politically correct' way of being lesbian/gay to take seriously anything that comes from the cruel and usually punitive churches.

The irony, of course, is that there are many lesbians in the field of religion. We have given leadership to the feminist critiques which have emerged as feminist theology. Now we are giving voice to our own insights as we shape religion for the 21st century.

CONTEXT

The ferment among lesbian/gay people in the 1970s coincided with several religious shifts. Among Catholics, the Second Vatican Council and the meeting of Latin American bishops in Medellín, Colombia, signaled a time of new openness to experimentation and change. Many of the gains made through feminist, Black and Latin American liberation theologies have been overturned under the present papacy, but the fact is that lesbian/gay concerns arose in the midst of other liberation struggles toward a renewed church.

Among Protestants the major inroads of the past twenty years have come from the dual concerns of women's participation in ministry and an upsurge in peace and justice work. The ordination of women in the Episcopal Church in the mid-seventies and the growing number of women in seminary and in the ministry has caused a paradigm shift in the understanding of the role and person of the minister. Likewise, through the efforts of national and global bodies like the National Council of Churches and the World Council of Churches, progressive mainline denominations in the U.S. have come to realize the privilege of their own place in the international economic order, as well as the negative effects of excessive nationalism. It is in this context that lesbian/gay issues have arisen in religion.

It is important to point out that some of 'the best and the brightest' of the feminist and liberation leadership in mainline churches has come from lesbian/gay people. Equally, it is interesting to note that some of the most skilled leaders of the women's movement, for example, Charlotte Bunch, have come from a church background. This is no coincidence, since the message of the Jesus movement, which Elisabeth Schüssler Fiorenza refers to as 'a discipleship of equals', was focused on loving one's neighbor without regard for sexual preference.[4]

For many people the churches' own positions against lesbian/gay rights drove them to bring their Christian values to bear but in the secular arena. Hence a disproportionate number of 'ex-Catholics' are members of groups like the National Organization for Women and other secular women's groups.

The women-church movement has arisen out of the efforts of progressive Catholic women, who, finding that ordination was not imminent, have begun to form small local base communities for worship and solidarity. It is in that context, today a growing movement of hundreds of such groups, that some of the most creative lesbian work is being done. The Conference for Catholic Lesbians, founded in 1983, is one such group that provides support and networking for members.

Women-church, though rooted in Catholic women's experience of frustration in changing the institutional church, is quickly becoming something of an umbrella which covers the many movements for justice among women from various Christian denominations. It is a fruitful locus for constructive work on lesbian issues, since, on the one hand, lesbians have been among its leaders, and on the other, heterosexually identified women in that movement are sympathetic to and supportive of our work.

These influences, as well as the churches' own claim to represent values of love and justice, inclusivity and mutuality, make it obvious that lesbian insights are inherently religious, i.e., looking at ultimate meaning and value. Likewise, feminist commitments to keeping the personal and the political connected and to bringing about equality overlap with these concerns. It was only a matter of time before lesbian issues were brought to religion.

HISTORY OF RELIGIOUS LESBIANS: CONTRADICTIONS

Lesbian Christian history is not yet recorded as men's is in the impressive, now classic *Christianity, Homosexuality and Social Tolerance* by John Boswell.[5] But we are beginning to unearth our history collectively. There are already a few sources on lesbians in church history. I would recommend a careful reading of the work of Bernadette Brootan who is researching the relational patterns of women in the early church. Reports of preliminary findings indicate that lesbians in the 20th century are not a new phenomenon, but that they were a part of the Christian community virtually from the beginning. She focuses on Paul's view of women as it relates to homoeroticism, finding much that scholars have passed over.[6]

Judith Brown's work in the medieval period on lesbian nuns is equally revealing. The celebrated case of Benedetta Carlini and Bartolomea Crivelli, 17th-century nuns whose love affair has now seen the light of day, is but one example. Their rather strange self-understanding (their sexual adventures were ripe with angels assuming human form and being part of the action) should in no way obscure the fact that they were lesbians, that they loved each other, and that they considered sexual behavior to be a part of their relational repertoire.[7]

My focus, however, is on contemporary sources which are shaping the future of institutional churches because lesbian issues are part of the larger agenda of women-church. In the modern period, especially in the 19th century, waves of immigrants came to the United States, including many women in religious orders.[8] I suspect that some of those who came so willingly two by two from Europe to start a new life and a new mission may have had some personal stake in starting over where no one knew them, especial-

ly in situations where women could be together without censure
and for religious goals. Who knows?

Turning to what we do know, the past twenty years where the
most obvious changes have taken place, I will focus on three
arenas: the ordination movements in the Catholic and Episcopal
churches, a brief review of the literature in the academic arena,
and a mention of groups that are now bringing this work to
expression in liturgical and support communities.

Ordination

No one knows how many of the pioneer women ordained in
various denominations were lesbian. But it is safe to say that there
were enough to claim that lesbians were there from the beginning. More to the point, the Episcopal Church, which began
ordaining women in 1974, had its first scuffle over ordination in
the late seventies when Rev. Ellen Barrett was presented as a
candidate for Holy Orders. It was not as if the Episcopal Church
had never ordained a gay person. Rather, it was that Barrett was
open about her sexual preference. The church is still hassling over
its policy, but Barrett broke the silence over sexual preference.

Later, already ordained priests like Carter Heyward, who was
one of the eleven women who were said to have been ordained
'irregularly' since their ordination took place before the church
passed legislation to sanction it, made their sexual preference a
matter of public record.[9] This too has touched off a controversy
that rages as we speak. Ironically, it is women who are most
marginal to the power structure of the church, albeit ordained
women, who have triggered much of the stir. Many of their gay
brothers remain closeted.

In the Catholic movement for ordination the lesbian concern
emerged rather early. The movement began in 1975 with a conference which later became an organization, the Women's Ordination Conference (WOC). By 1978, when the group had its
second national gathering, it had already begun to explore 'renewed priestly ministry' as part of its vision. As one of the speakers
at that meeting in Baltimore, I know that lesbian experience was
clearly a part of the analysis, even if it was not articulated as
overtly as it has been since.

WOC currently supports lesbians as well as heterosexual women who are interested in ordination. While there has been some talk among a minority of members about mixing agendas, the general flavor of WOC's analysis is that until all women can be ordained no women should be ordained. Some will say that this is easy when no one is in any danger of being ordained, but the fact is that such a posture spells real change as well as solidarity between and among women.

In October 1987 in the United Methodist Church a lesbian, Rose Mary Denman, an ordained minister who lives with a lover, underwent a ecclesial trial. The church requires 'fidelity in marriage and celibacy in singleness' of its pastors. At the nine hour trial, the jury of 13 Methodist ministers determined that Denman did indeed live in violation of the Book of Discipline. She was suspended until the next meeting of her General Conference (June 1988). The sentence was considered light since she could have been expelled from the church or asked to turn in her ministerial credentials. The fact that Denman had already made clear her intentions to join the ministry of the Unitarian Universalist denomination may have played a significant part in the jury's decision.

These three cases, with many more available, give evidence of the fact that lesbian women are involved in significant roles in the churches. When and how prejudices around sexual preference will disappear is anyone's guess, but it is safe to say that lesbians are on the forefront of change.

Academic Sources

The academic work that grounds the theology of these women is varied, if limited. Most significant is the development of a consultation on Lesbian-Feminist Issues in Religion at the American Academy of Religion annual meeting. I do not mean to suggest that lesbians need the imprimatur of the academy, but I do mean to suggest that work has become so sophisticated and of such widespread interest that it warrants scholarly attention. Indeed in the past two years some have suggested that among the liveliest sessions at the AAR are the lesbian ones!

This work was foreshadowed by the first writing by and about lesbians in religion by Sally Miller Gearhart. Her famous essay 'A Lesbian Looks at God the Father' (in a volume edited with William Johnson, the first openly gay man ordained by the United Church of Christ[10]) paved the way for other such considerations of how theology looks different through the lens I call 'the lesbian hermeneutic'.

The lesbian hermeneutic is a way of refining the perspective from which we understand the world. It focuses sexism, racism, classism and sexual preference as oppressive, cloudy films that block our vision of a just future. It is properly the subject of another essay but I mention it to reinforce the seriousness with which we need to attend to analysis of homophobia and heterosexism as they have pervaded the entire religious realm.

Mary Daly, in her later work such as *Pure Lust* and the recently released *Wickedary*, provides other insights.[11] She makes clear that dykes and lesbians are among the panoply of powerful women who people her pages (one even becomes Dalyesque just thinking about her creative reweaving of the English language). But Daly has not done the kind of systematic work that Carter Heyward and I attempted in our round table discussion 'Lesbianism and Feminist Theology'.[12]

Daly prefers to state her own reality while Heyward and Hunt tried to deal with the common context of lesbian feminists in the academy, namely the double bind we experience between the prurient interest of some on what lesbians do and our own sense of how deeply passion informs our work. All of these are efforts in the direction of a more adequate and meaningful articulation of lesbian insights.

Another approach has been taken by Rosemary Curb and Nancy Monahan in *Lesbian Nuns: Breaking Silence* which certainly did just that.[13] The book contains dozens of stories of Catholic lesbians who entered and (mostly) left religious life. While uneven in quality, the essays present an interesting array of experiences, including those of women who remain as lesbians in vowed religious life today.

The book was sensationalized in the media, not to mention the fact that it was the subject of serious concern in the feminist community over the way in which rights to certain essays were sold to publications of dubious repute. But even the sensationalization teaches us that lesbian nuns are the most untouchable. On the one hand, they fulfill a society's fantasy about what really goes on behind the walls. But on the other hand, the fact that nuns are sexually active, even women who have left the convent, is simply unthinkable to many.

A more sedate but no less interesting book is a collection edited by Barbara Zanotti entitled *A Faith of One's Own*.[14] In this collection Catholic women voice a range of concerns about living in the contradiction of being part of a religious tradition that despises us, yet loving the church in a strange and some would say masochistic way.

What the Zanotti collection reveals is that whether it is the founder of the Conference for Catholic Lesbians (Karen Doherty) telling her faith story, or the editor writing a poignant and powerful letter to her children, the message is the same. Religious faith has played a part in who we are. We can fight it or change it, but we cannot deny it.

We await the voices of lesbian women of color who are just beginning to make inroads in this territory. Here the perspective will be described, as by Alice Walker and Delores Williams, as 'womanist' rather than feminist. Womanist signals Black women's experience of oppression and liberation on its own terms, especially with regard to survival and nurture of dependent children.

The place of the church in the lives of some Black and Latina women is clear in the excellent collection *This Bridge Called My Back*.[15] But the strong censure and added oppression (on top of racism and sexism) of coming out as a lesbian keep many women of color from speaking or writing freely about their religious experiences. Making this safe is the task of all of us.

The Zanotti collection and *Open Hands*, a Methodist gay/lesbian publication, have carried essays which contain specific reference to the experience of women of color.[16] Unfortunately, the Argentine woman who wrote in the Zanotti collection had to choose a pen name, 'Fulana de Tal' (Jane Doe), since reprisals are real in her setting. Margarita Suarez's piece stands on its own as a beckoning to other women of color to 'speak the truth in love' though the stakes for them are unbelievably high.

Support Groups

Much of the work which is being done by religious lesbians is being done in groups like the Conference for Catholic Lesbians. Liturgies, rituals, prayer forms, new modes of spiritual expression are all being developed in small groups around the country. We await their publication so that they can be shared widely.

More remains to be unearthed of our proud history, especially about the contribution of non-Western and non-English-speaking women. But as a partner in the contemporary debate let me add a constructive approach to lesbian identity that emerges from religious thought as an example of one approach.

LESBIAN IDENTITY FROM A FEMINIST THEOLOGICAL PERSPECTIVE

Part of the excitement of lesbian feminist theology is our contribution to the theoretical debates among scholars from our theological perspective. We have long since abandoned traditional definitions of what it means to be a lesbian through patriarchal eyes. But I am equally suspicious of reductionistic approaches by sociology and psychology, or historical constructs which do not take account of the whole person as she is understood theologically. Therefore, I borrow from the phenomenological approach and focus on the quality of experiences, not the quantity of them. Likewise, I take women's own word for what we experience, allowing us to name ourselves on our own terms.

In this approach I use five elements which determine what I mean by lesbian rather than relying on one litmus test, be it sexual activity, self-identity or whatever.

First, I assume that *context* plays a key role in our self-understanding. Heterosexist patriarchy is an oppressive context in which to call oneself a lesbian, yet ironically it is because of heterosexist patriarchy that we must make such statements. Knowing oneself as a lesbian in our society is knowing oneself as outsider, outlaw, or even outcast.

Second, *eros* is a dimension of being a lesbian. Fantasy, touch, dreams, and attraction all aimed at women are part of what it means to love women in a context which tells us not to. Audre

Lorde has written about the power of the erotic, how it fortifies us for living in an often cruel world.[17] Her analysis makes clear that eros, far from being a privatized experience, has deeply political consequences.

Community is a third dimension of being a lesbian. Historically it was hard to determine what a lesbian community might look like, and even today in places outside of major metropolitan areas it is hard to find such a community. But it is obvious than when we say 'we' about a group of people we are talking about our community. Likewise, when we are held accountable for our behavior, including sexual conduct, fidelity to friends, use of resources, etc., it is clear we are part of a community.

Sexual experience is undoubtedly a component of lesbian identity. However, there are women who identify as lesbians who have had no sexual experience (e.g. lesbian nuns who are celibate for their entire lives). But this aspect highlights both the active, creative dimensions of sexual expression in the context of female-female relationships, as well as the healthy orientation or openness toward such experiences in a culture which considers them taboo. All of these dimensions, from genital sexual activity to casual sexual feelings, constitute part of lesbian identity.

Finally, I sense that there is another dimension which I call *spirituality* which is part of lesbian identity. It is hard to define and even harder to nurture, but it begins with a low tolerance for boredom and a concern for and attentiveness to the quality of human life. Spirituality involves celebration of relationships and the goodness of our woman love. It can involve commitment or covenant ceremonies for long term relationships, and it certainly encompasses our efforts to honor and recall the lives of our fore-sisters.

This five-part model begs further discussion. But for now let it stand as an antidote to the reductionistic ways of answering the question 'is she' or 'isn't she' which rely on one dimensional approaches.

ESSENTIALISM VERSUS SOCIAL CONSTRUCTION

Elements of both essentialist and social constructionist positions can be found in the above model. There is, for example, the assumption that there are such persons as lesbians in the world, that some of us are born with a greater propensity toward same-sex attraction than others. But there is also a heavy dose of social construction in the assumption that heterosexist patriarchy and the liberation movements which seek to overcome it have been formative in the identity of many contemporary lesbians.

However, it is important to point out that the theological approach used above does not belabor the seeming contradiction between these two approaches. Rather, I detect two tendencies among lesbian feminists in religion. The first is to see the debate as posed to be, frankly, rather uninteresting. At least it is not the question that many, myself included, are asking. We do not see the essentialist perspective as reflecting, for the most part, anything of our essence. The male models on which it is based and the extrapolation from male experience to female simply do not wash.

In a similar way the social constructionist position is based on men's view of the world. Few lesbians have been vocal and influential in the construction of even the contemporary lesbian/gay community which is in most manifestations a men's world. Thus our approach is to acknowledge the implications of both lines of debate but to pick and choose from them what is most helpful in answering the questions which we see as crucial, namely, what is it that religious lesbians contribute to a larger project of understanding ultimate meaning and value. This is not to say that we eschew the rigorous debate. It is simply that to the extent that it does not arise from our constituents we do not feel obligated to engage in it.

CHALLENGES OF LESBIANS TO RELIGION

In conclusion I wish to underscore some of the future questions that are pushing the horizons of lesbians and religion. After all, the work is just beginning but the critical edge needs to be maintained if this study is to be a contribution to the theological enterprise as well as a help to lesbian and gay religionists.

First, just as sexism raised a challenge to the essence of Christianity, so too does the lesbian/gay critique. If Christianity is inherently patriarchal, as Mary Daly argued, then one must leave it in order to achieve women's well-being. Likewise, if it is essentially heterosexist, then, for our own health lesbian/gay people and those who support us may have to leave as well.

Obviously in this essay I have not necessarily drawn that conclusion. I understand it to be a part of Mary Daly's critique, but I note with interest that Carter Heyward is still a priest, that a denomination like the Metropolitan Community Church has sprung up especially for lesbian/gay Christians, and that many Christian churches are making strides toward overcoming the problem.

However, I consider the academic jury to be out still when it comes to a rigorous answer to this question. The issue seems to be whether heterosexism is a subset of sexism or whether it is an analytic construct all its own. Elisabeth Schüssler Fiorenza seems to take the former position while I am inclined toward the latter. But discussion is in the early stages.

Second, the churches' homophobia and heterosexism are such that a new question arises as to the churches' moral authority. Can organizations which discriminate in so vicious and shameless a way claim any moral authority? AIDS seems to be the test case here.

This major medical pandemic that has hit gay men so hard has been ignored by many churches. Even recent pronouncements, like the controversial one by the Roman Catholic bishops in the United States which mentioned condoms in a highly nuanced way, seem hopelessly inadequate in light of the disease. As Kevin Gordon has stated so clearly, 'It is not that the churches will judge AIDS, but that AIDS will judge the churches.'

Some efforts to provide support and help for persons with AIDS and their families have come from church groups, often with women in the lead. But the general public posture ranging from indifference to hostility has made this a scandalous chapter in church history.

Third, lesbian experience provides us with new insight for the moral life. According to my lesbian hermeneutic, the essential shift needed is from a marriage norm to a friendship norm.[18] Friendship is a human experience available, at least potentially, to all. It may include sexual expression, though it need not. But most important, it is a challenge to the coupling syndrome of our society which is essentially dualistic.

More needs to be said about friendship, but for now it is enough to indicate that it grounds a new moral vision. Rather than base our ethical concerns on how those in coupled relationships work out their lives, we can begin to think about constellations of friends and what is appropriate to their collective well-being. Further, we can see how love and power, sex and spirituality all fit into the well grounded friendships that we need for social change and the nurture of the next generation.

Friendship is not a panacea, but it is a constructive start toward something more adequate than our current relational patterns. As such, lesbian feminist theology of friendship is a promising next chapter in the ethical discussion.

Finally, lesbian feminist theology is providing some tentative new ways of imaging the divine. Here I do not mean that Goddess as girlfriend has replaced God as father. Rather, we are thinking about the divine in relational terms, since friendship is the most adequate human experience to describe the essence of love.

While a divine being with breasts is more compatible to our view than one with a beard, this is not the point either. We look for the reflection of the divine in human beings, beginning with ourselves as lesbian women who have been marginalized by a heterosexist society and yet still have found ways to love well. There is much to be learned about love, faith and forgiveness from those who are oppressed.

CONCLUSION

The foregoing analysis of the history, sources, contemporary expressions and next steps emerging from lesbian religious experience in the Christian community is intended to spark further work. Some readers will think of people, works, events that should be included. Other will recognize their own efforts in a larger context. And still others will be surprised by the extent to which we have made an impact despite the overwhelming odds.

It is safe to say that the field of religion will never be the same again as the lesbian feminist critique is incorporated. It will reflect the presence of faithful, frolicking lesbians, and in so doing it will be a clearer reflection of human and divine cooperation.

NOTES

1   Evelyn Torton Beck (ed.), *Nice Jewish Girls*. New York: The Crossing Press, 1982.

2   Cf. Carter Heyward and Mary E. Hunt, 'Lesbianism and Feminist Theory'. *Journal of Feminist Studies in Religion* 2:2 (Fall 1986) pp. 95-99.

3   Cf. Elisabeth Schüssler Fiorenza's forthcoming book *Claiming the Center*.

4   Elisabeth Schüssler Fiorenza's *In Memory of Her* (New York: Crossroad, 1983) is a landmark book in feminist theology. It has provided enough of a reconstruction of the early Christian period to permit critical feminists to affirm some aspects of Christianity.

5   John Boswell, *Christianity, Homosexuality and Social Tolerance*. Chicago: University of Chicago Press, 1980.

6   Cf. Bernadette Brootan, 'Paul's View on the Nature of Woman and Female Homoeroticism'. In C. Atchinson, C.H. Buchanan, and M. Miles (eds.), *Immaculate and Powerful*. Boston: Beacon Press, 1985, pp. 61-87.

7   Judith C. Brown, *Immodest Acts*. New York: Oxford University Press, 1986.

8   Cf. Mary Jo Weaver, *New Catholic Women*. San Francisco: Harper & Row, 1985. Even though Weaver gives no attention to the lesbian possibilities I detect, the book is a useful source on Catholic women's history in the United States.

9   See for example Carter Heyward, *Our Passion for Justice*. New York: Pilgrim Press, 1984.

10   Sally Gearhart and William R. Johnson, *Loving Women, Loving Men: Gay Liberation and the Church*. San Francisco: Glide Publications, 1974.

11   Mary Daly, *Pure Lust*. Boston: Beacon Press, 1984; Mary Daly, *Websters' First New Intergalactic Wickedary of the English Language*. Boston: Beacon Press, 1987.

12   Cf. Carter Heyward and Mary E. Hunt, *op.cit.*

13   Rosemary Curb and Nancy Monahan (eds.), *Lesbian Nuns: Breaking Silence*. Tallahassee: Naiad Press, 1985.

14   Barbara Zanotti (ed.), *A Faith of One's Own*. Trumansburg, New York: The Crossing Press, 1986.

15   Cherrie Moraga and Gloria Anzaldua (eds.), *This Bridge Called My Back*. Watertown, Massachusetts: Persephone Press, 1981.

16   *Open Hands* is published by Affirmation: United Methodists for Lesbian/Gay Concerns, Inc. See especially Margarita Suarez, 'Reflections on Being Latina and Lesbian', *Open Hands* 2:4 (Spring 1987) pp. 8-9.

17   Cf. Audre Lorde, 'Uses of the Erotic: The Erotic as Power'. In *Sister Outsider*. Trumansburg, New York: The Crossing Press, 1984.

18   Cf. my forthcoming *Fierce Tenderness: Toward a Feminist Theology of Friendship*. San Francisco: Harper & Row, 1989.

THE CONTEXT OF GAY WRITING AND READING

Maurice van Lieshout

Thomas Mann's novel *Death in Venice* seems to have a large gay readership. In his survey of reading habits of Dutch gay activists Page Grubb found that almost one third had read this novel.[1] Most of them considered the subject matter to be in some way 'homosexual'.[2] Grubb did not ask whether they regarded *Death in Venice* as a gay novel. I confronted a (largely gay) audience with this question, and it caused some confusion.[3] Though it is not unusual nowadays to talk about 'gay literature' in general, labelling a specific work of art as 'gay' or 'lesbian' causes many eyebrows to be raised. To illustrate the confusion of many readers, I will point here to some of the pros and cons people put forward in response to the question 'Is *Death in Venice* a gay novel?'[4]

'Yes, of course it is', some people will say, 'because Aschenbach gets obsessed by the beauty of the young boy Tadzio. He even whispers he loves him.'

'Nonsense', others will argue. 'Aschenbach's feelings have nothing to do with homosexuality. Tadzio symbolizes the pure and untouchable beauty Aschenbach is searching for but cannot achieve in his art.' (This is, of course, only one of many possible interpretations).

'Yes, it *is* a gay story, because we know now that Thomas Mann had homoerotic feelings himself and was very impressed by the beauty of his son Klaus.'

'But Klaus was only five years old, when Mann wrote *Death in Venice*', an opponent objects, 'and furthermore, where an author's genitals are wont to keep house, is in most cases irrelevant for his literary work.'

'Be that as it may, *Death in Venice* gives gay people a special thrill, and therefore it is a gay novel.'

'Okay, but how special is that thrill compared with the emotions of non-gay readers?'

It seems necessary to confront ourselves with the question of what we are talking about when we use terms such as 'gay and lesbian literature', 'literature on homosexuality', 'gay and lesbian studies on literature', and so on. What is the determinant factor to call a novel, a poem, a play, or a movie homosexual, gay, lesbian, homoerotic, or whatever word you might prefer? The gayness of literature: is it hidden in the writer's sexual feelings, in his inspiration, in his skill, in the publisher's presentation of a book, in the reader's reception of it, in the subject matter, in the language and composition of the literary work, in some or all of these elements together, or is it wrapped in a shroud of mystery?

AN OUTLINE OF GAY WRITING AND READING

To say somthing on this subject that will hold water, we have to consider all elements of the *literary communication process*. To make things more clear I will make use of a simple outline of this process, a variation on the following outline:

sender -----> message -----> receiver
or:
writer -----> work of literature -----> reader

Of course, things are not as simple as this. Certainly not in the case of literature and homosexuality. To know how we read and why we read a book the way we do, we have to take into consideration the *context of reading*, and the same is true for the *context of writing*. For an outline this means we have to give both the writer and the reader a place in a context composed of three levels. I will call them the *sociohistorical*, the *literary*, and the *biographical* context.

I will further distinguish two kinds of readers: the professionals and the laymen, and I will call them 'Reader Number 1' and 'Reader Number 2'. In many cases the distinction between these types of readers is not important. But often it is, when Reader Number Two is informed by Reader Number One before himself becoming acquainted with the literary work.

To complete this outline we have the publisher, who influences the reader by his presentation of literary products. Sometimes he also tries to influence the writer's presentation of homosexuality. We must not forget that the act of publishing also occurs in a context. Here, for example, censorship comes into the picture, but to avoid making things too complicated I will not dwell on that aspect here. For the same reason I will leave the bookseller unmentioned.

Of course, such an outline is always an abstraction of reality, but it proves useful to understand what is going on when we deal with gay and lesbian literature.

THE CONTEXT OF GAY WRITING

Let's have a closer look at the elements in this communication process. I will first take the writer and his context. To illustrate what I mean, I quote from a Dutch play, from a dialogue between a mother (M) and son (S):

M: It's all right, son, you can trust me. Just tell me everything.
S: Everything? But, what if you don't understand? I don't really know what to make of it myself.
M: I'll understand, son, and otherwise I'll make sure I do.
S: Do you remember how Charles and I were in former days?
M: What do you mean? ... Yes, something offended me in your friendship, something excessive.... Is that what you mean?
S: Yes, we often quarrelled about it.
M: Well, son, it's just ... I ... I think a comradeship like that where you can't leave each other for one minute ... is ...
S: Unnatural?
M: Well, to say...
S: That's what you called it, and do you remember how angry I got?
M: Yes, I can't blame you. You had no ... no immoral thoughts.
S: No, I hadn't, at least not then. At least ...
M: Son, you're trying to say you have ... immoral thoughts at present?
S: Mother, I'm burning with shame. You don't know what this means to me. And I'm, I'm innocent....

M: What do you mean?

S: It isn't my fault. It was born in me.

M: Born in you?

S: I don't know how to express it. It's a crime of nature. A curse resting on me.

M: But, son, I don't understand.... What makes you think like that? You didn't do anything wrong?

S: No, of course not. Whatever gives you that idea? It's not a matter of thinking. It's ... nature, ... or rather unnature. It's something not only in thoughts and acts, but it permeates my whole being, something that is obviously in me since the day I was born.

M: Child, what utter nonsense!

... et cetera, et cetera.

I hope it's obvious I'm not quoting from one of the high points of Dutch literature. This is a fragment from the play *Things Not Allowed* (Wat niet mag) written by Ms. Yssel de Schepper-Becker and dating from 1922.[5]

The Sociohistorical Context of Writing

The image of homosexuality presented in this play is not the writer's invention. It is important to know what images of homosexuality were available to her at the moment of writing. A Dutch writer in the 1920s had a wide assortment to choose from. There existed scientific concepts of homosexuality: medical, biological, criminological, and psychiatric. Besides these concepts there were others: theological, cultural-historical (such as the Greek way of loving and educating boys, or romantic comradeship), and vernacular images of homosexuality, like that of the effeminate pervert seducing innocent children.[6] If homosexuality was, more or less, tolerated as a theme in literature, you had quite a choice. Yssel de Schepper-Becker chose the biological concept of the third sex for her play because this concept was – we may assume – the best for illustrating her message that homosexual men represent a natural sexual variation. In her case the sociohistorical context seems more important than a literary or biographical one. On these I will only make a few remarks.

Things Not Allowed belongs to a small tradition of didactic, tendentious literature on homosexuality which was inspired by the pre-war Dutch homosexual emancipation movement.[7] We know also that Yssel de Schepper-Becker preferred writing on oppressed groups like Uranians. Perhaps she felt in this case a stage-play was best suited to achieve her aim.

It is obvious that today the sociohistorical context of writing on homosexuality is quite different. Let me nevertheless point to one remarkable possible similarity between the 20s and the 80s. The emergence of AIDS has led or can lead to a new growth of didactic and defensive literature on homosexuality. Dominique Fernandez's latest novel *La Gloire du Paria* (The Outcast's Glory), for instance, is a novel with didactic elements and themes, especially in the dialogue between Nicole, Bernard, and Robert.[8]

The Literary Context of Writing

No writer is ever the first to write on homosexuality in literature. Writing on homosexuality often means taking up a position in the homosexual canon of literary texts. A writer can be inspired by and can refer to his predecessors, and he works in a specific literary climate. From several sources – literary works, autobiographies, case stories – we know that a special corpus of books has been or still is very important to gay readers and writers.[9] To name a few members of the Gay Parnassus: Plato, Sappho, Socrates, Shakespeare, Whitman, Wilde, and from our century Gide, Mann, Kavafis, and Lorca. Not only the homosexual canon is important, but also – and this is particularly the case for literature before World War II – the place homosexuality occupies in a literary movement. When, for example, we consider the main characteristics of three important literary movements in the nineteenth century, *Realism, Naturalism, the Decadent Movement*, we can expect homosexuality to be a potential literary theme. In Realism a new literary hero is introduced: an 'everyday' hero, often originating in the lower ranks of society. In Naturalism the novelist tries to reveal every gradation and determining factor of human identity. Realism and Naturalism sometimes prefer the 'abnormal' hero, because he serves better to demonstrate the conditions of human existence.[10] The scientific currents that gave birth to the modern homosexual – Darwinism, genetics and Determinism – are the same that were of great influence on the doctrine of Naturalism, and namely on its striving to describe how humans are made by *'race, milieu et moment'*.

To understand literature on homosexuality it seems important to investigate the typical conditions of a literary movement that stimulate or discourage a homosexual content in literature. Emile Zola, who based his view on creating literature on Bernard's *Introduction à l'étudé de la médicine expérimentale* and who became the architect of Naturalism, had the opportunity to make homosexuality a current literary topic. In the 1880s he received a document written by a homosexual officer. It is the confession of a man who talks about himself in terms of a different sexual identity, which is inborn. Zola thought the story suitable to turn into a novel. Instead, he delivered it in 1895 to Doctor Laupts (an anagram of his real name St. Paul), who was an authority on sexual perversions. As title for this homosexual confession, Zola chose *Le Roman d'un inverti-né* (Novel of a Born Invert). In his accompanying letter to Laupts, he wrote that he could not find the proper literary form for the story, and that he furthermore doubted whether he could find a publisher for a literary work on homosexuality.[11]

The third 19th-century literary movement appropriate for homosexual subject matter is that of the Decadents, where morbidity, evil, deviation, artificiality, sensuality, and decay become aesthetically highly praised values. Praz compiled a catalogue of sexual perversions in Romantic and Decadent literature, but gave little attention to homosexuality.[12]

The Biographical Context of Writing

It is clear that many writers express their homoerotic feelings in their literary work. Gide and Forster stated that 'an inner force' made them write books on homosexuality like *Corydon*, and *Maurice*.[13] It is this autobiographical component that often adds something to the common view on homosexuality outside literature. In novels like Forster's *Maurice* (1914) and De Haan's *Pathologieën* (Pathologies, a Dutch novel from 1908), we discover a modern image of homosexuality not yet common in the sociohistorical context of the time. Forster, De Haan, and others present us with a hero whose biological sex is male, whose gender role is masculine, and whose sexual behaviour and the sexual meaning he attaches to it are homosexual.[14] The sociohistorical context in those days presents us with a predominating image of the homosexual as someone whose gender identity is ambiguous and whose gender role is feminine.[15] Futhermore, Forster and De Haan provide a description of a process consisting of consciousness-raising, rejection, acception, integration, and some sort of 'coming out' – all this resulting in a homosexual identity quite like that we know today.

The Context of Publishing

The role of the publisher in the literary communication process should be limited to publishing books in a decent way. The publisher has many facilities for influencing the readers' reception: a book's exterior, cover texts, advertisements, and other publicity. In case there is a wide gap between the sociohistorical contexts of the writer and the reader (or the publisher), publishers often try to bridge this gap by presenting the literary work in contemporaneous terms. The Dutch publisher (sociohistorical context: Holland 1984) who released a translation of Kuzmin's novel *Wings* (sociohistorical context: Russia, 1906) bade for the public's favour (and money) by presenting this novel as a modern story about a homosexual coming out.[16]

THE CONTEXT OF GAY READING

In considering gay reading, I will first concentrate on Reader Number One, the professional reader, the student or graduate in literature, the literary critic, and so on. Let me quote from a recent article on gay novels written by a literary critic: 'Although this novel is about men with homosexual tendencies, it is not a gay novel. It comprises much more than just homosexuality, and that, it seems to me, is exactly why we have here a far more decent and fair presentation of homosexuality. Homosexuality is not presented as a separate, isolated world, but as only one element in society.'[17] At least this critic makes explicit what he considers a fine example of literature on homosexuality. But his touchstone is a highly subjective one.

If we examine studies on homosexual literature, we will find many pre-scientific and unscientific statements and approaches. I will distinguish the following[18]:

1. A non-historical approach to homosexuality (and sometimes even to literature). The critic divorces literary work, or at least its homosexual element, from its sociohistorical context.

2. The use of an anachronistic or culture-bound terminology for literature of all times and places. For instance, the critic speaks of 'gay poems in the Middle Ages' and 'homosexual plays in 18th-century Japan'.[19]

3. The reconstructions of homosexuality in literature in terms of the writer's sexuality. We then get something like: 'We know this writer had problems with his homosexual feelings, so we know how to evaluate to sexuality of his literary heroes.'[20]

4. The reconstruction of a writer's sexuality by means of an interpretation of his literary work. That can lead to something like, 'This homosexual hero commits suicide, so the writer must not accept his own homosexual feelings.'

These last two methods of literary interpretation presume the biographical context of a writer to be transferred with no major alterations to his literary work. Of course, analogy between biographical context and art is found in many cases, but we need verifiable information to prove it. Especially among scholars from disciplines other than literature, we find staggering examples of 'biographical fallacy'. [21]

5. The assumption of a separate corpus of gay or lesbian literature, while neglecting all differences in genre, literary background, and style. I already pointed out that something like a homosexual canon exists in literature, but that does not mean it forms a specific kind of literature in *literary* terms. There is no 'Homosexualism' in literature like there is Symbolism or Expressionism.

Reader Number One, the professional, can (provided he avoids the five methodological pitfalls I just mentioned) play an important role for Reader Number Two, the layman, in helping him bridge gaps in context, gaps not only in sociohistorical context, but especially in literary context. To give one simple example, Kuzmin's novel *Wings* is partially situated in Petersburg, where in some cultural circles a tolerant atmosphere for same-sex relationships exists. A limited examination of the sociohistorical context in which this novel was written yields following results: The aristocracy and the high officers' school in Petersburg were, according to Hirschfield, known for their tolerant climate for homosexual relations.[22] In Kuzmin's time homosexual activities in Russia were punishable only in cases of anal intercourse or when minors under 16 were involved.[23] Petersburg then was a cultural metropolis where people from all over Europe met. Knowing these facts can elucidate the meaning of *Wings* for the reader. The same is true when we take notice of all explicit references to the homosexual canon, in this case mostly to classical literature.[24]

Gay reading acquires more and more realistic dimensions if we are aware of the context of writing, our own context of reading, and the differences and the similarities between them. The way I read books on homosexuality when I was 15 years old is much different from the way I read them now. In my biographical context then, I was heavily involved with my search for homosexual heroes to identify with. In my sociohistorical context there was no place for gay people, or if they were mentioned it was only in negative terms. Not till I had read many, many books did I become aware of the existence of a literary context in which homosexuality figured.

In many cases gay readers call a work a literature 'gay' because it means something special for them as homosexuals. The question then arises if a straight reader can have any authority in calling literature (or art in general) gay. If he makes that statement, it seems to have a different meaning. He can say a novel is 'gay', meaning 'It's not meant for me', or 'It gives me an inside look into another world'.

The distinction between gay and non-gay books leads almost inescapably to a distinction between gay and non-gay readers. Woods refers to the reader and the literary work when he states, 'A gay text is one which lends itself to the hypothesis of gay reading'.[25] It is the reader who forms the decisive element in making a potential gay content active. We may assume gay readers possess a greater capability to do so. And Readers Number One, the 'professionals', can aid both one another and Readers Number Two in enjoying the gay content of literature.

STUDYING GAY LITERATURE

In my view studying literature and homosexuality, or studying homosexual, gay, or lesbian literature, means we first have to deal with literature, and only in the second place with homosexuality. This is a brazen statement that promptly needs subtle modification. I made it brazen because in many studies it is really the other way round. Not the literary work is the object of research, but the homosexuality expressed or anticipated in the work. Literature is then explained not using the tools of literary criticism, but the tools of psychology, sociology, and other disciplines.

If we concentrate on the literary work itself, we must forget just for one moment all elements that are not specifically literary. Then the main question remains: is it possible to talk about gay literature in literary terms? Can we distinguish the composition and style of, let us say, fifty novels on homosexuality when we compare them with fifty novels that are not on homosexuality? Is the rhythm in poems on homosexuality manifestly different from that in other poems? Is there a difference in the use of metaphor? Is stream-of-consciousness neglected in novels on homosexuality? Is homosexual literature, seen from a literary angle, in most cases conservative? Are the majority of novels on homosexuality a bit didactic or moralistic? Do writers on homosexuality prefer a specific literary genre and style? And to make things even more complicated: supposing we *can* find such differences, can they only be found (to employ American gay chronology) mostly in the pre-Stonewall period?

There has not been much research yet on these kinds of questions. Stockinger suggests a kind of specific *homotextuality*, such as the use of slang or the way in which the image of the mirror is used.[26] Others have pointed out that poets like Kavafis, George, and García Lorca make use of specific signals to clue readers that they are referring to same-sex affairs.[27] More research in this field of literary inquiry is needed to elucidate literature on homosexuality and to give answers to questions as 'What are we talking about when we talk about gay literature?' or 'Literature on homosexuality, literature on which homosexuality?'

NOTES

1 Page F. Grubb, *You Got It from All Those Books. A Study of Gay Reading.* Amsterdam: University of Amsterdam, 1984, p. 287. Only two non-Dutch novels achieved a higher score: Baldwin's *Giovanni's Room* (45%) and Wilde's *The Picture of Dorian Gray* (30%).

2 *Ibid.*, p. 194.

3 The audience concerned was that present at my lecture held at the *Homosexuality, Which Homosexuality?* conference. This article is a slightly altered version of that lecture.

4 See also Grubb, *op. cit.*, p. 191-200.

5 J.M. Yssel de Schepper-Becker, *Wat niet mag. Drama in 3 bedrijven.* Amsterdam [1922].

6 Maurice van Lieshout, 'Wetenschap, cultuurhistorie en homoemancipatie'. In Hans Hafkamp and Maurice van Lieshout (eds.), *Pijlen van naamloze liefde. Pioniers van de homoemancipatie* (forthcoming), pp. 9-23.

7 The *Nederlandsch Wetenschappelijk Humanitair Komitee*, founded in 1912 as a branch of Hirschfeld's Scientific Humanitarian Committee.

8 Dominique Fernandez, *La gloire du paria.* Paris, 1987.

9 Wim Hottentot, '"Ons geheim is een van woorden niet?" Een hineininterpretatie'. *Bzzlletin* 16:147 (1987), pp. 41-54.

10 G.J. Becker, 'Introduction: Modern Realism as a Literary Movement'. In G.J. Becker (ed.), *Documents of Modern Literary Realism.* Princeton, 1963, pp. 3-38.

11 'Le roman d'un inverti-né (Document communiqué par M. Emile Zola)' and 'Au Docteur Laupts, à Lyon'. In Pierre Hahn (ed.), *Nos ancêtres les pervers. La vie des homosexuels sous le Second Empire.* Paris, 1979, pp. 232-66.

12 M. Praz, *The Romantic Agony* (2nd ed., with a new foreword by F. Kermode). London and New York, 1970.

13 R. Martin du Gard, *Notes sur André Gide.* Paris, 1951, p. 45; E.M. Forster, *Maurice* (with introduction by N. Furbank).

Harmondsworth: Penguin, 1972. 'Terminal Note', pp. 217-22.

14 Maurice van Lieshout, 'De "ondergangen" van een "een zuiver homosexuelen jongen". De Haans *Pathologieën* als homoseksuele en decadente roman'. In E. Eweg (ed.), *Deugdelijk vermaak. Opstellen over literatuur en filosofie in de negentiende eeuw.* Amsterdam, 1987, pp. 136-50.

15 John Marshall, 'Pansies, Perverts and Macho Men: Changing Concepts of Male Homosexuality'. In Kenneth Plummer (ed.), *The Making of the Modern Homosexual.* London, 1981, pp. 133-54.

16 Michael Koezmin, *Op vleugels.* Amsterdam, 1984. (Mikhail Kuzmin, *Wings.*)

17 James Brockway, 'Homoseksuele romans'. *Bzzlletin* 16:142 (1987) pp. 75-81.

18 In detail: Maurice van Lieshout, 'Homosexuelle zwischen Fiktion und Wirklichkeit. Grundüberlegungen zur literarhistorischen Beschäftigung mit Homosexualität'. *Forum Homosexualität und Literatur* 1:1 (1987) pp. 73-86.

19 For example: S. Coote (ed.), *The Penguin Book of Homosexual Verse.* Harmondsworth: Penguin, 1983, pp. 48-49.

20 In fact, this is the underlying hypothesis of many interpretations in J. Meyers, *Homosexuality and Literature 1890-1930.* London, 1977.

21 J. Stockinger, 'Homotextuality: a Proposal'. In L. Crew (ed.), *The Gay Academic.* Palm Springs, 1978, p. 137.

22 Magnus Hirschfeld, *Die Homosexualität des Mannes und des Weibes.* Berlin, 1914, p. 591.

23 *Ibid.,* pp. 591 and 846.

24 Hottentot, *op.cit.,* p. 48.

25 G. Woods, *Articulate Flesh. Male Homo-Eroticism and Modern Poetry.* New Haven and London, 1987, p. 4.

26 Stockinger, *op.cit.,* pp. 135-51.

27 See for example: Marita Keilson-Lauritz, *Von der Liebe die Freundschaft heisst. Zur Homoerotik im Werk Stefan Georges.* West-Berlin, 1987; and
P. Binding, *Lorca. The Gay Imagination.* London, 1985.

FIGURE I

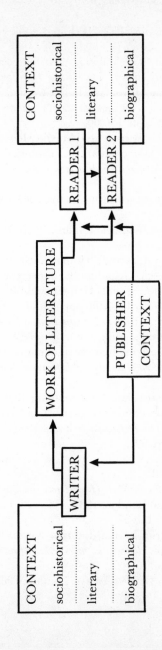

GAY THEOLOGY, WHICH GAY THEOLOGY?

Guy Ménard

I intentionally chose to give this lecture a title both broad and closely related to the conference theme, in that this paper was designed to offer a basis for reflection on the relationships between theology and homosexuality, as well as on the prospects for a gay theology. In doing this, I also hope to contribute to the debate surrounding the major issues being dealt with in this conference, especially around the 'dilemma' of the essentialist and constructionist approaches to homosexuality.

In recent years, theological thought on homosexuality and, more importantly, the efforts toward development of what could be called 'gay theology' have made great forward strides. This advance had occurred on both the *theoretical* (theological) and *practical* (pastoral) levels, and is even more remarkable considering that not so long ago homosexuality was considered 'a sin too horrible to mention among Christians'.

In fact, the evolution of the theology of homosexuality and gay theology has in many regards been comparable to that observed in other 'scientific' approaches to homosexuality. These approaches, dating from the end of the 19th century, featured the development of a new frame of reference which first saw homosexuality transferred from the category of 'sin' to that of one type of 'sickness' or 'disorder' or another, until one other variant appeared among the rest, a possible and legitimate one: homosexuality as a human 'sexual orientation'. This 'progression' is of course not at all linear or inevitable. In fact, if I may indulge in an ironic aside, some viewpoints on the subject seem to be bogged down in stages of thought at least as 'primitive' as those at which they place homosexuals....

But let us rather keep in mind that, around the 1950s and 60s in a number of Western countries, we began to see here and there on the part of the clergy new signs of openness and welcome toward homosexually oriented individuals. Holland immediately comes to mind, considering for example the work of Overing,

Kempe, Vermeulen and Ruygers[1] (following the researches of Trimbos and Ridderbos) which also had considerable impact in French-speaking countries; or the work of Father Marc Oraison[2] in France, for example. Initiatives in the area of critical rereading of the biblical sources of the official teaching of the Churches on homosexuality also come to mind – namely Canon Bailey's work[3] in the mid-50s, which also opened the door to rethinking the relationship between Christian faith and homosexuality.

More recently in the wider wake of the gay movement, even more daring theological arguments have emerged (here I refer in particular to the former Jesuit John McNeill[4]) which attempt to affirm the positiveness of homosexuality, as do gay and lesbian Christian groups and organizations[5] that want to create a space where they could live their dual reality as both homosexuals and believers, at the same time to contributing to the evolution of the mentality and attitudes held by mainstream Churches. We know, moreover, that some protestant denominations went so far as to ordain openly gay clergy.

I take the liberty of mentioning, in addition, that in the wake of the gay liberation movement of the 70s, a few theologians, including myself, had the opportunity, about ten years ago, to lay some groundwork for a 'gay liberation theology'.[6] In this we were inspired by the approach and methods of Latin American liberation theology[7], the import and richness of which, especially during the 70s, is well known, not only among politically involved Latin American Christians but also among other groups involved in various liberation movements.

Of course, the value of this type of approach was not always obvious – not only in traditional Christian circles, but even to the more 'progressive' Christians. The latter were themselves involved with liberation theology, but they often hesitated to recognize the relevance or even the 'dignity' of a reality as 'futile' ('decadent' and 'bourgeois'!) as homosexuality among the justifiable 'noble causes' for which one should fight politically and theologically. This line of thought met reticence as well on the part of certain gay Christian groups which were not radicalized or closely linked to the gay liberation movement but were more centred on spiritual matters or a desire for acceptance by the established Churches. Still we can say that the theological ideas of gay liberation did make major inroads and score many points in Christian consciousness and in the Christian community. It must nevertheless be added that the context of the 1980s and the new political issues which have emerged (most notably the critical scrutiny of the entire subject of the liberationist approach or ideology itself) in all likelihood today demand a reappraisal – or rethinking – of this gay theology in categories more adequately tuned to our present circumstances and the evolution in thought that has occurred.

And yet here we are, at just the right moment to pursue our efforts to renew, to update this gay theology, regarding liberationist thought more critically, with more awareness of recent research done in the social sciences (notably around the debate on essentialism and constructionism). We are once again faced with the brutal reality of an almost total lack of openness in certain sectors of the Christian world and in particular, but not only, in the Roman Catholic hierarchy. This fact is witnessed eloquently by the example of the 'Pastoral Letter' published last year by the Vatican and signed by Cardinal Ratzinger, prefect of the Congregation for the Doctrine of the Faith, a declaration which seems to bring us despairingly back to square one[8], or at least twenty or thirty years backward....

It is indeed discouraging, especially when one considers the great strides achieved during the past few decades, to find oneself again in the position of the travelling salesman who is tired of selling vacuum cleaners – dealing in apology rather than theology. 'No, the social sciences, contrary to what the eminent cardinal upholds, are not unanimous in their judgement on homosexuality....' 'No, it is not at all certain that the people of Sodom and Gomorrah were punished by God because of the threat of their transmitting AIDS to the angels....'

It is very disturbing to see arguments of this kind coming out of Rome barely a few months after the Pope had himself solemnly rehabilitated Galileo and expressed the regrets of the Church for this tragic misunderstanding – let us call it a misunderstanding! – in the history of the Church. One begins to think that clergy and theologians alike would gain from showing a bit more historical awareness – and modesty, like Sherlock Holmes, who, following one of the rare failures of his career, the *Case of the Yellow*

Face[9] (which took place in the tiny English village of Norbury),
asked his inseparable companion, Dr. Watson:

> Watson, if it should ever strike you that I am getting a little
> over-confident in my powers, or giving less pains to a case
> than it deserves, kindly whisper 'Norbury' in my ear, and
> I shall be infinitely obliged to you.

Be that as it may, there certainly is a temptation to attribute
this blunt refusal on the part of the traditional Christian world
to the powerful resurgence of the 'Right' in the West with
Reagan, Thatcher and John-Paul II. However, I prefer to leave
this type of explanation to others (to my mind it is much too
simple anyway), keeping in mind nonetheless that it does at least
provide confirmation of constructionist arguments – if not in the
area of homosexuality, at least with regard to theology itself!
What the last twenty or thirty years of theological debate around
the issue of homosexuality, as well as around other moral, social,
cultural and political issues, have brought out is indeed the eminently *plural* nature of theological debate in general and of the
theology of homosexuality in particular. What this plurality confirms – if confirmation was needed – is that theology is never
conceived from the perspective of Sirius or the North Star, and
even less from God's point of view, but, as the Latin American
liberationist theologians used to put it, always from the place
where one's feet are planted on the ground.

But we can also hark back to a very interesting assertion of the
French sociologist Michel Maffesoli[10] on sociology which, it
seems to me, applies equally well to theology. He suggested that
we could consider at least two types of knowledge. One could be
called *paranoiac*, hanging above our heads (which is of course an
illusion, in that it is never really above the melee but always
somewhere in the middle of it). The other he called *metanoiac*[11] in
the sense of 'conversion' of the subject matter from which the
theology is created and in the sense of knowledge of companion-
ship (*meta-noia*) instead of overbearing domination. If gay theologies have been able to see the light of day, it is essentially because
believers who have their two feet – and a few other parts of them
as well! – in homosexual desire have brought it out, in contrast

to theological debates (often even liberal ones) which continue to speak of it from the outside (that is, from above).

The theological issue of homosexuality appears to me, however, much wider than the classic and rather unoriginal debate taking place between progressives and conservatives in the Churches and the Christian World. It far surpasses the concerns only of gay and lesbian Christians, in that religious experience seems here, at the end of this century, to be put into a different and, up to a point, unpredictable light. The 'Radical Sixties' and the 'Revolutionary Seventies' – to put it bluntly – gave us the feeling (or the naïve illusion) that there was a conflict to settle between *religion* and *reason*, between the 'obscurantism' of another age and the 'light' of progress in a culture which had finally *come of age*. The West so firmly believed this that even its theologians were proclaiming the death of God. From this viewpoint, in consideration of our main interest here, it is certain that in many sectors of homosexual life, given the traditional teaching of the Churches, homosexuality as a theological issue often appeared at best a sympathetic oddity or an anachronism which was only of interest to a few homosexuals, the majority having detached themselves from the alienating oppression of religion.

But here we are today seeing our times in a rather different light. Not only does God seem to be not as dead as all that, but He – or perhaps She! – appears on the contrary to be alive and doing very well thank you.... We could, of course, once again be tempted to reduce this phenomenon to the revival of the Right and conservatism pretty much all over the world. But this would, once again, be too simple, I'm afraid. First of all, because we are seeing today that a good number of our peers – and among them many gays and lesbians – are relating positively to old or new religious roots: to Christianity, certainly, but also to others – of Eastern origins, Gnostic, or Neo-Pagan. Secondly, and perhaps more importantly, a glance at the religious anthropology of our culture reveals that many existing realities which at first sight are not of a religious nature have in fact been invested with religious meaning and lived as religious by many of our peers, and have become for all practical and even theoretical purposes 'secular religions', as some suggest calling them. We might in all likelihood consider the political and revolutionary involvement of the

60s and 70s (including, of course, feminist, gay, and other liberation movements in that perspective). We might also think of realities such as ecological awareness, sensitivity, and spirituality, so important today in many Western circles. And, of particular interest and importance to us here, sexuality, eroticism, that 'sex' which Michel Foucault[12] suggested has become for many the main avenue of self-fulfilment, the carrier of all expectations, to the point of believing that beyond sex there is no salvation.

In this wide but fundamental sense we could say that the theological issue of homosexuality involves everyone in his or her own religious experience, whatever it is labelled or however it is lived. And the tools of theology, like those of religious anthropology (which is at heart a sort of general linguistics of specific theological grammars) seem to be very useful for clarifying certain aspects – at first glance purely secular – of present homosexual reality. Thus, to take one brief example, it might be useful to distinguish between *religion* as an experience of ecstasy (i.e., an experience which allows escape from the limits of the secular human condition) and *morals*, whose essence would be more geared toward self-management of secular space – the direct opposite of the ecstatic nature of religion. Religious history reveals that religions are often born of the immorality of religious fervour and die of the most secular overmoralization. We may well wonder if this pattern of transformation does not throw light on the gay experience of sexuality in recent years. It seems to have evolved from an ecstatic and almost religious quest to an era of growing moralization – and I'm not only thinking of Reagan, or John-Paul II here, but of the gay world itself – notably under the impact of a phenomenon as AIDS. The emergence of the concept of 'safe sex' which would have given Georges Bataille[13], who considered eroticism an affirmation of life even unto death, a discomfiting start.

In any case this line of thinking seems to me to offer very fertile grounds for further inquiry.

I would now like to readdress directly the theological issue of homosexuality. It might be said that it involves anyone in the sense – the very classical sense – of St. Anselm's famous definition: *fides quaerens intellectum*, faith (adhering to a meaning which gives life and direction to existence and to the world) in quest of self-understanding. This, then, is the way in which theology appears as a kind of a quest for knowledge as related to a total experience of faith, analogous in this way to the proposition of philosophy as it relates to life: *primum vivere, deinde philosophare* (live first, philosophize later).... We adhere, first and foremost, vitally, wholly, emotionally to a life-giving meaning, and we then submit this adherence, this total experience to reflection which, to paraphrase the first Letter of St. Peter, renders us 'ready to account for our faith'. To believe is to affirm our direction and stick to it. 'Doing', or even 'making' theology (as one says 'making love') is becoming aware of the existential relevance of this direction for our life today.

Moreover, any theological act must be presented essentially in terms of *hermeneutics*. What matters here is the restatement, translation, interpretation for today – that is, for men and women in the here and now – of a way offered, a meaning affirmed which is usually rooted in the language and culture of other times and other worlds – be it in the Bible, an oriental religion, or a mystical or mythological tradition. I don't know how it is here in the heart of winter, but in my country, at 40° below zero, Krishna disciples have to wear something under their saffron robes – even though there is no provision of this kind in the *Baghavad Gita*.... Few Christians today, for example, are capable of reading the Bible directly form the original Hebrew or Greek. In order to have access to the source of the beliefs to which they want to adhere, they have to navigate the perilous seas of translation. Now we know that any attempt at translation is fraught with risk: *Traduttore, traditore*, says the Italian proverb: Translator, traitor! The claim, the risk, the wager of theology as a hermeneutic of faith exists in the present (and not as the simple exegesis of a dead text). This task is not only to affirm the present-day relevance of these beliefs but to be faithful to them as they are situated in the present through a translation – that is, a change which actually causes a *rupture* of the original text. The purpose of any theological act as an interpretive act is to affirm faithfulness to what is the same through that which is often different.

But this exercise is still not without risk or peril. Imagine this one example alone: the use in many translations of the Bible of the term 'homosexual' (a term first coined as we know in the second half of the 19th century in Europe) to designate certain behaviour and certain individuals condemned in the Old or New Testament. And here we really hit upon the heart of the theological issue and the debate on essentialism and constructionism. The *kadeshim* held so in contempt in Leviticus, those men who had sexual relations with other men in the ceremonies often interpreted in the term (itself problematic) 'sacred prostitution' – can they really be called 'homosexuals'? And the attitude the Biblical text displays toward these individuals and their behaviour – is it relevant to the reality of those whom *we* call 'homosexuals' *today*?

Let us take another example from Biblical tradition, one which is often used to illustrate this difficult exercise in interpretation: the example of the Biblical interdiction of the spilling (and consuming) of blood. We know that this inderdict is the basis for refusing blood transfusion – even on pain of death – for certain Christian sects practicing today. We see here the confrontation of two different concepts of faithfulness to the fold: one that is literal and consists of reproducing the materiality of certain acts or teachings; and another that, while distancing itself from the materiality of these acts (at times to the point of contradicting them radically), still claims to carry them out in the name of the same (or even a more authentic) faithfulness. In doing so they gauge the Biblical interdict as referring fundamentally to a respect for the sacredness of life, and the 'technique' of transfusion as one important way of assuring it in our modern world (though this particular example may have become problematic since AIDS appeared on the scene!).

Thus, interpretation aims at achieving faithfulness to the fold through a breaking with the codes that encase it. The interpreter, as translator, must master the language that gives access to the text in which he wants to convey the message, as well as the language of those to whom he wants to transmit this message (beginning with him- or herself, of course). Interpreting – and, of more precise concern to us here, 'doing' a theology of homosexuality – finds the theologian moving between the two great 'texts': the one a believing tradition looks to as the source of its belief (the Bible, for instance, but it would also be true of other founding sacred writings); and secondly, the immense text which is the present reality of homosexuality – that is, the reality of the men and women who concretely live a homosexual experience in a particular culture which has little to do with the Biblical times. It is in the language of these men and women that the message of the way to follow must be translated and transmitted, under pain of not being understandable at all.

This view of things is, if we think about it, eminently traditional. It is exactly what has been done by the entire Christian tradition. From St. Paul, who dropped circumcision to bring the Gospel to the Gentiles, to John-Paul II who has urged native peoples of Canada to embody their Christian faith in their own culture. And let's not forget some of the greatest and most orthodox theologians like Thomas Aquinas, who scandalized the Ratzingers of his day by undertaking the task of trying to reach understanding of the Christian faith using the philosophical categories of Aristotle – a 'pagan' thinker whose writings had moreover come to be known in Europe through Islam! – as these seemed to him to constitute the most useful and fruitful intellectual tool available to him in his days.

The challenge of the theology of homosexuality – gay theology – is to try to deliver the Christian message using the language, culture, and awareness through which homosexual experience is manifested today, and in which this experience tries to think of and understand itself. This 'text' is of course a vast, immense, and cacophonic entity; it is neither unanimous nor static. And of course it cannot claim dogmatic exclusivity. It also includes the debate over the conceptualization of homosexuality and how it is understood, as well as the multifarious life experience of gays and lesbians.

'Official' contemporary theology seems at times to be open to this hermeneutic necessity, in that, for example, in developing its thesis it takes into consideration some of the scientific findings and statistics based on experience. The problem is that the extremely selective and dogmatic use of these data compromise the possibility of truthful and fruitful interpretation. Thus, when a particular theology uses psychological or psychoanalytical data to 'assess' homosexuality as a 'disorder' (be it neurosis or regression), it is certainly using the context of present-day culture in viewing homosexuality. But in doing so it selects only *one view* among many others in a complex, ever evolving debate, not a definitive and indisputable truth.

It is quite obvious that 'doing' gay theology does not automatically guard against the risk of such bias. Actually, there is not much to be gained – except perhaps cheap sensationalism – by suggesting a gay relationship between Jesus and John, the 'Beloved' disciple.... However, when gay and lesbian Christians scrutinized the Biblical text from the text of their own involvement in life and liberation, they were highly sensitive to the fact that the God of the Bible appears as the God of Exodus, of *Liberation*. It is indeed to this God and His will that they are faithful when, as believers, they struggle for the historic emancipation of 'homosexual desire'. When gay and lesbian believers fought for the right of men and women to be different in their culture and society, they perhaps understood better than most others the message and profound logic of the old Biblical exhortation: 'Welcome the stranger! Not by virtue of any particular merit on the part of the stranger himself, but because you yourselves have been strangers in the land of Egypt. And I have taken you away from it, and given you a land of freedom and prosperity.' But it could also be that gay and lesbian believers, confronted today with the tragedy of AIDS, have come to see with new eyes not so much the old malediction of Sodom and Gomorrah, but rather the old wisdom of the Ecclesiastes who stated that if there is a time to embrace, there is also a time to abstain from embracing....

Truthfully, it is not only homosexual reality which needs to be theologically interpreted, it is the religious traditions themselves, notably the Christian one, which have to be read, interpreted, and, in a sense, enriched in a new way through the 'text' of homosexual reality, just as it has to be read through the 'texts' of women and other groups.

Undertaking a theological interpretation of homosexuality leads us back to the homosexual text in its totality – which is itself complex, full of contradictions, made up of sub-texts and dialects often unintelligible to one another: male and female, gay or closet, political or playful, etc.

It is very clear that the development of a 'gay identity' through the enormous gay liberation movement of the last fifteen years has encouraged certain ways of looking at homosexuality, of understanding it and above all living it, to the detriment of other ways which often found themselves excluded, banished, delegitimized, and this often in good faith, in the name of a liberationist ideology which fell in its own way into a reductionist essentialization of homosexuality. In so doing it neglected other possible forms that homosexual desire could take in the surrounding gloom of oppression, from which the movement claimed to liberate, or of inauthenticity, for which the movement wanted to substitute a more authentic truth.

The hermeneutic essence of theology (faithfulness to meaning through rupture in its interpretation) shows us perhaps the fruitfulness – or even the necessity – of a similar method of interpretation, of movement among the multiple texts of present-day homosexuality in order to overcome the dilemmas of essentialism and constructionism. If we see, for example, that Greek pederasty, where everything came to an end at the first sign of a beard, has little to do with today's gay *macho* homosexuality – where, on the contrary, nothing happens without a moustache! – we also must acknowledge the capacity of human beings to somehow transcend sociocultural structures and put themselves in touch with phenomena which, though in one sense completely different, are also, in some mysterious way, essentially the same.

NOTES

1   Overing *et al.*, *Homoseksualiteit.* (*Pastorale Cahiers*) Hilversum and Antwerp: Paul Brand. (French translation, Tours: Mame, 1967.)

2   Marc Oraison, *La question homosexuelle.* Paris: Seuil, 1975.

3   D.S. Bailey, *Homosexuality and the Western Christian Tradition.* Hamden, Connecticut: Shoestring Press, 1975. (London: Longmans, Green & Co., 1955.)

4   John McNeill, *The Church and the Homosexual.* Kansas City: Sheed Andrews and McMeel, 1976.

5   For example: *Dignity* (Catholic), *Integrity* (Anglican/Episcopal), *Lutherans Concerned for Gay People, David & Jonathan, Communauté du Christ Libérateur* (France), *European Forum of*

Gay Christians, etc. Cf. also the 'gay churches' (such as the Metropolitan Community Church).

6   *De Sodome à l'Exode. Jalons pour une théologie de la libération gaie* (with a preface by G. Baum). Montréal: l'Aurore, 1980. (G. Saint-Jean, ed., 1983.) Cf. also M. Marcourt (ed.), *Towards a Theology of Gay Liberation*. London: SCM Press, 1977.

7   Cf. for example G. Gutierrez, *A Liberation Theology*. Maryknoll, New York: Orbis, 1973; J.L. Segundo, *The Liberation of Theology*. Maryknoll, New York: Orbis, 1976.

8   And which the American feminist theologian Mary Hunt refers to – very convincingly! – as 'theological pornography'. (See her contribution elsewhere in this volume, as well as her paper 'Justice-Seeking Friendships' in *Homosexuality, Which Homosexuality? Conference Papers*, Theology. Amsterdam: Free University and Schorer Foundation, 1987.)

9   Arthur Conan Doyle, 'The Yellow Face'. In *The Penguin Complete Sherlock Holmes*. Harmondsworth: Penguin, 1981, p. 362.

10 Cf. M. Maffesoli, *La connaissance ordinaire*. Paris: Méridiens, 1986.

11 It is interesting to find a major concept of Paulinian theology in the writings of a sociologist from the Durkheimian school of thought in the French tradition!

12 Michel Foucault, *La volonté de savoir*. (*Histoire de la sexualité*, Vol. 1.) Paris, Gallimard, 1976. (English translation *The History of Sexuality*, Vol. 1. New York: Random House, 1978.)

13 G. Bataille, *L'érotisme*. Paris, Minuit, 1957.

HOMOSEXUAL IDENTITY, ESSENTIALISM AND CONSTRUCTIONISM

Jan Schippers

INTRODUCTION

Political and cultural doctrines about homosexuality have always had their influence on psychology and psychotherapeutic practice. Where homosexuality is seen as an illness, psychotherapists work to diagnose and cure it. Where it is conceptualized as being equal to heterosexuality, they have tried to help gay men and lesbian women to accept it and to find a satisfying lifestyle, based on sexual preference.

The recent debate between essentialism and constructionsm has placed helping professions in another difficult position. Essentialists say that homosexuality is universal and that it is a fixed and stable characteristic of the persons involved. Constructionists claim, on the other hand, that homosexuality is a cultural invention, or construct, designed to define and regulate sexual behaviour. They feel this construct is restrictive, since it posits a fixed relation between homosexual behaviour and homosexual identity.

Which theory is true and what are the consequences for psychotherapeutic practice? In this contribution I will first describe a model for (homosexual) identity formation. Having looked at how an identity is formed, I will proceed to take a critical look at essentialism and constructionism. I still try to explain why I believe that, for the helping professions, a synthesis between essentialism and constructionism is needed. Finally I will discuss some of the implications of this point of view for psychotherapeutic practice, especially for gay therapists working with gay clients.

Since I mainly work with homosexual men, I have chosen not to include female homosexuality, so generalizations concerning the position of women should be made with care.

THE FORMATION AND CHANGE OF AN IDENTITY

The concept of identity is extremely complex. Why and how do people form an identity, and why/how do they change it? Before discussing how an identity might be formed, I would like to stress that people do need one to be able to function. Identity seems to have a twofold purpose:
1. It enables a person to see him/herself as distinctive and separate from others.
2. It allows people to see themselves as self-consistent, with a workable integration of their own needs, motives, and pattern of responding.[1]

An ego identity consist of many parts, and in our society sexual identity appears to be one of them. As Moses and Hawkins point out, sexuality 'encompasses much more than genital functioning or methods by which orgasmic release is attained. It also includes attitudes towards relationships with people of both the same and the opposite gender, toward touching and being touched, and toward general physical closeness.'[2]

Now, let's take a look at how a (homosexual) identity might be formed. To stress the fact that identity formation is, in every person, a unique and individual process, I will not use one of the usual psychodynamic or developmental models. Instead I will present an adaptation of an *informational* model, developed by Lydia Temoshok.[3]

Figure 1 (see page 184) offers a simplified representation of this model. At the left side of the figure, information comes into the system and is then processed through hierarchically organized subsystems or filters which, when necessary, amplify it and pass it on to the next system, until it reaches the 'appositional' and 'propositional' consciousness. *Appositional* consciousness is probably located in the right hemisphere of the brain, which is non-dominant for language. It compares and fits in new information by way of associative and symbolic ordering. It knows no negatives and has no sense of time. It can be compared to what has been called *un*-consciousness. Western society does not know very much about the way it works, but those who are interested are referred to the work of Carl Jung.

As Temoshok notes, 'representation at the level of appositional consciousness involves the encoding of a gestalt, a patterning of stimuli that includes a distinctive perceptual quality of the particular emotional state associated with that pattern'.[4]

The *propositional* consciousness processes information by way of syntax, semantics, and mathematical logic. It is probably located in the left cerebral hemisphere (dominant for language) and is self-reflexive and verbal.

An identity image is first of all formed by certain individual characteristics of the four subsystems, but the core is represented in the appositional and propositional consciousness. From now on these two structures will be called 'emotional gestalt' and 'cognitive structure', respectively. Information leading to the formation of a homosexual identity might include: social and cultural messages, genetic information, experience in adult life, information from prenatal hormones, and so on. All this information leads up to the two basic structures: the emotionally loaded gestalt and the cognitive structure. Both structures interact and are to a certain extent protected from change by a phenomenon we might call 'cognitive and emotional dissonance'. That is, incoming information contradictory to the already established self-image will be transformed into information that does fit. Repression is one of the protective devices. It splits information into content (remaining in the propositional area) and meaning (which is repressed or sent back to the appositional area). It is clear that the brain will go to great lengths to protect identity images from fundamental change. It also seems clear that the emotional gestalt is more difficult to change than the cognitive structure.

A homosexual self-image is no different from other identity structures. Once formed, it becomes important for the homeostasis of the total personality, and it becomes resistant to change.

At this point I would like to postulate that, as far as homosexual identity is concerned, the formation of an emotional gestalt seems to precede in many cases the formation of the corresponding cognitive structure. This would explain why so many gay men report feelings of being different at a very early age or report a strong emotional reaction to the first confrontation with the word 'homosexual'. (As many of my clients say, 'I immediately felt this word and its definition had something to do with me'.)

One might say that many men and women who call themselves homosexual have formed a homosexual identity, with both appositional and propositional qualities. This part of their personalities is best described by essentialism. To date constructionism appears to remain in most cases a cognitive system that can and sometimes does challenge the cognitive structure, but which fails to change the emotional gestalt and thus the total identity image in large groups of people.

Keeping our model of identity formation in mind, we will now move on to a critical discussion of essentialism and constructionism.

A CRITICAL LOOK AT ESSENTIALISM AND CONSTRUCTIONISM

It is quite obvious that essentialism has been widely accepted and used by most psychotherapists and counsellors in the Western world. Even those who still see homosexuality as an illness that can and must be cured underline the important role of sexual identity in the formation of a self-image.

Essentialism has also greatly influenced (if not *made possible*) the gay liberation movement. Indeed many gay men and women themselves have stressed that the formation of a positive homosexual identity is important in the struggle for equal rights in and acceptance by society. In terms of our model: homosexual men receive an increasing amount of information that reinforces the appositional and propositional representations of homosexuality.

Let's look at essentialism more closely, because it has been pretty successful lately. This theory seems to have some considerable weaknesses, of which I will mention a few I consider important.

First, it seems extremely difficult to define 'a homosexual'. Research done by Kinsey[5] showed that heterosexuality and homosexuality are not separate categories, but that a continuum exists between the two extremes. Other clinical and scientific findings force essentialists to adopt additional categories, such as 'latent homosexuality', 'situational homosexuality', or 'egodystonic homosexuality'.[6]

Moses and Hawkins even resort to using six dimensions to evaluate the extent of homosexual orientation.[7] Essentialism seems to offer a procrustean bed, a bed which is too small. Individual images and structures labelled as homosexual seem to have, in reality, a broad range of different contents.

In the second place, essentialism does not explain cross-cultural differences in homosexual role and behaviour. These clearly do exist.

Thirdly, it has never been able to find a clear-cut aetiology for homosexuality. It gives no satisfying answer to the question of why some people *do* change their sexual identity in the course of their lives.

Finally, the essentialist theory is said to be repressive and limiting. It would force people into sexual categories that do not correspond to the desires and needs they might originally have.

Constructionism does seem to have answers to the questions and remarks made above. Nonetheless, it has its own weaknesses.

In the first place, it fails to account for the way many gay men feel (and deeply so) about their homosexuality. Most of my clients, for example, say they already felt 'different' before they ever heard of the word homosexual. This is also true for men who did not show any signs of cross-gender behaviour as a boy. As has been said before, many men report having had a strong emotional reaction when first confronted with the word 'homosexual'.

Secondly, there is the question of identity change. Most homosexuals have been very resistant to change – overwhelming pressure from the outside world and efforts of priests, therapists, etc., notwithstanding.

Finally, constructionism seems to have a threatening ring to it, perhaps because it disturbs the emotional gestalt of homosexuality I mentioned earlier. Many people fear constructionism will be applied to homosexuality only, leaving the construct of *heterosexuality* unchallenged. In this way it could take away the long-fought-for security a supportive gay subculture provides. Theoretically, it could also lead to a revival of therapies aimed at changing sexual preference, thereby threatening the self-image many gays have built up with pride.

It is quite clear that both constructionism and essentialism have some strong and some weak points. Both theories have not been proven in a scientific way and they probably never will be. At this moment in time it would probably be best to interpret both theoretical systems as two different ways of asking questions about homosexuality, without becoming dogmatic about either one.

For psychotherapists, the core of the problem has to do with the concepts of identity and self-image. As I have explained, homosexuality is represented in the brain both as a logical system and as an emotional-symbolic system. Most gay men seem to have representational systems about homosexuality which are more or less in line with essentialism. Constructionism can certainly challenge the logical system, but does that mean that psychotherapists should encourage their gay clients to try to change the whole configuration that is called 'homosexual identity'? Let's proceed to examine this question.

PRACTICAL IMPLICATIONS FOR PSYCHOTHERAPISTS AND COUNSELLORS

Homosexual men visit a therapist because they suffer. Some want to change because of the suffering, others do not. For some a good deal of change is possible, others have to learn to accept limitations.

Many gay men suffer and seek therapy because they have not been able to form a consistent and harmonious homosexual identity. Problems arising might have to do with logical construct, with the emotional gestalt, or with both. Some may have internalized negative cultural messages about homosexuality, while others have never learned how to relate intimately to other men, possibly due to a heterosexual socialization.[8]

All of these clients, however, call themselves homosexual, because they feel sexually attracted to men and have learned this is called homosexuality. It is my view that these clients should be helped to build a positive, homosexual identity, using, besides therapeutic procedures, the existing gay community. For many gay men, such an identity is a prerequisite for survival in a society founded on heterosexuality.

Other clients, possibly in growing numbers, suffer because of the restrictions homosexuality imposes upon them. For these men, constructionism offers a logical cognitive system that might help in making the corresponding emotional gestalt more flexible. This gestalt, however, will only change if there is an emotional pressure (e.g. suffering) to change it. This may partially clarify my observation that quite a lot of people, having accepted constructionism as a sound and logical theory, continue calling themselves gay and do not make any corresponding changes in their lifestyles.

As regards the feeling of emotional pressures, it is the client who is the expert, and therapists must try and follow the client's lead. I agree with John Hart, who wrote, 'I would suggest that we retain our basic belief in the privacy of the individual explanation of his or her own world. Consciousness-raising should be in our repertoire of helping strategies, but of course people will make their own choice.'[9]

I think that therapists at this time and in this culture need a theory of homosexuality that is a synthesis of essentialism and constructionism. Roughly, *my* synthesis would be as follows. Sexuality and friendships between men have historically taken on many forms in different cultures. The form most common in Western society (i.e. homosexual identities) has many positive sides, like the advent of a gay liberation movement, gay lifestyles as positive identification models, the existence of a subculture, and a homosexual discourse on homosexuality. The history and sociology of homosexuality can also make us aware of the restrictions such a construct can impose on an individual and on society at large. This awareness can and should change some aspects of therapeutic practice. It might be important to add that this is not only so for therapeutic work with gay men, who often have done a lot of thinking and feeling about their sexual preference. It seems to me that the 'constructionist message' is much more important for those who have never questioned their sexual feelings at all, as is the case with many heterosexuals.

In another publication[10] I have elaborated on some of the practical consequences constructionism has had for my work with gay clients, and I would like to repeat them here.

1. I take more time to explore what clients mean when they talk

about homosexuality, because I am no longer sure we mean the same thing with the same word. I try to get an idea of the cognitive structure and the emotional counterpart that form, for that client, his homosexual identity. Once again I would like to stress that quite many gay men have, at some point in their lives, also explored their sexual feelings towards women, and most of my clients find it quite easy to discuss sexuality beyond the strict homo-hetero dichotomy.

2. The acceptance and self-appreciation process that many gay men go through when they discover their feelings towards other men should be seen as continuous. Once a homosexual identity is established, it can be useful for some clients to explore the possibilities and limitations of such a label. They can subsequently decide if they want to challenge these limitations or just accept them.

3. In group therapy with homosexual men, I focus more on the different ways one can express homosexuality, sometimes using examples from other cultures. I always find it important to challenge notions that begin with 'all gays are...', and for some clients it is important to focus more on the non-sexual aspects of relationships with other men.

4. Transference can and should be used for psychodynamic interpretations. I additionally find that transference feelings, both in individual and group therapy, can be used as examples for the large variety of feelings that are possible between men.

The central theme of these practical consequences is that I try to incorporate some of the constructionist ways of asking questions about (homo)sexuality, without losing contact with the way my clients and I myself see and interpret reality.

CONCLUSION

To conclude, I would like to stress one more point. Constructionism has made us aware of the tremendous impact that the discourse on sexuality has had on our personalities and on those of our clients. It is therefore very important that homosexuals themselves are becoming more and more involved in the present discourse on homosexuality. If, however, heterosexuals indeed continue to avoid asking questions about their own sexuality, constructionism might easily become a boomerang that can turn against us. The first and most important oppression that is felt by men who feel the desire to engage in sexual and intimate relationships with other men emanates from the almost universal norm of heterosexuality, and not from the construct of homosexuality itself.

NOTES

1   P.H. Mussen, J.J. Conger, and J. Kagan, *Child Development and Personality*. New York: Harper & Row, 1969.

2   A.E. Moses and Robert O. Hawkins, Jr., *Counseling lesbian women and gay men*. St. Louis: C.V. Mosby, 1982.

3   Lydia Temoshok, 'Emotion, Adaptation, and Disease: A Multidimensional Theory'. In *Emotions in Health and Illness. Theoretical and Research Foundation*. New York: Grune & Stratton, 1983.

4   *Ibid.*

5   Allen P. Bell and Martin S. Weinberg, *Homosexualities. A Study of Diversity among Men and Women*. New York: Simon & Schuster, 1978.

6   Mary McIntosh, 'The Homosexual Role'. *Social Problems* 16 (1968) pp. 182-91. Reprinted in Kenneth Plummer (ed.), *The Making of the Modern Homosexual*. London: Hutchinson, 1981.

7   Moses and Hawkins, *op.cit.*

8   Jan Schippers and Mart van Werkhoven, 'Homoseksualiteit en hulpverlening'. *Handboek seksuele hulpverlening*, 5 June 1984.

9   John Hart and Diane Richardson (eds.), *The Theory and Practice of Homosexuality*. London: Routledge & Kegan Paul, 1981, p. 65.

10 Jan Schippers, *De identiteit van de categoriale hulpverlening. De verhouding tussen essentialisme en constructivisme.* (forthcoming)

figure I

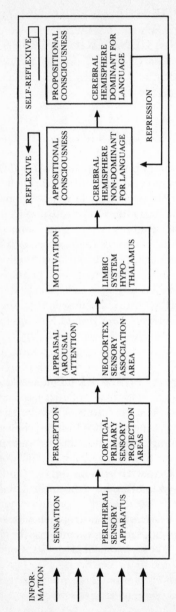

INFORMATIONAL PATHWAY

GENDER AND THE HOMOSEXUAL ROLE IN MODERN WESTERN CULTURE: THE 18th AND 19th CENTURIES COMPARED

Randolph Trumbach

FINDING THE RIGHT MODEL

In the last ten years the history of homosexual behaviour has become established as one of the new and vital branches of social history. But because it has often been written as the history of a despised minority, it has been less accepted by historians in general than have the histories of the family, women, and the poor. The fact than the history of homosexual behaviour has been so heavily tied to the history of apparently powerless minorities, has not, however, necessarily helped the field to achieve conceptual clarity. The connection has probably held back the making of those linkages between homosexual behaviour and the histories of the family and of gender for which most historians in the field have called. The conceptualization of this history as minority history has also caused historians to apply anachronistic analogies.[1]

Historians have used three different kinds of analogies drawn from the social sciences to help them organize the fragmentary information that survives on the history of homosexual behaviour. The first analogy has been drawn from psychology and its distinctions of 'the homosexual' and 'the heterosexual'. The second analogy has come from the sociological study of gay life, and the key terms in this case are subculture, role, and identity. The third analogy has been taken from the anthropologists, and it distinguishes between societies that organize homosexual behaviour around differences in age and those that have an adult male transvestite role. The psychological model is the oldest, but it is decreasingly used. The sociological model is the one that has most frequently been used in the new work of the last ten years. The anthropological model has barely begun to be used. There is a major difficulty, however, in using the psychological and the sociological models to study homosexual behaviour in any society other than that of the modern Western world. They are both deeply tied to the transformation in homosexual behaviour that accompanied the emergence of modern Western culture after 1700. The psychological model brings the heaviest freight of misleading judgements. The sociological model has been heavily used, but it is peculiarly misleading when applied to European culture before 1700; and it therefore obscures the nature of the changes in homosexual behaviour after 1700. The anthropological model in fact holds the greatest promise. But this can be difficult to see since its presumptions in some ways go against the grain of the Gay Liberation movement, out of which much of the most vital work of the last ten years has come.

It is very important, however, to be able to characterize the differences in homosexual behaviour before and after 1700 since that year may conveniently stand for the beginnings of modern Western culture. And it is only after that year that the use of the model of the gay minority, with its subculture and its roles, becomes appropriate in the study of Western societies. It is the insistent argument of this paper, however, that the minority model was fully established by 1750, at least in northwestern Europe, that is, in the Netherlands, France, and England.[2] But I mean to controvert the excessive importance that has been attached to the late-19th-century discourse on homosexuality, especially as it applied to the homosexual behaviour of men. For women, on the other hand, it is probable that the late-19th-century discourse did signalize the beginning of the formation of a new gender role for those who engaged in homosexual behaviour; and as a result there was by the late 1920s a recognized lesbian role, as there has been for men a new sodomite's role by the 1750s. The transition between Western homosexual behaviour before and after 1700 would be much easier to understand if we possessed an adequate model of cultural variations in homosexual behaviour that to some degree matched at least the density of the existing sociological and psychological models. But the anthropologists who are best situated to construct such a model have, till very recently, either ignored homosexual behaviour, or viewed it either in the light of the Western folk model of contemptuous dismissal that emerged around 1700, or in the light of the high cultural model of minority perversion that has developed since 1880. They have at least not gone looking for gay subcultures among the New Guinea tribes, although Frederick Whitam seems to be on the verge of doing just that.[3] But a historian is able to construct for himself from anthropological materials a model of cultural variations. I tried to do this myself, ten years ago, without seeing the full significance of what I had found as means to explain the shift in Western homosexual behaviour around 1700.[4] I have, however, had the satisfaction of having the organizational differences that I had observed confirmed by the anthropologists themselves; though, I must also say, they have sometimes used my work without the acknowledgment of priority usual in scholarship.[5] What I saw was as follows. Outside of Western culture, homosexual behaviour seemed to fall into one of two patterns. Adult men, who also married women, had sexual relations with males, who in some cultures were adolescent boys, and who, in others, were adult men who had permanently adopted a transvestite role situated somewhere between the other two genders. But the active adult male partner in these acts maintained his dominant gender status; adolescent boys left behind their passivity at manhood; and only the transvestite male undertook a permanent new gender role as a result of his sexual conduct. The passive male, according to the culture, might play the role of wife, concubine, lover, or prostitute. It seemed to me, in 1977, that neither of these patterns was discoverable in Western culture since the 12th century. Instead, drawing on the sociological model, I read the evidence to show a permanent pattern of effeminate males who met each other in illicit urban subcultures.

I was wrong on two counts. First, it is now clear that Western homosexual behaviour has always operated within the terms of the two worldwide patterns. And second, while it is the case that homosexual behaviour in the West was never legitimated, and therefore was always enacted within an illicit subculture, both before and after 1700, it can also be shown that the appearance of the adult effeminate male as the dominant actor in the subculture occured only after 1700.

In short, the matter can now be restated as follows. Around the year 1100, a distinctive Western European culture began to emerge. It produced its own pattern of family structures, sexual behaviour, and gender roles. Patrilineal ties were grafted on to existing kindreds. Marriage was late and monogamous, and divorce was forbidden. Many in the general population never married, and priestly celibacy began to be enforced. Sexual relations outside marriage were forbidden but tolerated in the form of regulated prostitution. But all sexual acts which were not procreative were viewed as sinful, whether they were solitary, between men and women, between persons of the same gender, or between men and beasts. Nonetheless, homosexual acts between males occurred. They were usually between an active adult male and a passive adolescent. In most cases, the adult male also had sexual relations with women. Some men openly declared their equal attraction to boys and girls. The adolescent boy, provided that he switched to an active role as manhood came on, did not suffer any loss of gender status. The only males who suffered in their status as a consequence of these acts were the very small group of men who took the passive role as well as the active, and were consequently sometimes stigmatized as hermaphrodites. Adult sodomites who took the active role probably actually increased their standing as dominant males. Their behaviour was nonetheless illegal, since it occurred outside of marriage. They could therefore most easily find their partners in the anonymity of the urban subcultures.

These subcultures were most developed in Italy, where urbanization was most advanced. The same was true of the world of female prostitution. The urban libertine might go equally to boys and whores. Aquinas himself noticed the equivalence when he said that if prostitution were not allowed, the world would be overrun with sodomy. Italy probably had the highest percentage of males who were sodomites: Michael Rocke estimates that one in ten boys in 15th-century Florence was arrested for sodomy.[6] But even in the more rural European north, as in the North American colonies, men could be found into the early 18th century who married women and had as well a career of seducing the local boys, without any risk to their status as dominant males. It is, in fact, a pattern that survived in English working-class culture well into the 20th century. One of John Marshall's respondents in the 1970s recalled that 'opinion generally was that homosexuality consisted of older men taking younger boys as female substitutes. When a man seduced a youth I don't think people regarded it as a homosexual act. It was a homosexual situation satisfying a heterosexual need.' Or in other words, the respondent justified the survival of one of the customs of old Europe before modernization, in the terms that the late 19th century had developed to describe, in the language of high culture, the new sodomite's role that had first appeared around 1700.[7]

The sodomite of the traditional European culture which existed between the 12th and the 17th centuries had been a man who had sex with boys and with women. Around 1700, with the emergence of modern Western culture, homosexual behaviour came to be defined around the role of the other worldwide pattern of the transvestite male. This is, in some ways, a difficult thing to say. Some anthropologists have already begun to deny that there is any similarity between the modern gay man and the transvestite male of many traditional cultures. The push in the Gay Liberation movement for social respectability has in some ways made it as difficult to talk about effeminacy as it is to talk about sex between men and boys. There is a desire to make the modern homosexual role *sui generis*, no matter at what point in time after 1700 one claims that it appeared.

Nonetheless, I would propose that the most salient characteristic of the homosexual role from about 1700 to the present day has been the presumption that all men who engage in sexual relations with other men are effeminate members of a third or intermediate gender, who surrender their rights to be treated as dominant males, and are exposed instead to a merited contempt as a species of male whore. This differs from the European pattern before 1700 in two important respects. After 1700, it seems to make little difference whether a man takes the active or the passive role, or whether his partner is an adult male or a boy – any sexual desire by one male for another leads to categorization as an effeminate sodomite. The second difference is that adolescent boys are no longer allowed a period of sexual passivity. The seduction of adolescents by effeminate sodomites, whatever the roles played in the sexual act, therefore becomes very dangerous to both the boy and the sodomite.[8] The European sodomite after 1700 also does differ significantly from the transvestite of non-European societies, since the transvestite is able to seek legitimate active partners among the general male population. But the sodomite and the transvestite do not differ (despite some claims to the contrary) in the degree to which they become women. In both cases some behaviour, but not all behaviour, from the other two genders is combined to form a third gender role. The North American berdache was described in Indian languages as he who was 'not-man, not-woman'. The European sodomite was described in the English sources of the early 18th century as a 'he-whore'; and Proust in the early 20th century still spoke of the 'homme-femme'.[9]

Why did the new role appear around 1700? Probably for reasons very similar to those that had led to the emergence of the old role six hundred years before. The modern Western culture, in which we still live, had begun to emerge around 1700, and with it came a distinctive pattern of family structures, sexual behaviour and gender roles. The early 18th century saw what I have called the rise of the egalitarian family, and what Lawrence Stone has described as affective individualism and the companionate marriage.[10] I think that what we are both describing is the beginning of a major cultural shift, which is still far from complete, in which a patriarchal morality that allowed adult men to own and dominate their wives, children, servants and slaves, was gradually challenged and partially replaced by an egalitarian morality which proposed that all men were created equal, that slavery must therefore be abolished, democracy achieved, women made equal with men, and children with their parents.

The older morality of patriarchy had produced both of the worldwide patterns of male homosexual behaviour: the adult male had remained dominant with the women, the boys, and the transvestite males with whom he had taken the active sexual role. But some traditional societies, while remaining within the bounds of patriarchy, had allowed a relatively greater degree of equality between men and women than had others. The variations had usually grown out of the differences in kinship structures and economies. These variations, in turn, probably explain why in some societies men had sex with boys, but in others with transvestites. It is likely that adult gender roles were more pronouncedly different in those societies where men had boys, since in these societies no adult man could ever be legitimately passive. But in societies with less differentiation between adult men and women, some males were allowed to be passive and transvestite. Walter Williams had suggested therefore that the transvestite male served as a bridge to join the other two genders.[11] But it seems more likely to me that the transvestite was a wall that guaranteed the permanent, lifelong separation of the majority of men and women, in societies where their relative equality must have been a perpetual danger to patriarchy. A minority of adult males were allowed to be passive, but the overwhelming majority of males can never have had the experience of being sexually submissive in their boyhood. The transvestite was the dike that held back the flood of a true equality between men and women, where both genders would experience power and submission in equal degrees. All women in societies with transvestites experienced sexual domination all their lives, but only the transvestite minority of males ever did so.

If this analysis of the role of the transvestite is correct, it will explain why in modern Western culture the effeminate sodomite and the rise of the egalitarian family came together at the same moment after 1700. The degree of equality between men and women, and parents and children, that resulted from companionate marriage and a closer attachment to one's children, raised profound anxiety in both men and women. The anxiety resulted in a compromise with full equality that historians have called domesticity. Men and women were equal, but they were supposed to live in separate spheres, he dominant in the economy, she in the home. Women were no longer supposed to have bodies which were inferior copies of men's; instead, as Thomas Laqueur has shown, their bodies were now seen to be biologically different[12]; and of course, on those differences could be founded supposedly inescapable differences in gender role, despite the morality of equality.

It was in this context that the effeminate sodomite played his role. In other societies, similar roles maintained differences between men and women in the face of relative equality. But the moral demand of modern society with regard to equality is absolute, and therefore the separation of the sexes, if it was to lessen anxiety, had to be stronger. Consequently, it was now supposed that only the effeminate sodomite felt desire for men. The majority of males were thought to feel no kind of desire toward other males, in contrast to traditional societies where they desired to take the active sexual role with transvestites. Men now were guaranteed to live, in still another way, in a sphere completely separated by biological nature from women. In the majority of human beings, only women desired men. The condition of the effeminate sodomite demonstrated that most men did not. But it was not until the late 19th century that women were drawn fully into this world where individuals did not sexually desire persons of their own gender.

In the remainder of this paper, I would like to ask why this was so. But I would also like to precede that question with a more detailed consideration of the transition from the old to the new model of sodomy between men, by looking at the two most modernizing societies of that day, namely the Netherlands and England, drawing on the work of Noordam for one, and on my own work for the other. Then in conclusion, I will try to show the sorts of difficulties that can arise when analogies drawn from the modern homosexual role are used to bind together the fragmentary evidence for homosexual behaviour in Europe between the 12th and the 17th centuries.

THE NEW MODEL SODOMY AFTER 1700

First, then, the old sodomite versus the new in England. In the late 17th century the sodomite was the most outrageous sort of rake, and in a real sense the most daringly masculine of men. He was not at all effeminate. It was the fop, instead, with his elaborate clothes, his soft ways, and his preference for the social company of women, who was called effeminate. (Simon Shepherd's paper on tailors makes a similar point.[13]) But though effeminate, the fop sexually desired women; what he would not have had the nerve to do was to have a boy also. The rake preferred masculine company with its drinking, brawling and foul language. The rake was eager for sexual experimentation: anything from anal intercourse with a whore to defecation in her mouth. But the most outrageous act of all was sodomy with a smooth-faced apprentice boy. Men of this kind were even likely to be atheist in religion (in the 17th-century sense) as well as republicans in politics. Still they could be affectionate with their boys, kissing them, and calling them Ganymede and Hephaestion.

In the late 1680s, the beginnings of the new relationship between men and women produced the new figure of the beau, who combined the dash of the rake with the softness of the fop. The beau, like the rake, pursued boys as well as women. In the 1690s the unchecked spread of venereal disease among London's prostitutes led the wives of that city to demand more thorough policing, but it also led men to seduce young girls and adolescent boys in an unprecedented way, since they were thought not to be infected, and it was even supposed that sex with a virgin would cure one's own venereal disease. Beaus, some with friends in high places, were arrested for sodomy. And in the public mind, effeminacy in dress began to be associated with sodomy between males.

But it was a series of arrests in 1707 and 1709 that suddenly revealed the existence of the new style sodomite, whose role must have been in formation during the previous decade. By the end of the 1720s it had quite displaced the old-style sodomite who had had sex with boys and women. The new effeminate sodomite was labeled a 'he-whore', when whore referred primarily to a married woman who was unfaithful to her husband. They called themselves mollies, which was a term first applied to female prostitutes. The sodomite was now no longer a rake but a species of outcast woman of the lowest standing. In the relative privacy of their clubs they enacted their status. Some took the masculine role and some the feminine. They kissed each other and danced together, as men did with whores. They addressed each other as women, and every man took a woman's name. They sometimes dressed as women. They went through marriage ceremonies with bridesmaids. But more often they simply called their partners husbands, and when they went into a back room to have sex, they said they had gone into the chapel to be married. When they came out, they enacted the role of women in labour and gave birth to wooden dolls. The occasional molly (who was usually involved in male prostitution) passed most of his time in women's clothes, and like the Princess Seraphina was referred to by all his acquaintances, both men and women, as 'she' and 'her'. But even the Princess sometimes wore men's clothes and sometimes took the active role in sex. The new role was a combination of male and female patterns of behaviour.[14]

Noordam has shown a similar pattern of development during the 17th and 18th centuries in the Dutch Republic. Between 1600 and 1690 there were few persecutions for sodomy, but most cases involved the seduction or rape of an adolescent boy by an older, married man. In the second stage, from 1690 to 1725, there appeared a subculture with a new kind of sodomite who was effeminate in speech and manner, took women's names, and sometimes dressed in women's clothes. But many of these men were also married to women. After 1780, however, increasing numbers of men appeared who declared that they were interested only in men and that they had been born that way.[15]

By 1750 then, in England, in Holland, and in France (as Michel Rey has shown[16]), men who had sex with men had usually conformed to the new role of the effeminate sodomite. And 1750 is also significantly the date by which a considerable part of the European elite had come to accept the ideals of the new domesticated family. But in 1750 there was for women who sexually desired women not yet any role parallel to the new role for male sodomites. Instead, women were presumed to be capable of having sex both with men and with women. They were sinful if they did the latter, but a woman did not lose her gender status for having had sex with a woman. That occurred only if she was one of those few women who dressed as a man, married a woman, and used an articial penis made of rags or leather. The system at mid-century is neatly demonstrated in two works of John Cleland's. In *Fanny Hill*, he sympathetically presented a female prostitute who also had sex with women, and roundly condemned the effeminate male sodomite. But when he published the translation of an Italian case of a cross-dressing woman who married women and used an artificial penis, he condemned her as harshly as he had the effeminate sodomite. Cleland's attitude towards sex between woman was an old one; and it was, as Lillian Faderman's evidence can show, part of a European tradition that went back at least to the 16th century.[17]

Between 1750 and 1880 this attitude towards female homosexual behaviour was modified significantly, without yet producing anything like a lesbian role. There was first a general change with regard to women's sexuality. Before the 18th century, women, as irrational creatures, has been seen as extremely vulnerable to sexual passion. But the role of women in the domesticated family tended to present them as faithful wives and mothers who did not feel passion. This change is sometimes viewed as something men did to women, but it is as useful to see it as a situation created by women to permit themselves to disregard the sexual demands of men. In any case, the doctrine of passionlessness changed the public perception of erotic friendship between women. Women in the early 19th century, as Carroll Smith-Rosenberg has notably shown, could kiss and cuddle, sleep together, and make passionate declarations to each other without arousing the disapproval that such behaviour between a man and a woman, or between two men, would have brought on. One or both of the women in these affairs usually married, since economic independence for women was impossible. But after 1850, when opportunities for women to have careers increased, passionate friendships could lead to lifelong domestic commitments between two women, or Boston marriages as they were called in New England. And this, it has been argued, led to an increasingly negative judgement of female friendships, especially after 1880.[18]

For many historians, the late-19th-century medical psychologists at this point became the villains in the story. But the psychologists have been presented as the oppressors of men as well. It is the psychologists who forged the homosexual role and eventually promoted the distinction between the heterosexual and the homosexual: they constructed thereby the foundations of the oppression of the gay male in the contemporary world. These psychologists also entered the Edenic world of female friendship and labelled it perverted and lesbian. It all makes for a splendid melodrama but is somewhat unconvincing history.

The question of the male homosexual role is the one more easily disposed of. It has been well described in the pioneering work of Jeffrey Weeks on England, and more recently by Gert Hekma for the Netherlands.[19] The doctors, however, were not creating the behaviour they observed and tried to describe in the categories of their science. The behaviour of sodomitical men in their sub-

culture existed independently in a complexity (as George Chauncey has shown[20]) that the doctors never fully observed or described. Effeminate sodomitical behaviour was the consequence
of a social role that modern society had created two hundred
years before the doctors attempted to describe it. It is also the case
that many homosexual men (as perhaps we may now call them)
since the middle of the 19th century had been looking for a
language that was not the language of the gutter, in which to
describe their experience. Walt Whitman tried to use the
doctrine of adhesiveness which he found in phrenology. But as
late as 1891 Symonds still complained that 'the accomplished
languages of Europe in the 19th century supply no terms for this
persistent feature of human psychology without importing some
implication of disgust, disgrace, vituperation.'[21] What of course
was needed was a social rather than a psychological description,
but late-19th-century psychology with its biological bias could
hardly encompass that. The consequence was that homosexual
men themselves, after observing the behaviour of their fellows,
produced a biological theory of an intermediate sex, rather than
a social analysis of the function of a third gender role in modern
society. The ban on the polite discussion of male sodomites had
nonetheless been broken. And the long process of justifying their
gender role had begun. This is a point wonderfully confirmed by
Frederic Silverstolpe's paper for the conference.[22]

   The question of the lesbian role is harder to analyze. It is as
unlikely that the doctors *created* the behaviour they described in
women as that they had done so with homosexual men. But in
the case of men, they were describing behaviour that had existed
in folk culture for nearly two hundred years; whereas with women
they seem to have been describing the new form of erotic attraction between women which was eventually labelled lesbianism.
Their descriptions centred especially on the role of transvestism
in the case of the more masculine of the two women in a couple.
For two women to conceptualize their love affair as a relationship
between a man and a woman (or between a mother and a daughter), was not in itself new: Smith-Rosenberg showed this occur-
ring in the platonic relations between the women of the early 19th
century. But female transvestism had traditionally been used to
allow a woman to pass safely in an all male world like the army

or the navy, which would otherwise have been dangerous to her. Or it had been used to attract men, as actresses had done when they took male roles on stage. Female transvestism had not been used to attract other women, not even (as Faderman points out) by those women who had married women. But now transvestism, as well as other masculine mannerisms, were being used by one woman to attract another, when neither woman desired a relationship with a man. It looks very much as though a lesbian role for women had emerged by 1900, and that it paralleled the effe minate sodomite role for men that had appeared as long ago as 1700.[23]

It is very likely that the new role among women is, like the male role, to be explained in terms of the effect of equality on the structure of the family and on gender roles. It meant, first of all, that the majority of women were now likely to conceive of themselves as incapable of desiring women, just as most men since the late 18th century has come to consider themselves as incapable of desiring men. The equality of men and women had now progressed to the point where psychosexual development in the individual was thought to be relatively the same in men and in women, even though women were still to be subjected to the indignities of theories of penis envy and all the rest. But the theory of the asexual woman was now discarded. Female friendship therefore became suspect. But as Martha Vicinus has said, it was a step in discarding the doctrine of separate spheres.[24] Separate worlds have, after all, never been equal worlds, whether the segregation is structured by gender or by race. It is still the case, however, that the extension of the homosexual taboo to women guaranteed a difference in experience between men and women which was conceived of as founded in biology and not in social mores. Human biology was now supposed to be so structured that the majority of persons did not know what it was like to desire persons of the same gender. And this belief was guaranteed by the outcast status of the homosexual man and the lesbian woman.

USING THE WRONG MODEL: SODOMY BEFORE 1700

Once these two deviant roles of the effeminate sodomite and the lesbian established themselves, it rapidly became impossible even for reflective and educated people to understand that their own culture had been differently organized only two generations before. By 1750 the English critic was convinced that the effeminate fop of Restoration plays (who had actually desired women) was in fact an effeminate sodomite who despised women. By 1950 the knowing American critic was also convinced that the two women in Henry James's *The Bostonians* were in fact lesbians. Historians who are trained to avoid anachronism as the crying sin of their profession ought to do better, but in this area they have not.[25] I therefore mean to conclude with a brief demonstration of the difficulties that have arisen in the last ten years when historians have tried to apply the model of homosexual behaviour that evolved in their culture between 1700 and 1900 to the materials of the earlier, traditional culture of the European middle ages and Renaissance.

Historians must use analogies whether they are analyzing anecdotal and literary evidence, or statistical series. But the analogies must be carefully chosen, and in this area they have not been. It will be useful to take up seven historians in the rough order of their periods of study: John Boswell on the 12th and 13th centuries, Guido Ruggiero and Rafael Carasco on Renaissance Venice and Valencia, Luiz Mott on 17th-century Portugal, and Jonathan Katz, B.R. Burg, and Alan Bray on 17th-century English-speaking societies.[26] All seven historians have to some degree been misled by their knowledge of the contemporary gay male urban subculture, as I confess I was in my time. It is therefore as a fellow sinner that I urge repentance.

Boswell, of course, has found a gay subculture even in ancient Rome where there was surely no need of one. But in his medieval material, while he does notice that the sexual relations were usually between men and boys, and that some of the men clearly liked girls as much as boys, he hardly makes enough of this observation, probably because of the influence of the modern model. Ruggiero documents the emergence of a subculture of sodomites over two centuries. But he presumes that the men were rather like modern homosexuals. He likewise notices that the relations were between men and boys, and that the men were more severely punished when caught. But he then comments that this was unlike the usual situation where the passive actor suffers more. His model is clearly that of the effeminate adult male. This is confirmed when he regrets that the 15th-century subculture did not emerge a century earlier, for if it had, the 14th-century hermaphrodite, Roland, would have been able to find shelter among the men rather than among the female prostitutes when he left his wife and became Rolandina.

Carasco admits that most of the acts in Valencia were between men and boys, but he then speaks of the exploitation of youth, unaware that a patriarchal society would have approved their submissiveness. He also insists that there was a homosexual ghetto because there were meeting places and signals, some adult males were effeminate, and some men preferred boys to women. But he does not consider that active men met passive boys in the subculture, and that the men who preferred boys to women only knew this because they had slept with both. The effeminate adults would have been classified as hermaphrodites, but the active adults certainly suffered no diminution in their male prestige because they had boys. Luiz Mott builds his case for a gay subculture around the presence of male transvestism. But it was adolescent boys who dressed up, for the most part, and they had sex with adult men. This was in a culture in which boys legitimately appeared on stage as women, but women were not allowed to dress as men. There were a few adult transvestites, but these would have been classified as hermaphrodites, and most acts of sodomy were between active men and passive boys.

Burg studied pirates and sodomy. His evidence was meagre and he therefore thought to flesh it out with analogies drawn from men in contemporary total institutions like prisons. But he did not consider that 17th-century men confined in a ship would have felt no gender anxiety if they desired the cabin-boy, unlike the 20th-century prisoner. Alan Bray, on the one hand, could not believe that a subculture existed when there were no exclusive homosexuals to populate it; and on the other hand, he found quite unbelievable the evidence for the libertine who went with his whore on one arm and his boy on the other. Finally, Jonathan Katz is, of all these, the historian most acutely aware of the differences between 17th-century sodomy and 19th-century homosexuality. But because he was aware that 19th-century homosexuality was inextricably bound to gender deviance, he presumed that 17th-century sodomy could have had no connection to gender. He therefore remained unaware that the rake very much used his women and his boys to confirm his gender role.

In short, I hope it is apparent that the tendency to interpret traditional Europe in the light of the behaviour of modern Europe has retarded our understanding of both societies. A theory of cultural variation based on worldwide patterns would have better served all of these historians. They would have been less likely to interpret a society that organized homosexual behaviour around differences in age as though it had been a society that did so around the creation of a third gender.

NOTES

1   John Boswell in 'Revolutions, Universals, Categories' (*Salmagundi* 58-59 (1982-83) pp. 89-113) advocated the minority model, but its use made for a number of interpretative difficulties in his *Chrisitanity, Homosexuality, and Social Tolerance* (Chicago, 1980).

2   Randolph Trumbach, 'Sodomitical Subcultures, Sodomitical Roles, and the Gender Revolution of the 18th Century: the Recent Historiography'. *Eighteenth-Century Life*, 9 n.s. 3 (1985) pp. 109-21. Reprinted in R.P. Maccubbin (ed.), *'Tis Nature's Fault. Unauthorized Sexuality during the Enlightenment*. Cambridge, 1987.

3   Frederick Whitam and Robin W. Mathy, *Male Homosexuality in Four Societies*. New York, 1986. These societies are Brazil, Guatemala, the United States, and the Philippines. The first three are Western societies; the fourth is a Christianized Asian society. It is hardly surprising that one finds in all of them the pattern of homosexual behaviour dominant in Western societies since 1700. Such evidence cannot consequently be used to speak of a universal psychological minority in human nature. But not surprisingly Richard Green tries to use Whitam to argue that his own study is not a culture-bound, psychological investigation: *The 'Sissy Boy*

Syndrome' and the Development of Homosexuality. New Haven, 1987.

4   Randolph Trumbach, 'London's Sodomites. Homosexual Behavior and Western Culture in the Eighteenth Century'. *Journal of Social History* 11 (1977) pp. 1-33.

5   It would be unduly sour to cite the particular cases. Instead I might note those anthropologists who have taken up my point because they found it useful: G. H. Herdt (ed.), *Ritualized Homosexuality in Melanesia*. Berkeley, 1984;
Charles Callender and Lee Kochems, 'Men and Not-Men. Male Gender-Mixing Statuses and Homosexuality'. In Evelyn Blackwood (ed.), *The Many Faces of Homosexuality*. New York, 1986;
Walter L. Williams, *The Spirit and the Flesh*. Boston, 1986;
S.O. Murray, *Social Theory, Homosexual Realities*. New York, 1984.

6   M.J. Rocke, '"They Have Lost All Shame": San Bernardino on Sodomites in Fifteenth-Century Florence'. *Journal of Homosexuality* 16 (1988);
Kent Gerard and Gert Hekma (eds.), *The Pursuit of Sodomy*. New York, 1989.

7   Dirk Jaap Noordam, 'Sodomy in the Dutch Republic, 1600-1725'. In Gerard and Hekma, *op.cit.*;
G.R. Quaife, *Wanton Wenches and Wayward Wives*. New Brunswick, 1979, pp. 175-77;
David Rollison, 'Property, Ideology and Popular Culture in a Gloucestershire Village, 1660-1740'. *Past and Present* 93 (1981) pp. 79-90;
Jonathan Katz, *Gay/Lesbian Almanac*. New York, 1983, pp. 111-18;
John Marshall, 'Pansies, Perverts and Macho Men: Changing Conceptions of Male Homosexuality'. In Kenneth Plummer (ed.), *The Making of the Modern Homosexual*. London, 1981, p. 136.

8   Randolph Trumbach, 'Sodomitical Assaults, Gender Role, and Sexual Development in Eighteenth-Century London'. In Gerard and Hekma, *op.cit.*

9   Callender and Kochems, *op.cit.*; Williams, *op.cit.*;
J.E. Rivers, 'The Myth and Science of Homosexuality in *A*

la recherche du temps perdu'. In George Stambolian and Elaine Marks (eds.), *Homosexualities and French Literature*. Ithaca, 1979.

10 Randolph Trumbach, *The Rise of the Egalitarian Family*. New York, 1978;
Lawrence Stone, *The Family, Sex and Marriage in England, 1500-1800*. New York, 1978.
Similar developments occurred in Holland (though Simon Schama plays them down) and France: Simon Schama, *The Embarrassment of Riches*. New York, 1987;
Cissie Fairchilds, *Domestic Enemies*. Baltimore, 1984.

11 Williams, *op.cit.*

12 Thomas Laqueur, 'Orgasm, Generation, and the Politics of Reproductive Biology'. In Catherine Gallagher and Thomas Laqueur (eds.), *The Making of the Modern Body*. Berkeley, 1987.

13 Simon Shepherd, 'What's So Funny About Ladies' Tailors'. In *Homosexuality, Which Homosexuality? Conference Papers*, History. Amsterdam: Free University and Schorer Foundation, 1987.

14 Randolph Trumbach, 'The Birth of the Queen: Sodomy and the Emergence of Gender Equality in Modern Culture, 1660-1750'. In Martin Duberman, Martha Vicinus, and George Chauncey, Jr. (eds.), *Reclaiming the Past*. New York, 1989; 'London's Sodomites', *op.cit.*; 'Sodomitical Assaults', *op.cit.* I hope to give a fuller description in my forthcoming book on the sexual life of 18th-century London.

15 Noordam, *op.cit.*; and Dirk Jaap Noordam, 'Sodomites in the Rural Areas of the Republic in the Early Modern Period'. *Homosexuality, Which Homosexuality? Conference Papers*, *op.cit.*, History. Noordam is at work on a general history of Dutch sodomy from the 14th to the 18th centuries. The authoritative work on 18th-century Amsterdam is:
Theo van der Meer, *De wesentlijke sonde van sodomie en andere Vuyligheeden, 1730-1811*. Amsterdam, 1984. An English summary appears in Gerard and Hekma, *op.cit.*, and a complete revised English edition is forthcoming.

16 Michel Rey, 'Parisian Homosexuals Create a Lifestyle, 1700-1750: the Police Archives'. *Eighteenth-Century Life* 9 n.s.

3 (1985) pp. 179-91. Reprinted in Maccubbin, *op.cit.*;

Michel Rey, 'Police et sodomie à Paris au XVIIIe siècle: du péché au désordre'. *Revue d'Histoire Moderne et Contemporaine* 29 (1982) pp. 113-24.

17 John Cleland, *Memoirs of a Woman of Pleasure*. Edited by Peter Sabor. New York, 1985, pp. 10-13.

Giovanni Bianchi, *An Historical and Physical Dissertation on the Case of Catherine Vizzani*. Translated with commentary by Cleland. London, 1751, pp. 51-63;

Lillian Faderman, *Surpassing the Love of Men. Romantic Friendships and Love Between Women from the Renaissance to the Present*. New York: William Morrow, 1981. See also: Lynne Friedli, "Passing Women": a Study of Gender Boundaries in the Eighteenth Century'. In G.S. Rousseau and Roy Porter (eds.), *Sexual Underworlds of the Enlightenment*. Manchester, 1987;

Diane Dugaw, 'Balladry's Female Warriors: Women, Warfare, and Disguise in the Eighteenth Century'. *Eighteenth-Century Life* 9 n.s. 2 (1985) pp. 1-20;

R.M. Dekker and L.C. van der Pol, *The Tradition of Female Transvestism in Early Modern Europe*. Basingstoke, 1988.

The role for women to avoid in the 18th century was that of the prostitute:

Randolph Trumbach, 'Modern Prostitution and Gender in *Fanny Hill*: Libertine and Domesticated Fantasy'. In Rousseau and Porter, *op.cit.*;

Erica-Marie Bénabou, *La prostitution et la police des moeurs au XVIIIe siècle*. Paris, 1987.

18 Nancy Cott, 'Passionlessness: an Interpretation of Victorian Sexual Ideology, 1790-1850'. *Signs* 4 (1978) pp. 219-36;

C.N. Degler, *At Odds*. New York, 1980, Ch. 7-12;

Carroll Smith-Rosenberg, *Disorderly Conduct*. New York: Oxford University Press, 1985;

Faderman, *op.cit.*

From the documentation it is apparent that by the 19th century the modern Western system of sexuality and its related gender roles were fully in force in the United States, as well as in northwestern Europe. At the end of the 18th century it is apparent, however, that Italy, and probably

most of southern and central Europe as well, had not adopted in the new system. J.W. von Archenholz noted that in
England men did not kiss each other, but that you might kiss
their wives in greeting: while in Italy the men kissed each
other but would consider it a deadly insult if you tried to kiss
their wives. (*A Picture of England*. London, 1789, Vol.2, pp.
102-04.)

19   Jeffrey Weeks, *Coming Out: Homosexual Politics in Britain from
the 19th Century to the Present*. London: Quartet, 1977;
Jeffrey Weeks, *Sex, Politics and Society. The Regulation of Sex-
uality Since 1800*. Harlow: Longman, 1981, Ch. 6;
Gert Hekma, *Homoseksualiteit, een medische reputatie*. Amster-
dam, 1987;
And for France and the United States:
Pierre Hahn (ed.), *Nos ancêtres les pervers*. Paris, 1971;
Jonathan Katz, *Gay American History*. New York, 1976;
Katz, *Gay/Lesbian Almanac, op.cit.*

20   George Chauncey, Jr., 'From Sexual Inversion to Homo-
sexuality: Medicine and the Changing Conceptualization of
Female Deviance'. *Salmagundi* 58-59 (1982-83), pp. 114-46;
George Chauncey, Jr., 'Christian Brotherhood or Sexual
Perversion? Homosexual Identities and the Construction of
Sexual Boundaries in the World War One Era'. *Journal of
Social History* 19 (1985) pp. 189-211.

21   Michael Lynch, ''Here is Adhesiveness'': from Friendship
to Homosexuality'. *Victorian Studies* 29 (1985) pp. 67-96.
J.A. Symonds, *A Problem in Modern Ethics*, 1891 (cited in
Weeks, *Coming Out, op.cit.*, p. 1). See also:
Symonds' Memoirs. Edited by Phyllis Grosskurth. Chicago,
1984; and Phyllis Grosskurth's biography of Symonds, *The
Woeful Victorian*. New York, 1964.

22   Frederic Silverstolpe, 'Benkert Was Not a Doctor. On the
Non-Medical Origins of the Homosexual Category in the
Nineteenth Century'. *Homosexuality, Which Homosexuality?
Conference Papers, op.cit.*, History.

23   Smith-Rosenberg, *op.cit.*; Faderman, *op.cit.*

24   Martha Vicinus, *Independent Women*. Chicago, 1985, pp. 158-
62, 187-210.

25 Trumbach, 'Birth of the Queen', *op.cit.*; Faderman, *op.cit.*
    pp. 190-96.
26 Boswell, *Christianity...*, *op.cit.*, especially pp. 247-50;
    Guido Ruggiero, *The Boundaries of Eros*. New York, 1985,
    Ch. 6. I comment more extensively on this work in *Journal
    of Homosexuality* 16 (1988); and in Gerard and Hekma, *op.cit.*;
    Rafael Carasco, *Inquisición y repressión sexual en Valencia. Histo-
    ria de los sodomitas (1565-1785)*. Barcelona, 1985;
    Luiz Mott, 'Portuguese Pleasures: the Gay Subculture in
    Portugal at the Time of the Inquisition'. *Homosexuality,
    Which Homosexuality? Conference Papers*, *op.cit.*, History (also
    published as 'Pogode português: a subcultura *gay* em Por-
    tugal nos tempos inquisitorias'. *Ciência e Cultura* 40 (1988) pp.
    120-39;
    Katz, *Gay/Lesbian Almanac*, *op.cit.*;
    B.R. Burg, *Sodomy and the Perception of Evil*. New York, 1983;
    Alan Bray, *Homosexuality in Renaissance England*. London:
    GMP, 1982, on which also see my comments in Trumbach,
    'Sodomitical Subcultures', *op.cit.*, pp. 116-18.

'THEY WONDER TO WHICH SEX I BELONG': THE HISTORICAL ROOTS OF THE MODERN LESBIAN IDENTITY

Martha Vicinus

In 1884, the aging French painter, Rosa Bonheur, wrote her sister from Nice where she had gone in her usual smock and trousers to sketch:

> 'It amuses me to see how puzzled the people are. They wonder to which sex I belong. The ladies especially lose themselves in conjectures about "the little old man who looks so lively". The men seem to conclude: "Oh, he's some aged singer from St. Peter's at Rome, who has turned to painting in his declining years to console himself for some misfortune." And they shake their beards triumphantly.'[1]

Bonheur's bemused description of the impact her androgynous appearance had upon the general public pinpoints many of the major difficulties historians face in reconstructing the history of the lesbian. Bonheur spent her adult life living with a woman and wearing male attire, but she used a specifically Victorian vocabulary, reveling in her gender-freedom, rather than her specific sexual identity. In describing her lifelong friendship with Nathalie Micas, Bonheur spoke appreciatively of those who understood that 'deux femmes peuvent sentir l'une pour l'autre le charme d'une amitié vive et passionée, sans que rien n'en altère la pureté'.[2] Did she or didn't she have an active sexual life with Micas? Was she or was she not a lesbian? Did she or did she not identify as a lesbian? Whom should we include and why in the history of the modern lesbian?

Lesbian history is in its initial stages, inhibited both by the suspect nature of the material and the small number of scholars willing and able to pursue half-forgotten, half-destroyed, or half-neglected sources. Nevertheless, the past ten years have seen an encouraging efflorescence of work, breaking from the old psychological paradigms and insisting upon the necessity of a historical understanding of women's same-sex sexual behavior. Like any new discipline, these studies have concentrated on issues of concern to those most deeply involved; for lesbians today the most important and controversial questions concern the origins of an individual and a group identity.

Contemporary lesbian history has been almost entirely written by lesbians, and often by women who are not trained and practicing historians. We have searched the past with an urgency that can only be felt by those who have been denied a history. Among the numerous and popular lesbian sessions at the *Berkshire Women's History Conference* in June 1987 were 'Love and Friendship in the Lesbian Bar Communities of the 1940s, 1950s and 1960s', 'The Evolution of the Contemporary Lesbian Community', and "Making History Bigger": Grassroots Lesbian Community History Projects'. Sessions on visual images and literature were also held, testifying to the continued interest in the cross-disciplinary and interdisciplinary study of lesbian life and culture. The eclecticism, enthusiasm and anger (a leaflet briefly appeared attacking the organizers for failing to provide large enough rooms for the lesbian sessions) surely demonstrated an inspiring level of commitment.

But I want to raise a problem: most of the panels seemed more concerned with finding heroines than with uncovering the often fragmentary and contradictory evidence which must make up the lesbian past. Too often the current fashion in appropriate behavior was used to judge the past. Thus, in one session those who organized the Daugthers of Bilitis and wrote for *The Ladder* in the 1950s were criticized for opposing butch/femme roles and for advocating assimilationist policies. At another session, after the alcoholism and violence of many of the working-class lesbian bars of the 1950s had been documented, this subculture was held up not only as the sole alternative for an 'out' lesbian, but also the best. At earlier history conferences, in contrast, I can remember praise lavished upon 19th-century romantic friendships as the ideal we should all strive to emulate. Now roles are in, romance is out; what will be next year's correct lesbian stance?

This modernist myopia, however satisfying for myth-makers, is ultimately condescending to the strengths *and* limitations of our foremothers. Although there is much to be admired in the pioneering studies of the past decade, the time has come for a more sophisticated history. Rather than raiding the past to find satisfactory models for today, we should look to the difficulties, contradictions, and triumphs of women within the larger context of their own times.

In a survey of the past three hundred years, I would like to trace the many roots from which the modern lesbian identity has grown. The defining of a person's prime identity through his or her sexual object choice has been an erratic and incomplete process that we still do not completely understand, and indeed, may never. Nevertheless, it is worth exploring the historical conditions that have led to this modern definition of an individual's identity. However critical I may be of past research in lesbian history, this essay is in many ways a summation of recent work.

Even as I call for a shift in the questions asked about women's same-sex relations, I too focus upon what has been seen as the single most important issue for contemporary lesbians, namely, the question of sexual identity. In 1984 the Editors of *Signs* pointed out that 'such a focus on identity may in fact limit inquiry to those cultures in which lesbian identity and survival as *lesbians* are crucial matters of concern; it may hinder cross-cultural analysis, for example, because it provides inadequate vocabulary for discussion of relationships among Third-World women.... Discussion of lesbianism in these terms has relevance only where identity and sexuality are intertwined and where personal identity is itself a cultural value.'[3] This bias in lesbian studies continues today, so that Third-World women's relationships remain stereotypically silent, mysterious and unknown. Perhaps as we gain a better understanding of the white, Euro-American past, so fully represented at the *Homosexuality, Which Homosexuality? Conference*, we will have the confidence and knowledge to move beyond our ethnocentrism. In turn, Third-World historians will bring new perspectives and new questions to bear upon the reconstruction of lesbian history.

PROBLEMS OF DEFINITION

The single most frustrating problem facing every historian of lesbianism is the historical suppression of female sexuality. All societies that I know of have denied, controlled or muted the public expression of active female sexuality. How and why they have done so, of course, varies enormously, and therein lies our particular task. We must first decode female sexual desire, and then within it, find same-sex desire. By necessity we need to be sensitive to nuance, masks, secrecy, and the unspoken. If we look to the margins, to the ruptures and breaks, we will be able to piece together a history of women speaking to each other. A closer examination of single women running their own schools, or actresses drinking after hours in male drag, or private costume parties for the initiated may reveal surprising continuities.

To date lesbian historiography has concentrated on three areas of research: 1) the retrieval and reconstruction of both lesbian couples and lesbian communities, 2) the exploration of the two major paradigmatic forms of lesbian behavior, namely, romantic friendships and butch/femme roles, and 3) the question of when the modern lesbian identity arose, and under what circumstances. Since scholars have spent so much time excavating a lost past, few cross-cultural or cross-national comparisons have yet been made. We also know all too little about the legal position of lesbians in comparison with the far richer documentation of the oppression of gay men.[4] In spite of the extensive debates about the influence of the late-19th-century sexologists, we do not yet have detailed studies of how their theories were popularized within and outside the medical profession.[5] Periodization remains an important issue. We are still woefully ignorant about women's sexual behavior before the early modern period.[6] The neglect of cross-class relationships seems inexplicable to me, except for the lack of obvious sources. If we knew more, would we find a similar idealization of the 'natural' working-class lover that characterizes so much 20th-century English gay male literature? Must we assume that women involved in romantic friendships were always and only middle class? Much still remains to be investigated.

One of the principal reasons why historians of lesbianism have had so much difficulty in defining a lesbian identity in the past is because our history is rooted in two very different kinds of female desire, both of which involve a self-conscious decision. On the one hand, we have women who passed as men, and as 'female husbands' were said to use a dildo to trick their 'wives'. These women, when discovered, were found guilty of homosexual *acts*. On the other hand, women who entered into long-term romantic friendships were presumed to be in *relationships* that involved no sex acts. Out of necessity we have coined the rather unsatisfactory word 'homoerotic' to describe the latter relationships, while reserving 'passing' or 'cross-dressing' for women who appeared by all accounts to be men. This latter definition ignores the lover of the passing woman. The 20th-century solution has been to call her a 'femme', but this hardly solves the problem for a historian.[7]

The difficulty of negotiating these two different worlds is compounded by the fact that sometime in the middle of the 19th century a third type appeared, namely the cross-dressed masculine-appearing woman whose primary emotional and probably also sexual commitment was to women – the Rosa Bonheurs, about whom society wondered to which sex they belonged. At the same time, both romantic friendships and passing women continued well into the 20th century. In 1929, for example, in the midst of the *Well of Loneliness* obscenity trial, a Colonel Barker was arrested after over a decade of passing as a World War I hero; she had been married for three years before deserting her wife.[8] Leila Rupp has documented the homoerotic relations of woman activists in the American Women's Party in the 1940s and 50s.[9] Neither sexual relations nor a self-proclaimed identity can define the history of lesbianism.[10]

None of these three well-recognized types includes a possible fourth type, the intermittent lover of women. Like the masculine partner in a gay male relation, this woman lacked a visible identity, but may have been quite common.[11] We probably have ignored this kind of woman because the little documentation we have about her is either gossip or pornography. She has sometimes been dismissed as either bisexual or as a dangerous dabbler. Alternatively, for those seeking evidence of lesbian activity in the past, she has been added to the list of heroines. George Sand dressed as a male student in order to sit in the cheap seats at the theatre, and into her forties she wore informal male dress at home. She was also for a brief period madly in love with the actress Marie Dorval. Given her reputation as a sexually free woman, rumors swirled around Sand, inviting different interpretations of her identity then and now. Her position at the center of 19th-century French Bohemia, however, is a clue to where we should look for examples of the intermittent lover of women.

If we turn to the larger historical context within which a lesbian identity may have grown, all the usual criteria used by historians to explain social change do not seem sufficient. A lesbian identity did not result from economic independence, nor from an ideology of individualism, nor from the formation of women's communities, although all these elements were important for enhancing women's personal choices. In 1981 Ann Ferguson argued that financial independence was a necessary precondition for the formation of a lesbian identity, but this does not seem to be the case.[12] We have examples from the 18th century to the present of professional and working-class women who earned their own living and lived apart from their families with women. Their lives were usually woman-centered, but this was often due more to the necessity of maintaining respectability than to overt sexual preference. Economic freedom created more choice for women, but not a new sexual identity.

The onset of the industrial revolution appears to have had little impact upon the formation of a lesbian culture, although it led to more occupational opportunities for women of all social classes. The development of a mercantile economy in 17th- and 18th-century northern Europe may have encouraged some women to think of themselves as individuals apart from their families. Both religion and politics united to emphasize the importance of the individual's soul; those women who found strength through belief to seek non-traditional roles may also have felt – and acted upon – non-traditional sexual desires.

The formation of self-conscious women's communities can be seen as a necessary precondition for a lesbian identity. But here again we find a tradition going back into the Middle Ages that yielded feminine and proto-feminist independence and bonding, but hardly anything one could recognize as a lesbian identity. During the 18th and 19th centuries women organized salons, artistic coteries, religious organizations and educational institutions, but these were not exclusively lesbian groups. Thus at every turn we seem to be baffled for an explanation of the sources of a lesbian identity. No wonder so many scholars keep returning to the late-19th-century sexologists. Did *they* define us, or did we define ourselves?

This question, or rather, the broader one about the formation of a lesbian identity, has been difficult to answer because there is no agreement about what constitutes a lesbian. The general lack of court records, which have provided gay male historians with such rich archival material, has forced women to think in broader, and consequently, vaguer terms. Following Faderman's pioneering work, *Surpassing the Love of Men. Romantic Friendships and Love Between Women form the Renaissance to the Present* (1981), some scholars have found romantic friendships to be the most characteristic form of pre-20th-century same-sex love. Blanche Wiesen Cook and Adrienne Rich have pointed to the historical suppression of homosexuality, and argued for the essential unity of all woman-identified women. Cook's definition, for example, has been influential in encouraging women to rethink the broader social and political context of their own lives and of women in the past: 'Women who love women, who choose women to nurture and support and to create a living environment in which to work creatively and independently are lesbians.'[13] This general definition neglects both the element of sexual choice and the marginal status that was (and continues to be) so important in lesbian relationships. The woman who moved in and out of relationships and commitments to women is denied a place in this 'living environment'. Moreover, the very different patterns of sexual behavior in the working class and aristocracy are neglected in favor of a middle class that closely resembles the present feminist movement.

Not surprisingly, these broad definitions of the lesbian have met with a strong response from those who have felt that scholars were in danger of draining sexuality from lesbian women's lives. In an important special issue of *Heresies* (1981), several lesbians challenged the feminist vision of an egalitarian, 'mutually orgasmic, struggle-free, trouble-free sex'. Amber Hollibaugh insisted, 'I think by focusing on roles in lesbian relationships, we can begin

to unravel who we really are in bed. When you hide how profoundly roles can shape your sexuality, you can use that as an
example of other things that get hidden.'[14] In the same issue Joan
Nestle proclaimed, 'Butch/fem was [in the 1950s] an erotic partnership, serving as a conspicuous flag of rebellion and as an intimate exploration of women's sexuality.'[15] However valuable this
position has been in the political debates of the present, it has
sometimes served to limit the exploration of the past. Depending
as it does upon self-definition and active sexuality, it can become
insensitive to the very different lives of women in the past. How
are we ever to know definitively what someone born a hundred
or two hundred years ago did in bed? And as Cook had pointed
out, does it really matter so much?[16]

It may be easier if we avoid the psychological and sociological
labels of 'identity' and 'self', and return instead to the language
of the past. Our foremothers and forefathers appear to have had
a very clear sense of what we would call lesbian desire, but they
interpreted it rather differently from us. Their vocabulary,
drawn from the classical world, emphasized homosexual acts
rather than a lifelong identity. The Greek word *'tribade'* appears
only in the 16th and early 17th centuries in France and England.
Even then, only educated men used it. Far more common was
'hermaphrodite', but it was applied to both men and women, and
it too was largely used by the educated. *Sapphic*, the word used
most frequently in memoirs, does not even merit a sexual definition in the Oxford English Dictionary.[17] What is most striking,
however, is the lack of popular slang, in comparison with male
homosexuality, until the 20th century.[18] Female soldiers and
sailors, well known among the common people, appear to have
been categorized simply as curiosities.

In the late 17th and 18th centuries, when the traditional hierarchies of social order, private and public, were giving way to
ideas of individualism and egalitarianism, lesbian desire appears
to have been defined in three dominant ways, closely linked to
the social class of the women concerned. This correlation
between class, public appearance and sexual behavior suggests
an effort to categorize women's deviant sexual behavior in a
satisfactory manner that did not threaten the dominant heterosexual and social paradigms of the age.

At the risk of oversimplification, the most familiar model was drawn from the folklore of the people, in which a woman cross-dressed as a man. Virtually all of the examples of passing women that have survived (and many women must have died with their true identity unknown) are of working-class and peasant women who sought more job opportunities, better pay and greater freedom.[19] Contemporaries often reinterpreted this behavior to suit a more personal, even romantic, explanation. Many accounts of 'female warriors' or 'sailors' survive; 18th-century broadside ballads praised the brave woman who went into battle in order to find her beloved. Most versions excited the listener with the possibility of sexual transgression, but resolved matters in the final verse with a happy marriage or other appropriate female destiny.[20] Alternatively, the cross-dressed woman was an eccentric and flamboyant character. Wandering actresses, or even less reputable vagrants, made up most of this group. The most famous example was Charlotte Charke, whose 1746 memoirs robustly declared on the title page, 'Her Adventures in Mens Cloaths, going by the Name of Mr. *Brown*, and being belov'd by a Lady of great Fortune, who intended to marry her'.[21] However, she cast her autobiography in terms of a theatrical comedy, so as to mitigate the dangerous implications of her actions.

Rudolph Dekker and Lotte van der Pol have argued that in Holland women who dressed as men did so because they could conceive of love for another woman only in terms of the existing heterosexual paradigm. If this was so, the highly risky marriages that so many cross-dressed women undertook make sense, for they were 'the logical consequence of, on the one hand, the absence of a social role for lesbians and the existence of, on the other hand, a tradition of women in men's clothing.'[22] I find this interpretation to be convincing, especially since we have corroborating evidence from the 19th century. Nevertheless, most of our examples of cross-dressed women include too little personal information to generalize with confidence about the many and complicated psychosocial reasons why a woman might cross-dress in the past. Their reasons, in most cases, appear to have been for the freedom and advantages male clothing insured.

The second category of publicly-identified lesbian desire is what I would label 'porn and politics', that is, the many attacks on powerful women who could be seen as endangering the normal political hierarchies through their undue influence upon a ruler. It is here that we find much of our evidence for the intermittent lover of women. The connection between sexual deviance and political deviance is hardly unique to women; indeed, the libertine libertarian John Wilkes (1727-97) was the subject of an intense pamphlet war linking him with excessive freedoms of all sorts.[23] The most famous example of this kind of political linkage is Marie Antoinette, who was repeatedly accused of political intrigue and bisexual debauchery.[24] Although her female lovers were of her own social class, she was accused of taking on male lovers from the lower classes. The major difficulty in interpreting much of this material is that it was obviously generated by those with a particular political ax to grind. Moreover, it has close links with the long-standing tradition of male pornographic fantasies; indeed, in several cases Marie Antoinette was woven into pornographic plots with little consideration of historical facts. I believe that we should not dismiss this material, for such culturally influential male fantasies, derived from both pornography and high art, had a lasting impact upon the public image of the lesbian.

The third, and increasingly important, form that lesbian desire took was based upon, but subtly different from, the bourgeois family. This was, of course, the romantic friendship. Nancy Cott has documented the ways in which the definition of 'friend' changed in the 18th century to refer specifically to an elective, non-familial relationship of particular importance.[25] By the second half of the 19th century, these 'Boston marriages', with their strong erotic undertones, were obviously alternatives to, but strongly modeled upon, the heterosexual family. Most couples had one partner who was more active and public, while the other was more retiring. The 19th-century English educational reformers Constance Maynard and Louisa Lumsden, for example, spoke of each other as wife and husband respectively; as headmistress of the school, Lumsden expected her 'wife' to support her decisions and to comfort her when difficulties arose.[26]

Maaike Meijer in her description of the friendship of two famous 18th-century Dutch bluestockings, Betje Wolff and Aagje Deken, points to the importance of a shared interest in learning, often in the face of family and public opposition, as a crucial element in many romantic friendships.[27] A sense of being different, of wanting more than other young women, symbolized by a love of learning, characterizes many of the romantic friendships described by Faderman in *Surpassing the Love of Men*. Yet even here, women's friendships were tightly controlled by external definitions of respectability. All bourgeois families feared any emotions that would overturn the conventional hierarchies in the private and public spheres. It was hoped that the discipline of study might teach women friends to be rational, to control their love for each other. In actuality, it probably led to a desire for greater independence – and consequently, an increased labeling of such friendships as deviant.[28]

These three types were united less by the behavior or attitudes of the women than by the ways in which men interpreted women's same-sex desire. On the one hand, we have condescension, amusement and curiosity; on the other, we have horror, punishment and expulsion. In either response, however, women's same-sex behavior remained marginal to the male sexual and societal discourses. Only when a woman seemed to contravene directly masculine priorities and privileges was she punished. But even in these cases, sexual deviancy had to be compounded by a trespassing upon the male preserves of religion or politics in order to draw the full wrath of masculine authority. Lesbian sexuality remained a muted discourse except in those isolated instances when men felt threatened directly by it.

The most usual punishment for a woman who 'married' another woman was a public whipping and banishment. One notable exception, however, was the early 18th-century case of 'James How'. After suffering from years of blackmail, the respected innkeeper took her case to the magistrates; they did not arrest her for fraud, but imprisoned the blackmailer. All surviving accounts of How treat her sympathetically.[29] The most acceptable model for understanding her thirty-five year 'marriage' was the female-warrior ballad, and reports were circulated that she and her 'wife' must have decided to join together after they had been jilted by men.

The aristocracy were assumed, of course, to be especially cavalier about sexual morals. Havelock Ellis mentions an 18th-century Frenchman who told a friend in regard to his fiancée's lesbian relationship, 'I confess that that is a kind of rivalry which causes me no annoyance; on the contrary it amuses me, and I am immoral enough to laugh at it.'[30] In contrast, Carroll Smith-Rosenberg had documented the closeness of middle-class friends in America, where husbands obligingly let them sleep together on the long visits characteristic of an age without good transportation.[31]

This casual and seeming indifference to women's relationships needs to be contrasted with those occasions when women clearly threatened the dominance of men or of the traditional family. Charlotte Charke, in spite of her notoriety, was never a public threat because she remained a liminal figure, but the multifarious sins of the German Catharina Margaretha Linck led to her hanging. She had joined an egalitarian, woman-led religion, and later had converted to Roman Catholicism and then Lutheranism. Cross-dressed as a man, she served in a Prussian volunteer corps, worked as a weaver, and married a woman. After hearing complaints from her daughter, Linck's mother-in-law and a neighbor 'attacked her, took her sword, ripped open her pants, examined her, and discovered that she was indeed not a man but a woman.'[32] In her defense, Linck insisted she had been deluded by Satan, and that it was no sin for a maiden to wear men's clothes.

As befits their class origins, romantic friendships were generally accepted without question. But I think that we may have exaggerated their overall acceptability. A fear of excess – whether of learning or of emotion – may well have been a cover for opposition to the erotic preference implied by such close friends. The dangerous usurping of marital privileges can be seen in a famous English divorce case. In 1864 Admiral Henry Codrington petitioned for divorce on the grounds of his wife's adultery; in addition, the feminist Emily Faithfull (1835-95) was accused of alienating his wife's affections. Helen Codrington, in turn, accused him of attempted rape upon Faithfull one night when the two women were sleeping together.[33] Faithfull herself first signed an affidavit claiming that this incident had taken place, but in court she refused to confirm it. The scandal permanently damaged her standing with other feminists, and she never regained the position of leadership she had held as the founder of the Victoria Press and *The Victoria Magazine*.

Women who avoided a direct confrontation with male prerogatives, whether sexual or political, fared best. The most famous example of romantic friendship in the 18th century was the upper-class 'Ladies of Llangollen', who ran away from threats of marriage and the convent to live with each other in remote North Wales.[34] Eleanor Butler (1739-1829) and Sarah Ponsonby (1755-1831) succeeded because they each had a small income and made a determined effort to reproduce a happy marriage in rural retirement. (James How and his 'wife' had followed the working-class equivalent of this pattern in their moral probity, modesty and hard work.) Samuel Johnson's friend, the well-known gossip Mrs. Piozzi, throughout her life kept up a vigorous correspondence with the admired couple about the arts, literature and contemporary affairs.

Mrs. Piozzi, however, made a distinction that was typical of the age, in respecting the intellectual Ladies and loathing the sexual antics of the aristocracy. In 1789 she noted, 'The Queen of France is at the Head of a Set of Monsters call'd by each other *Sapphists*, who boast her example and deserve to be thrown with the *He* Demons that haunt each other likewise, into Mount Vesuvius. *That* Vice increases hourly in Extent – while expected *Parricides* frighten us no longer....'[35] The dislike of such behavior seems to have stemmed from the growing political hatred of the dissolute aristocracy as much as a distaste for their frolics. Nevertheless, the fear of active female sexuality in places of power was a potent threat, as Marie-Jo Bonnet reminds us. She argues that the Revolutionary crowd's decapitation and then mutilation of Mme. Lamballe's genitals was an effort to destroy lesbian friendships, and not just the friend of the imprisoned queen.[36]

EXPLORING IDENTITIES

By the early years of the 19th century we can see two changes in same-sex relations. First, male commentary on intermittent lesbian love-making, whether hearsay, journalism or literature, became much more common. Public gossip shifted from Marie Antoinette's bedroom politics to the overtly sexual women of

Bohemia. Now women who were not necessarily wealthy or well-connected could – at the price of respectability – choose to live a sexually free life. Second, a few middle-class working women began to wear masculine (or simply practical) clothing. They insisted upon their sexual respectability, but also asserted their right to enter many predominantly male arenas, such as medicine, literature, art and travel. The bohemians flaunted their sexuality, while the professional single woman strove for an asexual androgyny. George Sand (1804-76) is the most important representative of the former type, and Rosa Bonheur (1822-99) of the latter; not coincidentally, both were self-supporting artists.

The active, mannish woman from the middle classes can be found throughout Europe and America by the mid-century. One of the most famous was the American sculptor Harriet Hosmer (1830-1908), who led a group of expatriate women artists in Rome.[37] Charlotte Cushman (1816-76), an American actress of the period, frequently acted in male roles and wore men's clothes off stage. She and Hosmer, keen advocates of physical activity for women, took midnight horse rides, sat astride, and followed the hounds with the men.[38] The highly esteemed Rosa Bonheur had been granted special permission to dress in trousers when she visited abattoirs and livestock auctions in order to study the anatomy of animals. She wore her trousers and smock, however, on all but formal occasions.

Bonheur worked hard to keep the image of respectable independence which characterized romantic friendships. Nevertheless, her masculine features and wearing of men's clothes placed her in a suspect category. When French taste turned against her realistic paintings, she hinted to friends that the criticism was as much a personal attack on her life with Nathalie Micas as it was her artistry.[39] However proud she may have been of her androgynous appearance, Bonheur was also self-conscious enough to insist that her lifelong relations with Micas and Anna Klumpke were pure, and she wrote to Magnus Hirschfeld describing herself as a member of the 'third sex'.[40]

Bonheur's insistence upon her androgyny contrasts sharply with the behavior of the earlier George Sand. Bonheur appears to have separated her body from her clothes, or rather her masculine clothes represented her soul, and not her body. Sand, as

Isabelle de Courtivon has pointed out, fit into male fantasies of the devouring lesbian, of the woman who is all body. When this remarkable woman cross-dressed, it represented not her soul but her all-too-dominating body.[41] Sand symbolized the strong woman who devoured weak men, and found her pleasure in the arms of other women. The 1830s in France spawned novels about monsters, of whom lesbians were among the most titillating. This male-generated image of sexual deviance proved to be especially powerful, and one that would return repeatedly in 20th-century portrayals of the lesbian *femme damnée.*[42]

During the first half of the 19th century we can see the accelerating efforts of the medical and legal professions to define, codify and control all forms of sexuality, and thereby to replace the church as the arbiters of sin and morality. Women's deviant sexual behaviors, whether heterosexual prostitution or homosexual sex, continued to be male-defined transgressions dominated by male language, theories and traditions. The pioneering French medical hygienist, A.J.B. Parent-Duchâtelet, linked the lives of prostitutes with those of cross-dressed lesbians. Both represented possibilities and fears for men, for each embodied an active, independent, uncontrollable sexuality.[43] Underneath their veneer of scientific language, the medical and legal tracts betray many of the same interests and biases as pornography and literature.

It has become a truism that the sexologists, such as Richard von Krafft-Ebing and Havelock Ellis, did not so much define a lesbian identity as describe and categorize what they saw about them. Ellis drew his small sample of six lesbians from his bisexual wife and her friends; all his other examples are either historical or literary, many of them from the French writers who had been so shocked by George Sand's flamboyance. Like Krafft-Ebing, he identified lesbians by their so-called masculine behavior, such as smoking, speaking loudly and wearing comfortable clothes. Carroll Smith-Rosenberg has pointed out that 'Krafft-Ebing's lesbians seemed to desire male privileges and power as ardently as, perhaps more ardently than, they sexually desired women.'[44] However revolutionary these men may have thought their descriptions to be, both were simply confirming the long-standing representation of women's social transgression as both the symptom and the cause of their sexual transgression. What had changed, however, was the new biologism that insisted upon the primacy of the body as the definer of public, social behavior. The long-familiar descriptions of deviant sexual activity were now labeled innate characteristics, rather than immoral choices.

Several feminist historians in Britain, following the lead of Lillian Faderman, have argued that the sexologists created a climate of opinion that stigmatized single women and their relationships and favored heterosexuality.[45] Others have argued that the sexologists stimulated the formation of a lesbian identity[46] or that their influence has been greatly exaggerated.[47] All of these scholars have, to date, looked almost exclusively at the medical debates, rather than placing these debates in a wider historical context. A host of competing sociobiological ideologies and disciplines flourished at the end of the 19th century, including Social Darwinism, eugenics, criminology and anthropology; women's sexual relations could hardly remain unaffected by them.

Have we too readily categorized these early sexologists and their embarrassingly crude classifications of sexual behavior? Rather than labeling the sexologists' descriptions benighted misogyny, we might learn more from them about both contemporary lesbian mores and masculine attitudes. Esther Newton has suggested that Havelock Ellis's biological determinism at the very least made available a sexual discourse to middle-class women, who 'had no developed female sexual discourse; there were only male discourses – pornographic, literary, and medical – *about* female sexuality'.[48] I would also add that these three male discourses had long affected the traditional categories of passing women, romantic friendships, intermittent lesbian sexuality and androgynous women; all four types had already been defined as suspect before they were taken up by Krafft-Ebing and Ellis. In effect, women's sexual behavior has never been isolated from or independent of the dominant male discourses of an age.

By the end of the 19th century, Paris was known for its lesbian subculture, thanks not only to Sand's reputation, but also to the poetry and fiction of such notable male writers as Balzac, Gautier, Baudelaire, Pierre Louys, Zola, Maupassant and Daudet. Wealthy and/or intrepid women consciously migrated not only to Paris, but also to Berlin, Amsterdam, New York, San Francisco, Chicago and other cities, where they hoped to find others sympathetic to their sexual preference.[49] They were specifically attracted to cities with a reputation for bohemian freedom, which promised to give women space to explore their sexuality.

The self-conscious leaders of these 20th-century communities embraced all aspects of the mixed heritage of same-sex relations. Perhaps wealth (or an expatriate status) gave them the confidence to forge a new female-defined identity.[50] The passing woman was embodied in the cross-dressed Marquise de Belbeuf, Colette's lover, or in Radclyffe Hall, author of *The Well of Loneliness* (1928). The enthusiasm for learning, languages and the arts, so characteristic of earlier generations of romantic friends, continued. Renée Vivien (1877-1909) and Natalie Barney took Greek lessons in order to read Sappho in the original; both made numerous trips to Greece, and participated in Greek theatricals. The Sapphic parties of Marie Antoinette were revived in Barney's famous entertainments. The militant respectability of Rosa Bonheur was transformed into the militant demand for recognition, best embodied in Hall's decision to write a book defending the 'true invert'. The bohemian world of George Sand did not need to be recreated because these women were living their own version of it.[51]

The most striking aspect of the lesbian coteries of the 1910s and 20s was their self-conscious effort to create a new sexual language for themselves that included not only words, but also gestures, costume and behavior.[52] The parties, plays and masquerades of the wealthy American Natalie Barney (1876-1970) are the best known 'creations'. They are commemorated in Djuna Barnes's privately published mock-heroic epic, *The Ladies' Almanack* (1928), in which Barney appears as Evangeline Musset. Although a 'witty and learned Fifty', she was 'so much in Demand, and so wide famed for her Genius at bringing up by Hand, and so noted and esteemed for her Slips of the Tongue that it finally brought her in the Hall of Fame....'[53] Barney herself said, 'Men have skins, but women have flesh – flesh that takes and gives light.'[54]

It is this insistence upon the flesh, the very body of the lesbian, that distinguishes this generation. But if Barney celebrated the tactile delights of a woman's body, for Radclyffe Hall the lesbian body could be a curse because society refused to acknowledge its inherent validity. Without public, and especially family, acceptance, self-hatred was inevitable for her heroine Stephen in *The Well of Loneliness*: '... she hated her body with its muscular shoulders, its small compact breasts, and its slender flanks of an athlete. All her life she must drag this body of hers like a monstrous fetter imposed on her spirit. This strangely ardent yet sterile body.'[55] Moreover, contemporaries had the example of Renée Vivien to remind them of the psychic dangers of lesbian love. Vivien embodied the doomed lesbian by changing her name, her religion and her body, finally drinking and starving herself to death by the age of 31.

On the one hand, we have Barney's declaration that a woman's body was her greatest pleasure, and on the other, Hall's contention that a woman's body was her unavoidable destiny, sterile or fertile. Both positions have an altogether too familiar ring, for both had long been encoded in male discourse. This generation of extraordinary women could not escape a familiar paradox that feminists still confront: by privileging the body, positively or negatively, women necessarily become participants in an already-defined language and debate. Woman as body had been a male trope for too long to be overcome by a spirited or tragic rejection.[56]

Newton has argued that Radclyffe Hall chose to portray Stephen as a congenital invert, based upon Havelock Ellis's theories, because it was her only alternative to the asexuality of romantic friendships. Actually, by the late 1920s she had numerous other alternatives, including Natalie Barney's hedonistic lesbianism, Vivien's self-created tragedy, Colette's theatrical affair with the Marquise, and the many less colorful monogamous couples in Paris's literary world. For her, these women were either too closeted or too ostentatious, and therefore too close to heterosexual fantasies about the life of the deviant.[57] Hall's militant demand that lesbians be granted respect for who they were, and not who they might associate with or how they might live, made Ellis's congenital invert the most natural choice. Ironically, as soon as a woman's body – specifically Stephen's 'monstrous' body – became the focus of discussion, it was outlawed socially and legally. A book that proclaimed a woman's free sexual choice as overtly as *The Well* was as dangerous as Catharina Margaretha Linck's dildo.

The demand for respect, for acceptance of one's innate difference, assumed a kind of sexual parity with men which women have never had. Hall's radical message was lost, but her portrait of Stephen remained. The complex heritage of the first generation of self-identified lesbians seemed at first to come together to create a New Woman, but then collapsed into the single figure of the deprived and depraved *femme damnée*. The open-ended confidence and playfulness of the 1910s and 20s did not survive the court case against *The Well of Loneliness*. The politically and economically turbulent 1930s narrowed women's sexual options. The lesbian community in Paris certainly continued, but shorn of its former glamor. Those who could find work often had to support their relatives. The women's movement itself seemed increasingly irrelevant in the face of such competing ideologies as Communism and Fascism. Unfortunately generalizations are difficult to make, for we know little about the isolated lesbian of the 1930s. Our only evidence is fleeting references in popular psychology books, labeling her – like Krafft-Ebing – as dangerously independent.

The doomed lesbian was a remarkably durable image. By the 1950s everyone knew what a lesbian was; she had been assigned a clearly defined role. Defiance and loneliness marked her life, according to the pulp romances. The English Elizabeth Wilson has described how attractive this model was for her in the 1950s, providing as it did an alternative to bourgeois marriage.[58] But once again, the femme had disappeared. Although the American Joan Nestle has argued forcefully for her importance, Wilson experienced being a woman's woman as 'the lowest of the low' in the liberal heterosexual world she inhabited.[59] Both the general public and lesbians themselves privileged the figure of the mannish lesbian because she most nearly approximated their expectations of what a lesbian should be. Romantic feeling, forbidden desires and social marginality were all represented by her cross-dressing. But, as I have demonstrated, she was also the product of a tangled history which embodied the outlawry of passing, the idealism of romantic friendship and the theatricality of aristocratic play. What has adhered to her identity most powerfully, however, is the sense of being born different, of having a body that reflects a specific sexual identity.

But even as the tragic lesbian stalked the imagination of the 1950s and early 60s, the old playfulness of an earlier generation never completely died. Now it has returned not to recreate the past, but either to celebrate the identification of homosexuality with defined, and inescapable, roles or to imagine a utopian world of transformed women. Like the women of the early 20th century, many lesbians of our time have set themselves the task of creating a lesbian language, of defining lesbian desire, and of imagining a lesbian society. Monique Wittig, in *Les Guérillères* (1969), *Le Corps lesbien* (1973) and *Brouillon pour un dictionnaire des amantes* (1975), has presented the most sustained alternative language and worlds. Her wholesale rewriting of history, in which all mention of man is eliminated, makes it possible to imagine a woman's body outside male discourse. Even here, however, our history is incomplete. In their heroic comedy *Brouillon pour un dictionnaire des amantes*, Wittig and her co-author Sande Zeig, leave a blank page for the reader to fill in under Sappho. *Dyke*, *butch*, *amazon*, *witch*, and such 'obsolete' words as *woman* and *wife* are included. But *androgyne*, *femme*, *invert* and *friendship* are missing.[60] Rosa Bonheur, who so disliked rigid sex roles, is strangely absent from this world. And what about the intermittent lover of women? Historians are more confined to the evidence before them than writers of fiction, and cannot create utopias, but they can and do create myths. When we rewrite, indeed, recreate, our lost past, do we too readily drop those parts of our past that seem unattractive to us? Can (and should) utopian language and ideas help us recuperate a history full of contradictions?

NOTES

My thanks to Anne Herrmann, Claire Moses, Karin Lutzen and Anna Davin for their suggestions for revision; their probing questions and detailed suggestions have improved this essay immensely. Special thanks go to Alice Echols, who read and critiqued each version of this essay with such encouragement and good will.

1   Theodore Stanton (ed.), *Reminiscences of Rosa Bonheur*. New York: Hacker Books, 1976 [1910], p. 199.

2   Anna Klumpke, *Rosa Bonheur: sa vie, son oeuvre*. Paris: Flammarion, 1908, p. 356. I am indebted to Karin Lutzen for this reference.

3   Estelle Freedman *et al.*, 'Editorial'. *Signs* 9:4 (Summer 1984) p. 554.

4   See the case studies: Brigitte Ericksson (trans.), 'A Lesbian Execution in Germany, 1721: the Trial Records'. In Salvatore J. Licata and Robert P. Petersen (eds.), *Historical Perspectives on Homosexuality*. New York: Haworth Press, 1981, p. 33.
    For the notorious Miss Pirie and Miss Woods vs Lady Cumming Gordon, see Lillian Faderman, *Scotch Verdict*. New York: Quill Press, 1981.
    See also Louis Crompton, 'The Myth of Lesbian Impunity: Capital Laws from 1270 to 1791'. In Litica and Petersen (eds.), *op.cit.*, pp. 11-26.

5   But see George Chauncey, Jr., 'From Sexual Inversion to Homosexuality: Medicine and the Changing Conceptualization of Female Desire'. *Salmagundi* 58/59 (Fall/Winter 1982-83) pp. 114-46; and
    Myriam Everard, 'Lesbianism and Medical Practice in the Netherlands, 1897-1930'. *Homosexuality, Which Homosexuality? Conference Papers*, History, Supplement. Amsterdam: Free University and Schorer Foundation, 1987, pp. 73-84.

6   See Judith C. Brown's *Immodest Acts: The Life of a Lesbian Nun* (New York: Oxford University Press, 1986) for a case study of a 17th-century Italian nun.
    See also the preliminary study of Elaine Hobby, 'Seventeenth-Century English Lesbianism: First Steps'. In *Homosexuality, Which Homosexuality? Conference Papers*, *op.cit.*, History, Vol. 1, pp. 44-55.

7   Havelock Ellis described these womanly women as homelier than the average woman, and therefore 'this is the reason why they are open to homosexual advances, but I do not think it is the sole reason. So far as they may be said to constitute a class they seem to possess a genuine, though not precisely sexual, preference for women over men.' As Esther

Newton points out, this 'awkward compromise' did not suit his theory of congenital inversion, and so no more mention is made of the 'womanly' invert. See her essay, 'The Mythic Mannish Lesbian: Radclyffe Hall and the New Woman'. *Signs* 9:4 (Summer 1984) pp. 567-68.

8   Michael Baker, *Our Three Selves: The Life of Radclyffe Hall.* London: Hamish Hamilton, 1985, p. 254.

9   See her essay, Leila Rupp, '"Imagine My Surprise." Women's Relationships in Historical Perspective'. *Frontiers* 5:3 (Fall 1980) pp. 61-70.

10   Some of the issues raised here are also discussed by Lisa Duggan in 'Eleanor Roosevelt – Was She or Wasn't She? The Problem of Definition in Lesbian History'. In *Homosexuality, Which Homosexuality? Conference Papers, op.cit.,* History, Vol. 1, pp. 5-17.

11   For a discussion of this among gay men, see Randolph Trumbach, 'Gender and the Homosexual Role in Modern Western Culture: The 18th and 19th Centuries Compared,' elsewhere in this volume.

12   See her essay: Ann Ferguson, 'Patriarchy, Sexual Identity, and the Sexual Revolution'. *Signs* 7 (Autumn 1981) pp. 158-72.

13   Blanche Wiesen Cook, 'Female Support Networks and Political Activism: Lillian Wald, Crystal Eastman, Emma Goldman'. *Chrysalis* 3 (Autumn 1977) p. 48.
       See also my discussion of this debate in Martha Vicinus, 'Sexuality and Power: A Review of Current Work in the History of Sexuality'. *Feminist Studies* 8 (Spring 1982) pp. 133-56.

14   Amber Hollibaugh and Cherrie Moraga, 'What We're Rollin' Around in Bed With. Sexual Silences in Feminism: a Conversation Toward Ending Them'. *Heresies* 12 (1981) p. 58.

15   Joan Nestle, 'Butch-Fem Relationships: Sexual Courage in the 1950s'. *Heresies* 12 (1981) p. 21.

16   Blanche Wiesen Cook, 'The Historical Denial of Lesbianism'. *Radical History Review* 20 (Spring/Summer 1979) p. 64.

17   The Oxford English Dictionary, not always the most reliable source on sexual matters, records the first use of *tribade*

in 1601; *tribady* in 1811-19, in reference to the famous Miss Woods and Miss Pirie vs Lady Cumming Gordon. *Hermaphrodite* receives the most complete coverage, with the first reference to its use as 1398. *Sapphic* is defined simply as 'Of or pertaining to Sappho, the famous poetess of Lesbos', or 'A meter used by Sappho or named after her'. *Sapphism* is not mentioned. Marie-Jo Bonnet traces a similar linguistic development in French, beginning with the 16th-century use of *tribade*, in *Un choix sans équivoque* (Paris: Denoel, 1981) pp. 25-67. She gives three examples from the *Dictionnaire érotique latin-français*, a 17th-century erotic dictionary (published only in the 19th century) which mentions *tribade*, *lesbian*, and *fricatrix* (someone who rubs/caresses another person 'for pleasure or for health'). See p. 43.

18   Obviously the earliest usages of slang are difficult to establish, but Eric Partridge's *A Dictionary of the Underworld: British and American* (London: Routledge & Kegan Paul, 1949; 1961) dates the first use of *bull-dike* as ca. 1920 and *dike* [sic] as 1935; *lezo* ca. 1930; *lesb*, *lesbie*, *lesbo*, as 20th-century, '? by 1940 at latest'. *Sapphist* and *bull-dagger* are not mentioned.

19   The one obvious exception to this generalization is Dr. James Barry (1795?-1865), a well-known British army surgeon, whom contemporaries assumed was a hermaphrodite on account of her small stature, lack of beard, and high voice. Julie Wheelwright, who is completing a book on women who passed as soldiers and sailors, feels that Dr. Barry may not have been a woman. The only definite evidence we have is the claim made by the woman who laid her out. But see Isobel Rae, *The Strange Story of Dr. James Barry*. London: Longman, 1958.

20   The most complete discussion to date of these ballads is Dianne Dugaw, 'Balladry's Female Warriors: Women, Warfare, and Disguise in the Eighteenth Century'. *Eighteenth-Century Life* 9:2 (January 1985) pp. 1-20.

21   See the facsimile reprint of the second edition (1755), *A Narrative of the Life of Charlotte Charke*. Edited by Leonard R.N. Ashley. Gainesville, Florida: Scholars; Facsimiles and Reprints, 1969.

22   Rudolph Dekker and Lotte van der Pol, 'Cross-Dressing as

an Expression of Female Homosexuality in Early Modern Europe'. In *Homosexuality, Which Homosexuality? Conference Papers, op.cit.*, History, Vol. 1, p. 76. See also their *The Tradition of Female Transvestism in Early Modern Europe*. London: Macmillan, 1988.

23 See Richard Sennett's discussion of the ways in which Wilkes's body – and sexual freedom – came to represent political freedom, in *The Fall of the Public Man. On the Social Psychology of Capitalism*. New York: Vintage, 1978, pp. 99-106.

24 Bonnet, *op.cit.*, pp. 137-65. See also: Faderman, *Surpassing the Love of Men, op.cit.*, pp. 42-43.

25 Nancy Cott, *The Bonds of Womanhood: 'Woman's Sphere' in New England, 1780-1835*. New Haven: Yale University Press, 1977, p. 186.

26 Martha Vicinus, ''One Life to Stand Beside Me''. Emotional Conflicts in First-Generation College Women in England'. *Feminist Studies* 8:3 (Fall 1982) pp. 610-11.

27 Maaike Meijer, 'Pious and Learned Female Bosom Friends in Holland in the Eighteenth Century'. *Among Men, Among Women Conference Papers*. Amsterdam: University of Amsterdam, 1983, pp. 404-19.

28 These issues are touched on, but not completely developed, in Martha Vicinus, 'Distance and Desire: English Boarding-School Friendships'. *Signs* 9:4 (Summer 1984) pp. 618-22.

29 Faderman, *Surpassing the Love of Men, op.cit.*, p. 56; and Bram Stoker, *Famous Imposters*. New York: Sturgis & Walton, 1910, pp. 241-246. Similar revelations were always fair game for the prurient and pornographic. See for example Henry Fielding's titillating (and inaccurate) account of Mary Hamilton: *The Female Husband* (1746). The actual events are described by Sheridan Baker, 'Henry Fielding's *The Female Husband*: Fact and Fiction'. *PMLA* 74 (1959) pp. 213-24.

30 Havelock Ellis, *Studies in the Psychology of Sex. Part IV: Sexual Inversion*. New York: Random House, 1936. Vol. 1. p. 204.

31 Carroll Smith-Rosenberg, 'The Female World of Love and Ritual: Relations Between Women in Nineteenth-Century America'. In her *Disorderly Conduct: Visions of Gender in Vic-*

torian America. New York: Knopf, 1985, p. 61.

32   Ericksson, *op.cit.*, p. 33.

33   The known facts are briefly outlined in Olive Banks, *The Biographical Dictionary of British Feminists, 1800-1930.* New York: New York University Press, 1985, p. 74. I am indebted to Gail Malmgreen for reminding me of this example of the disruption of the nuclear family by an excessive friendship.

34   Their lives are recounted in Elizabeth Mavor, *The Ladies of Llangollen.* London: Michael Joseph, 1971.

35   *Thraliana: The Diary of Hester Lynch Thrale (Later Mrs. Piozzi),* 2nd ed. Edited by Katharine Balderston. Oxford: Clarendon Press, 1951. Vol. 1, p. 740.

36   Bonnet, *op.cit.*, p. 165.

37   See Emmanuel Cooper, *The Sexual Perspective: Homosexuality and Art in the Last 100 Years in the West.* London: Routledge & Kegan Paul, 1986, pp. 55-58.

38   *Ibid.*, p. 56. See also the biography by her special friend: Emma Stebbins (ed.), *Charlotte Cushman: Her Life and Memories of Her Life.* Boston: Houghton Mifflin, 1881.

39   Dore Ashton and Denise Browne Hare, *Rosa Bonheur: A Life and a Legend.* New York: Viking Press, 1981, p. 162.

40   Cooper, *op.cit.*, pp. 48-49. For the Saint-Simonian roots of Bonheur's androgyny, see Albert Boime, 'The Case of Rosa Bonheur: Why Should a Woman Want to Be More Like a Man?' *Art History* 4:4 (December 1981) pp. 384-409.

41   Isabelle de Courtivon, 'Weak Men and Fatal Women: The Sand Image'. In George Stambolian and Elaine Marks (eds.), *Homosexualities and French Literature.* Ithaca: Cornell University Press, 1979, pp. 214-16.

42   In addition to De Courtivon, see also Faderman, *Surpassing the Love of Men, op.cit.*, pp. 274-99; and Dorelies Kraakman, 'Sexual Ambivalence of Women Artists in Early Nineteenth-Century France'. In *Homosexuality, Which Homosexuality? Conference Papers, op.cit.*, History, Vol. 1, pp. 169-80. I am indebted to Dorelies Kraakman for discussing with me the importance of the 1830s and 40s in France for understanding the formation of a new public discourse about women's sexuality.

43   He claimed: 'Lesbians have fallen to the last degree of vice

to which a human creature can attain, and, for that very reason, they require a most particular surveillance on the part of those charged with the surveillance of prostitutes....'
A.J.B. Parent-Duchâtelet, *La prostititution dans la ville de Paris* [1836], Vol. 1, p. 170. (Quoted in Stambolian and Marks, *op.cit.*, p. 148.) I am indebted to Marjan Sax for pointing out the connection between prostitutes and lesbians in medical and legal texts.

44   Carroll Smith-Rosenberg, 'The New Woman as Andro-gyne: Social Disorder and Gender Crisis, 1870-1936'. In Smith-Rosenberg, *Disorderly Conduct, op.cit.*, pp. 271-72.

45   See: Lal Coveney *et al.*, *The Sexuality Papers: Male Sexuality and the Sexual Control of Women*. London: Hutchinson, 1984; and
      Sheila Jeffreys, *The Spinster and Her Enemies*. London: Pandora, 1985. I am grateful for the opportunity to discuss these issues and their current popularity in England with Alison Oram.

46   Sonia Ruehl, 'Inverts and Experts: Radclyffe Hall and the Lesbian Identity'. In Rosalind Brunt and Caroline Rowan (eds.), *Feminism, Culture and Politics*. London: Lawrence & Wishart, 1982, pp. 15-36.

47   See Chauncey, *op.cit.*; and Vicinus, 'Distance and Desire', *op.cit.*

48   Newton, *op.cit.*, p. 573.

49   Gayle Rubin has coined the phrase 'sexual migrations' to 'describe the movement of people to cities undertaken to explore specialized sexualities not available in the traditional family arrangement, and often smaller towns, where they grew up.' (Quoted by Rayna Rapp in 'An Introduction to Elsa Gidlow: Memoirs'. *Feminist Studies* 6:1 (Spring 1980) p. 106.)

50   The literary relations in the most famous lesbian subculture have been explored by Shari Benstock, *Women of the Left Bank: Paris, 1900-1940*. Austin: University of Texas Press, 1986. See also the numerous biographies of the most famous figures. Benstock follows the lead of Elyse Blankley in characterizing Paris as 'a double-edged sword, offering both free sexual expression and oppressive sexual stereotyping. It

might cultivate lesbianism like an exotic vine, but it would never nourish it. In front of [Renée] Vivien – and indeed, every lesbian – yawned the immense, unbridgeable chasm separating men's perceptions of lesbian women and lesbian women's perceptions of themselves.' (Quoted in Benstock, p. 49.) See Elyse Blankley, 'Return to Mytilene: Renée Vivien and the City of Women'. In Susan Merrill Squier (ed.), *Women Writers and the City*. Knoxville: University of Tennessee Press, 1984, pp. 45-67.

51 We have very little evidence of a working-class lesbian sub-culture at this time. Elsa Gidlow's memoirs seem to indicate a similar pattern of seeking out a bohemian artistic culture. During World War I she started a literary group in Montreal which attracted a young gay man who introduced her to the Decadent writers of the late 19th-century, avant-garde music and modern art. See Elsa Gidlow, 'Memoirs'. *Feminist Studies* 6:1 (Spring 1980) pp. 107-27.

52 In her essay 'The New Woman as Androgyne' (*op.cit.*) Carroll Smith-Rosenberg discusses the revolutionary nature of this project – and its failure, which she attributes to the writers' unsuccessful effort to transform the male discourse on female sexuality. See pp. 265-66, 285-96.

53 Quoted in Meryle Secrest, *Between Me and Life. A Biography of Romaine Brooks*. London: Macdonald & Jones, 1976, p. 335. See also George Wickes, *The Amazon of Letters. The Life and Loves of Natalie Barney*. London: W.H. Allen, 1977.

54 Secrest, *op.cit.*, p. 336.

55 Radclyffe Hall, *The Well of Loneliness*. London: Corgi Books, 1968, p. 217.

56 The feminist literature on this equation is vast, but see most recently Susan R. Suleiman (ed.), *The Female Body in Western Culture: Contemporary Perspectives*. Cambridge, Mass.: Harvard University Press, 1986.

57 This point is also made by Gillian Whitlock, '"Everything is Out of Place": Radclyffe Hall and the Lesbian Literary Tradition'. *Feminist Studies* 13:3 (Fall 1987) p. 576. See also Benstock's comment about this generation of lesbian writers as a whole: 'Without historical models, [their] writing was forced to take upon itself the double burden of creating a

model of lesbian behavior while recording the personal experience of that behavior.' Benstock, *op.cit.*, p. 59.

58 Elizabeth Wilson, 'Forbidden Love', in her *Hidden Agendas: Theory, Politics and Experience in the Women's Movement.* London: Tavistock, 1986, p. 175.

59 Nestle, *op.cit.*; and Elisabeth Wilson, 'Gayness and Liberalism'. In Wilson, *Hidden Agendas, op.cit.*, p. 141.

60 I am using the English translation: Monique Wittig and Sande Zeig, *Lesbian Peoples: Materials for a Dictionary.* London: Virago, 1980.

AGAINST NATURE

Jeffrey Weeks

I want to start with a simple statement: 'The only thing that one really knows about human nature is that it changes. Change is the one quality we can predicate of it.'

That's not me, Jeffrey Weeks, in the late 1980s. It's Oscar Wilde in the early 1890s.[1]

Put baldly like that, no one could dispute the words – I hope. But I am going to take this little quotation as my starting text because it seems to me that when we talk about sexuality we still do assume that whatever else changes, our sex does not. A man is a man, a woman a woman, a heterosexual is a heterosexual, a homosexual is a homosexual, beyond the bounds of history, social transformation, conscious choice and political will.

The question of the nature of our sexual natures is at the heart of the debate about 'essentialism' and 'social constructionism' around which this conference has been structured. The majority of papers have attempted to show that this dichotomy is an increasingly arid and false one. I agree. It is a polemical distinction that all the time needs to be tested against the empirical evidence and reevaluated in the light of our evolving theoretical sophistication.

At the same time I firmly believe that if we are going to be true to the protocols of an historical approach and to the methods of social science then we cannot afford to question everything else – conventional morality, oppressive social regulation, political prejudice and the like – and ignore what lies at the heart of all these things, the shaping and reshaping, in a complex and prolonged history, of the sexual categories we inhabit and the identities we bear. Before we can really understand and come to terms with who we are, and what we are to become, we need to understand how we are and why we are.

These sorts of questions, it needs to be said, are not peculiar to the growing but still relatively small world of lesbian and gay studies. They in fact pervade the whole debate about what we mean by modernity and post-modernity, how we characterize our age. If often seems to be suggested that a concern with the emergence and development of distinctive lesbian and gay identities – and with a problematization of these identities – is somehow the product of esoteric schools of thought, or the malign influence of this or that over-hyped philosopher. The real situation is that the debate within our own ranks is a reflection of a much wider realization that if everything else changes, why shouldn't sexuality.

What I want to try to do in this paper is show how our own local debates are shaped by, and in turn of course help reshape, a wider attempt to understand the flux and complexity of the modern world. To put it bluntly, we cannot understand homosexuality just by studying homosexuality alone. We would lack the language, concepts, and basic historical understanding to do so.

I started off with a quotation from Oscar Wilde. Before going on, I should like to complete it: 'The systems that fail,' he writes, 'are those that rely on the permanency of human nature, and not on its growth and development.'[2] As I argued in my book, *Sexuality and Its Discontents*[3], appeals to nature, to the claims of the natural, are amongst the most potent we can make. They place us in a world of apparent fixity and truth. They appear to tell us what and who we are, and where we are going. They seem to tell us the truth.

And yet, as we know, there are so many truths. The textbooks used to tell us that homosexuality was unnatural. Lesbians and gay men, on the contrary, assert that homosexuality *is* natural. Who is to tell us which of these two 'truths' is true? The fact is – I almost said the truth is – that, as Jonathan Katz has said, when we explore the histories of terms like 'heterosexuality' or 'homosexuality' we can only conclude that Nature had very little to do with it.[4]

This raises, to my mind, three types of questions: about the status of history; about the social and historical forces that shape subjectivity and identity; and about the implications of deconstructing the categories of nature, history and identity for contemporary politics. Each carries us beyond the confines of homosexuality in particular or sexuality in general. They pose critical questions about the character of the culture we live in.

HISTORY

Many of the political debates within the lesbian and gay movement, as we have seen over the past few days, are played out in terms of historical argument. These debates have stimulated historical work. In turn, historical investigation had fed into political controversy. This is very characteristic of political movements generally, and of the new social movements – movements such as those of blacks, women, gays – particularly.

But there is a paradox in this: this resort to history comes at a time when historical studies themselves are in crisis, when the very possibility of 'history' is itself being questioned. And the new social history, concerning, for example, women, blacks, and lesbians and gay men, is contributing to that crisis. Not only do the new histories pinpoint the omissions of past histories; they also challenge the fundamental categories by which the past has been understood.

Take for instance the impact of women's history. This not only provides evidence about those previously 'hidden from history'. It also asks difficult and challenging questions, about the sexual division of labour, about reproduction, about the categories of masculinity and femininity, and about the very dynamics of history.

In the same way histories of black people do more than provide the oppressed with an awareness of their roots or the continuity of their struggles. They also critically undermine the conventional histories of, for example, industrialization, the material base of our modernity. Once you realize that the slave trade was a major element in the capital accumulation that led to Britain's, and later the world's, industrial revolution, then it becomes impossible to accept conventional accounts of the inevitability of 'modernization'. Instead we must learn to accept that the modern world is rooted in exploitation and domination – and resistance to those forces.

Lesbian and gay history may seem, at first, less radical in its implications – especially if you are wedded to the idea that we are a 'permanent minority'. But not if you begin to see that our history is part of a much wider pattern of sexual regulation. Lesbian and gay history had led the way in challenging the conventional view that sex is a private, unchanging, 'natural' phenomenon, outside the bounds of history. On the contrary, patterns of alliances, sexual taboos, family formation, sexual identities are at the very centre of the historic process, constitutive and not derivative.

The histories that have emerged over the past 10 to 15 years have, then, broadened the scope of historical work and challenged its conventional categories. Within the area of gay and lesbian history we may not always agree on the interpretation of events or trends. We may argue about the evidence for the existence of subcultures in this or that city during this or that century, or the continuity of identities throughout the Christian era. We may disagree on the timing of major transformations. But there can no longer be to my mind, and I hope to yours, any dispute that these are legitimately historical questions.

Having said that, however, we are still left to decide what the purpose of this great endeavour of historical excavation is. We know it is popular, and widespread. There are many pleasures in delving in the archive, in reading old documents, in trying to find across the centuries the experience that echoes our own. But we surely do not do it for its own sake. That's the argument of the most conservative type of historian – though one, alas, currently resurging rapidly in Britain – who does not normally look very favourably on the sort of history we are interested in.

There are a variety of possible justifications. We could for instance see the past as a great romance, a story of great kings and especially queens. This appeals to many a gay heart. Or we could see in history a series of lessons, of opportunities lost and of chances to be grasped, a cautionary tale to bolster current struggles. Or there is the history that exhorts us to repay the sacrifices of the past by battling in the present in order to win the future.

Each of these, however, assumes a linear pattern, a grand narrative of history in which the present is the undisputed heir of the past.

What if, however, we can no longer trust the grand narrative? Lyotard has written: 'I define post-modern as incredulity towards meta-narratives'.[5] This implies that many of the old certainties – about the unity of history, about the inevitability of progress, about the possibilities of scientific understanding of the past and the present – no longer hold.

There are many reasons for this scepticism. Some are episte-
mological: a questioning of the very possibility of knowing something to be true. How do we know that what we think we know
is not 'ideology'? Some are political: the decline in the impact of
progressive and Marxist views over the past decade. Some are the
result of the emergence of the social movements themselves,
which, as I have suggested, challenge traditional notions, on left
and right, about the dynamics of history, the nature of subjectivity, and the configurations of power and politics.

These currents are reflected widely in our debates. The work
of Michel Foucault has, for example, been influential on lesbian
and gay writing precisely because his work addresses that scepticism and those problems.[6] He asks, for instance, whether it is
possible to see the history of sexuality as a history of progress.
Might it not be instead a history of invention of categories of the
sexual in order to regulate and discipline the population?

In the same way he queries the legitimacy of the category of
science. To what extent can the claims of medicine, or sexology,
the self-proclaimed 'science of desire', or of psychoanalysis be
regarded as neutral, value-free, precisely 'scientific', when you
know their dubious origins in the murky byways of power?

It does not matter whether you agree with all his interpretations. As it happens, I do disagree with many elements of his work.
My point is that he has been influential because he encapsulates
so many currents in our attempts to come to grips with the present, a present where so many of the old truths no longer seem to
hold.

It is here with the present that we find a crucial justification
of the new social history. Historians have always argued about
the degree to which the present is the source of the questions we
ask of the past, and the interpretation we impose on it. I think the
really interesting thing about the new histories, of women, blacks,
lesbians, and gays, is what it forces us to ask about the present.
Increasingly we can see the present not as the culmination of the
past but as itself historical: a complex series of interlocking histories whose interactions have to be reconstructed, not assumed.

This does not mean that we should only study the immediate
past. My point is that this historical present is the product of many

histories, some of which are very ancient, some very recent. But what we should use history for – whether it is the history of homosexuality in Tahiti or in ancient Rome – is to problematize the taken for granted, to question our own culturally specific preoccupations, and to try to see whether what we assume is natural is not in fact social and historical.

IDENTITY

The sort of history I am advocating is one concerned with attempting to understand the conditions – intellectual, moral, material – which made possible our present. It is an approach that both reflects and contributes to a sense of the extreme diversity and complexity of the present.

At the heart of this understanding is an awareness of the range of possible identities that consequently exist – based on class, ethnicity, status, occupation, gender, sexual preference, and so on. We can all identify with many of these categories simultaneously, but which we give priority to depends on a number of historical variables. In times of heightened industrial conflict we might emphasize our class positions – as working-class or middle-class, and make fundamental political decisions on that basis. In periods of racial conflict and intensified racism our loyalties, as black or white, might well come to the fore.

Nietzsche noticed a hundred years or so ago that the 'tropical tempo' of modernity was fragmenting traditional identities.[7] During the past generation the pace has speeded up dramatically. The effects can be seen throughout the West. It is no longer easy to predict in advance on what basis individuals or groups will make their fundamental social or political commitments. The decline of traditional working-class based political parties is one dramatic index of this.

What has this got to do with lesbian and gay politics? Over the past twenty years a number of conditions, products of the development of new social antagonisms and of new social movements, have made sexual identities critical battlegrounds. It is not an accident that the New Right throughout the West has targeted lesbian and gay movements and communities as sources of moral pollution and a measure of social decline. The new, openly gay identities proclaim the need for a new social space, for the primacy of sexual choice and for challenging the relations of power that fix us, like insects in a spider's web, in categories labelled 'natural' or 'unnatural'. This is deeply threatening.

Leaving aside for the moment the question of whether sexual orientation and preferences are inborn or not, it seems to me self-evident that these social identities based on sex are relatively new. They have not, could not have existed throughout the mists of time, because the conditions that gave rise to them just did not exist.

'Modern society is to be distinguished from older social formations,' Niklas Luhmann has written, 'by the fact that it has become more elaborate in two ways: it affords more opportunities both for impersonal and for more intensive personal relations.'[8] Put another way, the growing complexity of modern society has made possible the rise of a range of possible sexual identities and of sexual communities. At the same time, these have become sites of conflict, giving rise to important social movements of the oppressed against a social order that seeks to dominate. 'Community' provides the language through which the resistance to domination is expressed.

If we really want to understand and come to grips with the present, the crucial task is to unravel the tangled strands that made these things possible. Why has modern culture been so concerned with the details of individuals' sexual behaviour, seeking out in the way we look, the ways we dress, the ways we wave our hands or cross our feet, our ability or not to whistle, the true secrets of our being? Why does freedom of the individual, the cornerstone of Western values, always stop short of sexual freedom? Why do the main sufferers in the West from the effects of a particular virus get blamed for it?

We might disagree over our answers to these questions, but it is impossible to deny that these are critical questions to ask. In order to understand them we might need to explore the sustained rewriting of general sexual codes in the late 19th century as part of the response to urbanization and the transformation of traditional values, as I have tried to do in various studies.[9] Or we might speculate on how and why patterns of female friendship came to be transformed into pathological categories, as Carroll Smith-

Rosenberg and Lillian Faderman have done.[10] Or we might look at the gender revolution in the late 18th century as Randolph Trumbach is doing.[11] Or we might, like Alan Bray, explore the new language of friendship and desire, and the growth of the subculture of molly-houses in early 18th-century London.[12] Or we might even go back to the roots of our civilization in ancient Greece and Early Christian Rome to trace the source of our preoccupation with sex as truth, as Michel Foucault did in his last works.[13]

What we cannot do if we want to understand why we are where we are is simply assume that nothing changes, that gays and lesbians have always existed as we exist today, that homophobia has always remained constant, and that there is a mystical continuity between our desires and their desires across the ranges of cultures and histories. We do not do it for any other aspect of our social existence. We should not do it for our sex.

My arguments so far have been in terms of the historical evidence. But behind them are a number of theoretical assumptions that I want to spell out. The starting point is the sustained challenge in Western thought during much of this century to the naturalness of 'natural man', and to the constitutive centrality of the 'unitary subject'. The idea of the individual as a unified, preconstituted whole, the fount and origin of all things, has been at the heart of liberal ideology for centuries. The challenge to this concept has therefore been profoundly troubling. I suspect that much of the heat generated by the argument over sexual essentialism has its roots in a fear that respect for the individual will disappear in a welter of social explanations.

Nevertheless, challenged essentialism has been, in a wide variety of fields, and from a variety of sources – from radical sociology, structuralist anthropology, Marxism, and psychoanalysis, from the prophets of post-modernism, and from feminist scholars. Marx's view that the individual is a product of social forces, 'an ensemble of the social relations', is ambiguous, but very troubling.[14] Even more subversive is Freud's concept of consciousness constantly undermined by unconscious forces outside rational control. Freud's work is, in its implications if not always in its application, the most radical theoretical challenge this century to the fixity of gender and sexual identities.[15] These insights have been taken up in turn by feminist writers disinterring the intricate connections between our psychic structures and the play of male power.[16]

Two conclusions flow from this work: firstly, that subjectivity is always fractured, contradictory, ambiguous, and disrupted; secondly, that identity is not inborn, pregiven, or 'natural'. It is striven for, contested, negotiated, and achieved, often in struggles of the subordinated against the dominant. Moreover, it is not achieved just by an individual act of will, or discovered hidden in the recesses of the soul. It is put together in circumstances bequeathed by history, in collective experiences as much as by individual destiny. As Alasdair MacIntyre has put it, 'The unity of a human life is the unity of a narrative quest.'[17] The elements of that narrative we find around us as much as in ourselves.

None of this must be taken to mean that I reject the importance of lesbian and gay identities. On the contrary, it is because I have a strong sense of their contingency, of the conditions of their existence in concrete historical circumstances, and of their critical importance in challenging the imposition of arbitrary sexual norms that I am deeply committed to their value, emotionally, socially and politically. Lesbian and gay identities, and the communities that made them possible, and which in turn they sustain, are the precondition for a realistic sexual politics in the age of AIDS.

And notice in this that I stress the importance of collective activity and of self-making. Modern lesbian and gay identities are not the results of sexological or medical labelling, let alone the invention of historians. They are the results of that process of definition and self-definition that I described in my first book, and which has been the constant feature of homosexual politics over the past century.[18]

The word *community*, James Baldwin has written, 'simply means our endless connection with, and responsibility for, each other.'[19] This serves to remind me, at least, that the values of humanism, of collective endeavour, and of individual freedom do not depend on a supposed 'natural man' or 'woman', but on a politics and ethics that we shape for ourselves in this historic present.

POLITICS

Implicit in all I have said so far is a critique of an essentialist approach both to sexuality and to other social phenomena. By this I mean a method which attempts to explain the properties of a complex reality by reference to a supposed inner truth or essence, whether that essence is assumed to be the explanation of an individual, a class, a nation or 'society'. I believe that this is a reductionist method, in that it reduces the complexity of the world to the imagined simplicities of its constituent parts. It is also deterministic, in that it seeks to explain individuals as automatic products of inner propulsions, whether we dignify these as the products of the instincts, the genes, the hormones, or something altogether more mysterious.

Against this, I argue that the meanings we give to sexuality in general, and homosexuality in particular, are socially organized, but contradictory, sustained by a variety of languages, which seek to tell us what sex is, what it ought to be, and what it could be. Existing languages of sex, embedded in moral treatises, laws, educational practices, psychological theories, medical definitions, social rituals, pornographic or romantic fictions, popular assumptions, and sexual communities, set the limits of the possible. We, in our various ways, try to make sense of what we are offered.

The problem lies in their contradictory appeals, in the babel of voices. How can we make sense of these various languages, and translate them into a common tongue?

The pioneers of modern homosexual politics, from Ulrichs through Hirschfeld and Carpenter up to the early Mattachine leaders had no fundamental problem. They borrowed the common language of their contemporaries, especially the sexologists, and simply reversed their terms. The language of sexual science that, by and large, denied the validity of homosexuality, was turned into a language which asserted its naturalness.[20] This was supported by an optimism that the humane sciences would be able to convince people rationally of the justice of the cause. Through science to justice, Hirschfeld nobly proclaimed.[21]

The problem was, as I have suggested earlier, that science did not always see eye to eye with itself, let alone with the pioneers of reform. And today, with a clearer awareness that 'science' provides no ready-made, let alone consistent, guidelines, we are more reluctant to give it too much credence. Recent liberation movements, Foucault observed in a late interview, 'suffer from the fact that they cannot find any principle on which to base the elaboration of the new ethics ... [other than] an ethics founded on so-called scientific knowledge of what the self is, what the unconscious is, and so on.'[22]

If, as I have argued, we can no longer base our values on nature; if we are no longer quite sure what the self is; and if we do not really believe in the unconscious, on what basis do we elaborate any ethics at all? 'Where, after the meta-narratives', asked Lyotard, 'can legitimacy reside?'[23]

This question, I believe, is at the heart of our contemporary political and moral dilemmas. We have all witnessed, over the past decade, a number of issues that have torn our communities apart. Conflicts between men and women, between black and white. Divisions over pornography, sadomasochism, butch-femme, paedophilia, about lesbian sexuality. Arguments, even, over our response to AIDS.

These are genuine divisions of commitment and conviction. I do not want to argue that they could or should have been sub-sumed under some cosy consensus. What I do want to pinpoint, however, is that we lacked even a common language to talk to one another with, let alone common analytical tools. What we got was a language of assertion on all sides.

The reasons for this are rooted in the very conditions which have made our identities possible. Communities are always about both identity and difference: what we have in common, and what differentiates us. Over the past few years it has often seemed that we wanted to fragment our identities and commu-nities into even smaller splinters, each proclaiming its toe-hold on the truth.

This is, I suggest, a reflection on a smaller stage of a wider political crisis. Many of the old landmarks of progressive politics have been severely shaken during the 1980s. Liberal, radical, and socialist values have been under sustained assault, and have been further undermined by their collapse of confidence and failure of nerve. The New Right has been much more successful in capitalizing on signs of social strain than the Old or New Left. A powerful wave of political and moral fundamentalism has tried to reshape the moral contours that many of us were beginning to take for granted in the 1960s and 70s. In this context the new social movements have been thrown onto the defensive. Most tragically of all, at this very moment of political challenge, the AIDS crisis has provided the excuse and justification for a moral onslaught on the lives of lesbian and gay people.[24]

In the light of all this, how can we justify a theoretical position that problematizes sexuality and sexual identity? How valid is it to propose a history that offers no easy consolations? Is it right to argue that people have a choice of social and political identifications? I can only answer that there is only hope for the future if we are able to confront the past and the present dispassionately. We must learn the contours and hidden obstacles of this historic present before we can realistically face the future.

What my attempt at a dispassionate understanding shows is that the lesbian and gay identities are both constructed and essential, constructed in the sense that they are historically moulded and therefore subject to change, essential in the particular sense that they are necessary and in the end inescapable. Frank Kermode has made a distinction between 'myth' and 'fictions'. Myth, he says, 'operates within the diagram of ritual, which presupposes total and adequate explanations of things as they are and were: it is a sequence of radically unchangeable gestures. Fictions are for finding things out, and they change as the needs of sense-making change. Myths are the agents of stability, fictions the agents of change.'[25]

In that sense, gay and lesbian identities are fictions, the necessary ways we mobilize our energies in order to change things. The emergence over the past few decades of large gay communities is one of the signs of a major shift in the political geography of the West. New 'elective communities', or communities of interest and choice, have provided a focus for the growth of new sorts of social and political identifications. As Cohen has argued, people map out their social identities and find their social orientations in the relationships which are symbolically close to them, rather than in relation to an abstract notion of society.[26] Through these relationships we are able to negotiate the complexities of the modern world, come to some understanding of it, and contribute to changing it. I don't think that's an ignoble achievement for a necessary fiction.

'A title must muddle the reader's ideas', Umberto Eco argues, 'not regiment them.'[27] I chose a title, 'Against Nature', that was deliberately vague, and at the same time, I hope, provocative. Vague because I wanted an opportunity to range widely through a number of issues that have run through our discussions. Provocative because I wanted to challenge the idea that there is any solution to our current discontents in a search for what is truly natural.

That does not mean that I want to deny the importance of biology, let alone deny the body. But I do want to insist that we can only fully understand our needs and desires when we grasp the social and historical forces, the unconscious motivations, and the personal and collective responses that shape our sexualities. Understanding where we came from seems to me the starting point for thinking about both the politics and ethics of sexuality, and where we want to go.

I have introduced a word we do not often use, but one we should perhaps use more: 'ethics'. By this I do not mean a set of prescriptions on right behaviour, but rather a set of values that can help to shape the way we live. I don't want here to offer my own thoughts on what the contents of these should be. But I'll end with two quotations which might just show the way my thoughts are going.

The first comes from the English philosopher, Bernard Williams. 'No one', he writes, 'should make any claims about the importance of human beings to the universe: the point is about the importance of human beings to human beings.'[28]

I like that because it does not root its humanism in grand metaphysical schemes, let alone nature. Rather it stresses the ordinary, the commonplace, but the fundamental value we share, or should share: our need for one another.

The second quotation comes from Oscar Wilde again, in fact from the same essay from which the earlier quotes were taken, 'The Soul of Man Under Socialism'. Towards the end of it he writes: 'Pain is not the ultimate mode of perfection. It is merely provisional and a protest. It has reference to wrong, unhealthy, unjust surroundings. When the wrong, and the disease, and the injustice are removed, it will have no further place.'[29]

That was written nearly a hundred years ago. It has a poignant echo today. But its sentiments are no less true in the 1980s than they were in the 1890s.

That's the limit of my attempts to regiment your ideas.

NOTES

1   Oscar Wilde, 'The Soul of Man Under Socialism'. In *Complete Works of Oscar Wilde*. London: Book Club Associates, 1978, p. 1100.

2   *Ibid.*

3   Jeffrey Weeks, *Sexuality and Its Discontents*. London: Routledge & Kegan Paul, 1985.

4   Jonathan Katz, *Gay/Lesbian Almanac*. New York: Harper & Row, 1983.

5   Jean-François Lyotard, *The Post-Modern Condition. A Report on Knowledge*. Manchester: Manchester University Press, 1986, p. xxv.

6   Michel Foucault, *The History of Sexuality*, Vol. 1. London: Allen Lane, 1979.

7   Quoted in Elizabeth Wilson, *Adorned in Dreams*. London: Virago, 1985, p. 27.

8   Niklas Luhman, *Love as Passion*. London: Polity Press, 1986, p. 12.

9   See Jeffrey Weeks, *Sex, Politics and Society. The Regulation of Sexuality Since 1800*. Harlow: Longman, 1981.

10   Carroll Smith-Rosenberg, *Disorderly Conduct*. London: Oxford University Press, 1985.
     Lillian Faderman, *Surpassing the Love of Men. Romantic Friendship and Love Between Women from the Renaissance to the Present*. Junction Books, 1980.

11   See Randolph Trumbach, 'Sodomitical Subcultures, Sodomitical Roles, and the Gender Revolution of the 18th Century: the Recent Historiography'. *Eighteenth-Century Life*, 9 n.s. 3 (1985) pp. 109-121. Reprinted in R.P. Maccubbin

(ed.), *'Tis Nature's Fault. Unauthorized Sexuality during the Enlightenment*. Cambridge, 1987.
See also Randolph Trumbach's contribution elsewhere in this volume.

12 Alan Bray, *Homosexuality in Renaissance England*. London: GMP, 1982.

13 Michel Foucault, *The History of Sexuality*, Vol. 2: *The Use of Pleasure*; and Vol. 3: *The Care of the Self*. New York: Pantheon, 1985; 1986.

14 See Jeffrey Weeks, *op.cit.*, 1985, p. 120.

15 *Ibid.*, Ch. 6.

16 Jacqueline Rose, *Sexuality in the Field of Vision*. London: Virgo, 1986.

17 Alasdair MacIntyre, *Against Virtue*. London: Duckworth, 1985, p. 219.

18 Jeffrey Weeks, *Coming Out. Homosexual Politics in Britain from the 19th Century to the Present*. London: Quartet, 1977.

19 James Baldwin, *Evidence of Things Not Seen*. London: Michael Joseph, 1986, p. 122.

20 Jeffrey Weeks, *op.cit.*, 1985, Ch. 4;
Jeffrey Weeks, *Sexuality*. London: Tavistock, 1986, Ch. 6.

21 See Jeffrey Weeks, *op.cit.*, 1986, Ch. 6.

22 Michel Foucault, 'On the Genealogy of Ethics: an Overview of Work in Progress'. In Paul Rabinow (ed.), *The Foucault Reader*. New York: Pantheon, 1984, p. 343.

23 Lyotard, *op.cit.*, p. xxv.

24 Weeks, *op.cit.*, 1986, Ch. 5;
Simon Watney, *Policing Desire: Pornography, AIDS and the Media*. London: Methuen, 1987.

25 Frank Kermode, *The Sense of an Ending*. London: Oxford University Press, 1967, p. 39.

26 Anthony P. Cohen, *The Symbolic Construction of Community*. London: Tavistock, 1985.

27 Umberto Eco, *Reflections on the Name of the Rose*. Secker & Warburg, 1985, p. 3.

28 Bernard Williams, *Ethics and the Limits of Philosophy*. London: Fontana, 1985, p. 118.

29 Oscar Wilde, *op.cit.*, p. 1103.

AN ANTHROPOLOGICAL CRITIQUE OF CONSTRUCTIONISM: BERDACHES AND BUTCHES

Saskia Wieringa

INTRODUCTION

As papers, like love affairs, have their special place in a person's individual history, let me start by giving the background to this lecture. When in the beginning of the eighties I started coordinating the Institute of Social Studies research project 'Women's Movements and Organizations in Historical Perspective',[1] I was very careful not to make my own lesbianism known in the countries in which we worked. I was afraid of being accused of 'exporting Western lesbian values', not so much by the women in the groups participating in the research, but by their adversaries. After all, the time when my Third-World colleagues were denounced as feminists, and hence as decadent and capitalist, by their leftist male allies was not long past. Very soon, however, I came across groups of lesbian women, mainly in Indonesia and Peru. They led a marginal existence, very different from my own so-called 'political lesbianism' at that time. Their culture resembled more the butch/femme culture of the West, which at that time I regarded as rather outdated, as 'old lesbian' (to use Dutch feminist jargon). In 1984 I was witness to the confrontation of the butch/femme bar culture of Lima with the feminist movement in that city. The Peruvian feminists denounced this bar culture as aggressive and anti-feminist (these women are only fighting, and talking about sex, where are their politics?).

These encounters with the lesbian bar scenes of Jakarta and Lima made me realize how narrow my own so-called *political lesbianism* was.[2] This led me to pose certain questions both about these Third-World butch/femme bar scenes and about the history of butch/femme cultures in the West. Also, in trying to make sense of these lesbian cultures and get more insight into the

meaning of 'the lesbian' in various cultural settings, I found that I had to look beyond the confines of the current constructionist theories. I was specifically concerned about the following issues:
1. The way the 'lesbian' is lived shows some clear similarities cross-culturally, as well as some differences. The discontinuities can be understood from the different cultural contexts in which these women live. But how could I explain the transcultural and historical continuities? Is it possible that these elements which women who engage in same-sex unions have in common may be so vital in determining their identities that it may transcend their sometimes widely different historical and social circumstances? And what do these common elements consist of? Sexuality with other women?
2. In all cases the women involved have to show a sometimes considerable amount of individual courage to live the lives they want to live. How and why do certain women 'choose' for a particular lifestyle? In some cases there is a certain cultural niche available for women to live their desires; in other cases women have to become freaks, outcasts, passing soldiers or sapphic sailors to lead the lives they want. Again, in other cases, women 'choose' to become SM lesbians when the dominant lesbian culture prescribes vanilla sex, or butch/femme couples in a lesbian scene which regards these as old-fashioned, or berdaches against the wishes of their families. How could I conceptualize these individual drives? Would it be possible to speak of an individual constitutional temperament which shapes people's desires in such a way that it influences the social choices people make? But then again, how must I conceptualize the realm beyond the social, beyond the 'knowable', beyond the confines of structure and language? Within the boundaries of the constructionist discourse I found it was impossible to ask these questions. The dictates of the body itself and psychobiological processes are virtually ignored. This led me to a rethinking of the relationship between the biological and the social, in other words, to a reevaluation of some of the questions essentialists asked.
3. Lastly, while working on these questions I became concerned about the way a feminist discourse is able to influence women's lives, in other words, how normative feminism can be. To a large degree many feminist theories are influenced by constructionist

theories. For instance in the discussions about sexuality and the body a heavy emphasis is put on sociocultural factors.

I then began a search for older anthropological material on woman-to-woman relationships and learnt about the sisterhoods of the Chinese silk workers in the last century, about the woman marriages of Africa and about the berdaches among the North American Indians.[3] All these three forms of homosocial arrangements are institutionalized in their respective societies and are surrounded by the accepted rituals of those cultures. In these three cases one partner adheres more or less to the norms of male behaviour which are generally accepted in that culture. Accordingly, her status is determined by her performance in this role. She is socially accepted as having fairly strong characteristics which generally appertain to the male gender. Her partner is seen as belonging to the female gender and she is judged by how well she performs in that role. Just as in the present-day butch/femme bar cultures, the partners in these relationships are engaged in a relatively strict form of polarized role-playing. However, the ingredients of their roles differ widely. Those differences are to be found not only in the divergent interpretations of power, sexuality, and eroticism prevalent in the various cultural settings in which these forms manifest themselves, but also in the widely varying importance placed on the different elements the roles consist of. The social status of a female husband, for instance, is largely determined by her wealth, her skills as a provider, and the number of wives and children she has. The status of a butch, on the other hand, is judged by the way she is able to take erotic responsibility in her relationship – and it is this image of herself that she will try to project.

Both this review of anthropological material and my own observations in the lesbian bar cultures of Jakarta and Lima made me aware of the existence of the transcultural and trans-historical continuity of a certain type of same-sex lifestyle between women. I have long hesitated whether the concept of butch/femme is applicable in non-Western settings, because of its clearly Western connotations, complete with stereotypes pertaining to dress and specific social, erotic and sexual behaviour. Of course the actual women falling into this category will not always conform to these norms. Very little research has been done on the lives of butches and femmes, especially on the power of femmes and on the internal dynamism of their relationships.[4]

In other societies, 'dominant' members of same-sex unions as well as their partners have found ways of expressing their identities which are more in keeping with their own cultural values. I decided it would not be possible to use the same concept for a Buffalo stone butch[5] as for a female husband in a polygynous setting, even though both women can be seen as the 'dominant' partners in their relationships: the butch with her lover, the female husband as the head of the family of women. The way this dominance is expressed will be determined by the cultural and historical context in which the women live. It may be expressed in certain dress or behavioural patterns, there may be differences in wealth or social status, the women may use different speech patterns, different political positions may be involved, or different erotic games played. So I decided to use the general term *same-sex lifestyle* for all these relationships, also for those in which one partner is dominant. Dominance, too, remains to be defined. In the context of this paper 'dominance' refers only to a situation in which one partner takes on one or more of those aspects which are assumed to belong to the male gender. It does not necessarily imply an asymmetry in other aspects of the relationship, nor does it mean that the non-dominant partner is necessarily oppressed in that relationship. In fact, the non-dominant partner can be extremely powerful in other aspects of the relationship. That is also the reason why I refrain from speaking of a 'femme' as the *passive partner* in a relationship between women. Use of that term might de-emphasize definite aspects of power femmes have in their relationships. Neither the wives of berdaches or female husbands, nor femmes, can be equated simply with women in heterosexual relationships. How to find a term which would encompass both the (often very active) recipient of sexual attention (as in some Western settings, and in the bar culture of Jakarta) and the wife of a female husband in an African context? Therefore, in the context of this essay I will speak of same-sex lifestyles, of relationships between a dominant woman and her non-dominant partner(s).

After a short introduction to both essentialist and constructionist positions I will explore some of the issues that surround the lifestyles of butch/femme couples and of berdaches. I will point to the kinds of questions which to my mind should be asked in order to comprehend these lifestyles. In doing so I will plead for a more thorough exploration of transcultural issues surrounding lesbianism, and for more research into the internal dynamics of woman-to-woman relationships.

ESSENTIALISTS AND CONSTRUCTIONISTS

Essentialism as a body of theoretical constructs emerged in the wake of evolutionism at the end of the 19th century. Adherents of this theory posited 'homosexuality' as having a universal meaning. According to them human sexuality was rooted in biology, that is in a 'normal' heterosexual drive intended for procreation. Any deviation was considered to be pathological, either a symptom of a hereditary weakness or a consequence of other factors such as socialization and the influence of the family (Freud). Sometimes a combination of both factors was seen to be the culprit. Constructionist theorists later analyzed this process as the medicalization of homosexuality. Lesbians and gay men were seen in it as 'perverts' (passive women, active men), or as 'inverts' (active lesbians, or passive gay men). Closeting, the internalization of homophobia and guilt feelings and other negative effects were the result.

However, this body of theories is not the only kind of essentialism. In the fifties, Kinsey[6] came to another type of essentialism on the basis of his research on sexuality. According to his view the biological basis of sexuality can take on various forms, one of which is homosexuality. Thus, homosexuality is just as 'natural' an expression of sexuality as heterosexuality is. However, according to Kinsey's theories homosexuality is still defined within the medico-biological debate. And so it remained difficult to account for crosscultural and transhistorical variations in expressions of homosexual love.

Constructionism arose in the seventies. No longer are genetic or physiological factors sought to 'explain' a homosexual 'nature'. Gay scientists engaged themselves in studies on the social malleability of homosexual identities and lifestyles, on discontinuity in the concept of homosexuality, and on the history of the medicalization of homosexuality in the West. It was shown that historical and social processes determine the form in which a homosexual lifestyle is manifested. Apart from being a great theoretical step forward, this new approach also had great political consequences: not homosexuals were ill, but society, in its patriarchal, heterosexist form. Gay-affirmative actions were carried out and political lesbians became the vanguard of the feminist movement: weren't they the ones who were most truly liberated from patriarchal oppression?

I feel there are also a number of serious problems in constructionism. Carole Vance, in her opening address to this congress[7], already pointed out that there are many ambiguities in much of constructionist writing itself. In many cases it is not clear what kind of 'constructions' are actually being discussed. Are we dealing with the sexual and erotic components of a same-sex union? Or rather with the identities of individuals who are engaged in same-sex unions? Or maybe with the views and activities of specific sexual communities? Also, and Vance did not dwell on this aspect specifically, the importance and the cultural relevance of these three areas, for instance the way they relate to one another, may be very different in various historical and cultural settings. In addition to the above-mentioned problems, I see major difficulties with constructionist theories along the following lines:

1. What kind of essentialism is actually being attacked by constructionist scientists? I do not feel that essentialism is done justice to when only the theories around the turn of the century are being held up for scrutiny. Many social science theories which sprang up in those days are now considered to be outdated. Many present-day scientists are extremely aware of the inherent dangers of essentialism and make serious efforts to overcome them.

2. I find there is a serious amount of ethnocentrism in much of constructionist writing. Much of the history of homosexuality in the West in the last century has now to an important degree been charted. However, this is only a tiny fraction of the overall history of same-sex unions. Yet, sometimes far-reaching and general conclusions are presented on the basis of this limited material. This raises important questions. For instance, what is the relevance of

the debate between essentialists and constructionists for social settings where same-sex unions have always been institutionalized? where there has never occurred a process of medicalization of homosexuality? Many women engaged in same-sex unions have been and are highly respected members of their communities. They have never suffered from internalized homophobia; they have never considered themselves to be perverts or inverts. Neither do they have a lesbian identity in the present-day Western sense. Their identity may be formed by factors they themselves consider to be much more important than their choice of a sexual partner.

Another illustration of the difficulties inherent in the transcultural analysis of the relation between sexual acts and sexual identities is given by the differences in the *function* of concepts relating to homosexuality between Western and various non-Western settings. In the West an enormous importance is placed on the words *lesbian* or *homosexual* themselves. In many non-Western settings there does not exist one world for 'lesbianism'. It is either circumscribed (as in the Chinese: 'grinding bean curd') or it is referred to as 'love between women'. Very often the word 'lesbian' is imported.

3. Thirdly I feel constructionism has led to the sociologization of sexuality. Constructionist scientists have put such an emphasis on the analysis of social factors in relation to the construction of homosexual identities that the sexual and erotic aspects of same-sex unions have sometimes been played down. Psychobiological factors have been neglected in favour of the analysis of lifestyles and the cultural construction of identities. Also, social constructionists generally consider social elements to be the major determining factors in the individual expression of (homo)sexuality to such an extent that mainly groups of lesbians, bar cultures, lesbian or gay communities as a whole are being analyzed, not the differences within these groups, cultures and communities. It seems as if there is no room in these debates for the individual expression of sexual drives.

To conclude this section, although I feel constructionism is a great improvement over essentialist theories, I feel constricted in my analysis by the constructionist parameters. Just as essentialism cannot explain the historical variation in the expression of homosexuality, constructionism is not able to account for the individual variation of certain sexual patterns in specific social settings, nor for the historical or transcultural continuity of certain types of (homo)sexual behaviour. What is needed is, I feel, a theoretical approach in which there is room for a discussion on both continuity and discontinuity, on both individuality and the influence of social structures.

LESBIANISM IN ANTHROPOLOGY: A NOTE ON METHODS

Anthropology is a most useful discipline for pointing out diversity. To whatever social hypothesis posited, there is always some exception found, tucked away in a tiny corner of the globe. Early ethnologists like Karsch-Haack were able to collect so much material on homosexuality, that already in 1911, when Karsch-Haack published his book, it was made abundantly clear that homosexuality is in no way a purely Western phenomenon and that there is a great range of homosexual practices.

There is also another aspect to anthropology, which is admittedly much more risky, that is, trying to come to general abstractions on the basis on anthropological material. The dangers here are clear. If one is looking for something, one is apt to find it in the wealth of ethnographic data available. Also, as many specialists on one village or tribe will mutter, in this way one will explain away the social specificity of the data collected, and wasn't specificity one of the trademarks of anthropology to start with? Yet it is to generalization I will turn, focusing on female same-sex unions.

Now the next cluster of problems arises, that is, the collection and interpretation of data on female same-sex unions. For several reasons the amount of data on lesbianism is very scarce, and the information we do have is often heavily distorted. One reason is that many societies were oral societies. The mainly male historiographers or ethnographers who came to collect information about these groups did not pay much attention to what the women told them, or did not listen to what the women said. In other cases the women themselves had reasons of their own to keep their secrets.[8] Then again, most ethnographers were male, or, if they were women, they were heavily influenced by male views. Apart from this viricentrism, ethnocentrism has always been one of the central problems in anthroplogy. Ethnographers generally are only able to recognize features with which they themselves are familiar in their own cultures. Thus ethnographers are likely to be as homophobic as the societies they come from, and they have often not been able to recognize female same-sex unions where they saw them, or, if they did so, they didn't want to be associated with such a phenomenon.[9]

Non-Western women clearly would possess the best potential to write about their own cultures. Yet even they may not be the best informants on female same-sex unions if they are heterosexual themselves. An illustration is provided by the way the Nigerian sociologist Ifi Amadiume denounces Audre Lorde's assertion that African woman marriages may be considered as lesbian unions. According to Amadiume, Lorde bases herself upon racist sources and she then continues to 'prove' there are no lesbian elements involved in at least the woman marriages she is concerned with, those of the Nnobi women of Nigeria.[10] I agree with her that it is difficult to stick the Western label 'lesbian' with its present-day connotations upon these unions; yet there are also other sources which point to sexual elements pertaining to African same-sex unions. For instance it has been pointed out that the Surinamese *mati* unions are clearly in some ways African retentions.[11] And, as Wekker asserts, so have other female same-sex unions in the Diaspora of black people.

BERDACHES

Anthropological data point to a continuity in several aspects of same-sex unions between women, as for instance the polarization of role-playing between the partners in some settings, as well as to a discontinuity in social aspects of these relations. Although there is generally a lack of information about the internal dynamism of female same-sex lifestyles, some important issues can be noted. In comparison with butch/femme relations in the West it is striking to observe that central aspects of female same-sex lifestyles, such as labour, sexuality, occupation, and social status, differ markedly. The following quotation from Ifi Amadiume's

study on woman marriages in Nigeria shows that a female husband's social status and identity was not determined by her
choice of a sexual partner (as one of the main criteria for a butch/
femme couple is), but by her wealth, her cleverness or trading
skills, and the number of her wives or children: 'Among the wives
of Eze Okigbo was Nwambata Aku, who was said to have been
his favourite.... She is said to have had about 24 wives. Among
the qualities attributed to her were hard work and perseverance.
She was described as a clever woman who knew how to utilize
her money. As well as having her wives trade for her, she herself
sold kola-nuts, and would buy pots of palm-oil during times of
plenty and sell them at a high price when oil was scarce.... As well
as making money for their husband, Nwambata's wives also
made money for themselves through the palm-kernel trade.... In
those days, it seems, it was not enough for a woman to be merely
wealthy. She had to be known for something else as well, such as
the number of sons she bore, or the number of wives she married.... Another well-remembered wife was Iheuwa. In her case,
she had no children, but married a woman called Onudiulu, who
bore three sons.'[12]

In the following account I will focus on the American berdaches. *Berdache* is the concept used by ethnographers for those
individuals in certain native American groups who adopted the
occupation, the behaviour, the clothing and the marital status of
members of the other sex. The word itself is derived from the
French word for male prostitute. The most important characteristic of the female berdache is that she carries out tasks generally
done by the male gender. Ruth Landes observes about Sioux
berdaches: 'A few individual women in each village did drive
buffalo on horseback, and did stalk, scalp and mutilate the
enemy; often they were young women of childbearing age. Their
deeds were accepted simply by the men, who not only failed to
criticize them but even accorded them the honors of men.'[13]

A Gros Ventre woman who was captured by the Crow was so
skilled in warfare that she was elected to be a chief. Occupation
was the most important element of the identity of a berdache, but
also in behaviour and clothing a female berdache demonstrated
that she belonged to the male gender. A third characteristic of
a berdache is that she or he is allowed to choose a marital partner

of the same sex. This is not necessarily prescribed: female berdaches are known to have married men, and male ones to have
married women, in both cases without losing their berdache status. So the element which determined the identity of a berdache
was not the choice of a sexual partner, but rather her or his
occupation.

It is still being debated where and on what scale berdaches
were found. Whitehead asserts that there were far fewer female
than male berdaches, because it would be more difficult for
women to aspire to the 'higher' social status of the male gender,
than it would be for men to become social women. Blackwood
argues that these reasons are not valid for egalitarian societies as
the Mohave where there is hardly any hierarchy implicit in gender categories. She has counted 33 North American tribes where
members of the female sex have adopted the occupation and the
social status of the male gender. Female berdaches were found
in various groups of the Southwest Plains, such as the Mohave,
the Zuni, and also among the Apache and the Navajo. The Kaska
society had only the female form, whereas the Canadian Black-
foot Indians had an institution whereby women turned into berdaches after their menopause and were called 'manly-hearted
women'. The berdache phenomenon is not limited to North
American Indians. Karsch-Haack quotes the Portugese explorer
De Magalhanes de Gandavo who in 1576 wrote the following
account about the Brazilian Tupi tribe: 'They [the women] went
to war with bows and arrows. They also went hunting with the
men. Each of the women had with them another female Indian
and told that she was married to this woman; both lived together
as husband and wife.'[14]

Generally berdaches were highly regarded in their tribes.
They were often consulted in the tribal councils, and many of
them were supposed to possess special powers. Some berdaches
were shamans, or they fulfilled other important ritual tasks. Yet
accounts are found in the literature dealing with berdaches
whereby they were often ridiculed as well. This has to be ascribed
partly to the cultural prejudices of the white observers, who found
it hard to disengage themselves from the values in their own
societies which only allowed for a strict binary opposition
between the genders. They could hardly accept the existence of

a gender category which was not based upon anatomical characteristics. But they were not always incorrect. As Greenberg[15]
convincingly argues, many of those instances on which berdaches
were ridiculed should not be seen as a condemnation of the berdaches themselves. Sometimes they might be interpreted as part
of a 'joking relationship', an accepted way of teasing certain individuals to which a person is related in a special manner. In other
cases berdaches violated certain kinship rules, for instance taboos
on incest which no individual was allowed to defy.

In fact the berdache status allowed individuals to always stay
within the accepted heterosexual pattern. A berdache fell into a
third or *fourth* gender category, beside the more prevalent gender
categories 'man' and 'woman'. If a female berdache married a
woman, the social component of her berdache status was regarded as dominant. If on the other hand she married a man, she did
this referring to her original biological characteristics. In both
cases her partner was considered heterosexual. Not every sexual
relationship between partners of the same sex was institutionalized within a heterosexual pattern by this 'construction'. Homosexual behaviour was found also, and was accepted or ridiculed,
depending upon the various customs in the tribes in which it
occurred. In some tribes, among the Mohave for instance, homosexual behaviour was tolerated during puberty, but adult persons who chose a homosexual partner were condemned.

The literature about female berdaches yields certain vital data
which, on several aspects of these same-sex lifestyles, point to a
continuity with the relationship between the partners of the African woman-to-woman marriages, and with the sisters of the Chinese sisterhoods. First, in all these cases the same-sex unions are
fully embedded in their respective societies. They are neither seen
as pathological nor stigmatized in any other way. Also, in none
of these cases do these same-sex lifestyles attack the existing social,
religious or sexual norms. Secondly, the status of the partners in
these relationships is determined by values as wealth, occupation, or skills. The 'dominant' partner in these relationships is
judged according to how well she performs along the lines established for the male gender, the 'non-dominant' partner according to her 'feminine' skills. Choice of sexual object is not the most

important element in determining the status of either the berdache or the female husband. The Chinese sisters made their
rejection of heterosexuality and especially of a heterosexual marriage more clear.

There are major differences between these non-Western same-
sex lifestyles and the Western butch/femme couples. These differences are mainly in the areas of the conceptualization of these
relationships and in the periodization of their development. In
non-Western cultures the influence both of the medicalization of
homosexuality and of feminist discourse is felt mainly through the
mediation of a colonial and, at present, imperialist reality. Stigmatization of woman-marriages and of the institution of the berdache is an imported phenomenon, through colonialism, religion
and present-day governments. The Sisterhoods were branded as
'feudal remnants' by the victorious Red Army. Yet some similarities between butch/femme couples and the non-Western
same-sex lifestyles as mentioned in this essay can be noted as well.
This continuity lies mainly in the area of the polarization of
gender roles between the partners.

The analysis of the American berdaches allows us to illustrate
the different approaches of essentialist and constructionist scientists. Essentialist social scientists like Kroeber and Devereux were
mainly concerned with physiological issues.[16] Their argument is
that the gender category of the berdache allows the Indians to
accept people with 'deviant' or 'abnormal' sexual inclinations
within the social system. Whitehead convincingly argues that
this position makes it impossible to explain why a comparable
'solution' was not found for non-institutionalized homosexual
behaviour. Irrefutably she concludes that sexual object choice is
not the main criterion in determining one's gender identity, as
it is in white society. Her constructionist approach allows her to
ask other questions as well: about the meaning of gender in relation to identity, and about the relative importance of the various
elements which constitute one's gender identity. Both Blackwood
and Whitehead are concerned with the meaning of the institutionalized character of the berdache phenomenon, and as such
they are asking essential questions. However they are not able to
ask questions about the individual choices each berdache had to
make in order to reach berdache status. I will come back to this

problem after some remarks on the history of butch/femme relations.

BUTCH/FEMME RELATIONSHIPS

Butch/femme couples are another example of a same-sex lifestyle with a polarized division of roles between the partners. The history of the Western butch/femme culture is also an illustration of the censorship which may be exercised by a particular discourse. I will use here the concept butch/femme for those relationships between lesbian women in Europe and Northern America which are characterized by a clearly polarized role division in erotic and sexual patterns, clothing and behaviour. The butch/femme culture was essentially an urban bar culture, a lifestyle which made visible a certain pattern of lesbian eroticism. The concept butch/femme was mainly used in Northern America; in France jules/femmes was more commonly used, in Holland the Dutch equivalent of boy/girl or male/female was used.

These cultures prospered chiefly in the first sixty years of our century. The butches defined themselves in a terminology derived from those sexologists who had introduced the concept of the *third sex*. They described themselves as '100% gay', and had 'always been like that'. At a very early age they had known they were 'different', even if they didn't know exactly what that meant; but they had known they would always be like that. With the femmes all these things were less manifest. Even after a long lesbian life they might have doubts whether they were really 'like that'. They might have relationships with men, or they might become married later on. Sometimes femmes became butches at a later age. The butches often described the femmes as 'real women', with a mixture of passionate admiration and distrust. 'Butches were known by their appearances, femmes by their choices.'[17]

In the twenties and thirties of this century there was a rich butch/femme culture, especially in Paris and Berlin. The 'lesbo-look' and the 'lesbo way of life' had an influence on fashion, the stage, literature and other forms of art. This subculture was ignored by the feminist movement of those days. Feminists were mainly concerned with issues like the vote, education for women and birth control and did not concern themselves with female homosexuality. If sexuality was discussed their concern was with heterosexuality, and especially with those aspects of heterosexuality which were unpleasant to women. Besides this dominant feminist stream a smaller group of feminists preached 'free love'. Concepts like 'compulsory heterosexuality' and 'patriarchal power structures' were not used, not even by those feminists who had relationships with other women, such as Goldman and Sanger. The butch/femme culture was outside the range of feminist discourse and could flourish there.

In those instances in which there *was* contact between feminist discourse and the butch/femme culture, it was of a positive nature. The German feminist Anna Rüling, for example, praised the positive character traits of those feminists who belonged to the 'third sex'. In her view they were apt to be more energetic, objective and efficient, and should be considered an asset to any feminist group.[18]

The second wave of feminism developed a strong critique of 'heterosexist patriarchy'. The demands of the first wave, notably the vote, equality and education were seen as insufficient. The roots of women's oppression had to be unearthed more deeply, and these were found to lie in patriarchal societal structures. These in turn were founded on compulsory heterosexuality. Gay-affirmative groups joined the confrontation with heterosexist society. This critique of heterosexism and capitalist patriarchy seems an immensely valuable step forward when compared to the struggles of the first-wave feminists. Many lesbian women recognized the potential of these theories and political practices and eagerly put themselves at the forefront of the movement.

This discourse, however, put butch/femme relationships under great pressure. In feminist eyes these were regarded as 'copying' hetero patterns. This type of erotic behaviour was denounced in favour of soft, equal, and affectionate sexuality between women. In Holland the most important pressure group for gay rights, the COC, discouraged too openly 'male' behaviour for women. In Dutch terminology, 'new' (that is, politicized) lesbian behaviour became the fashion; women exhibiting 'old' lesbian behaviour were regarded as outdated. Butch/femme relationships disappeared from feminist discourse and butch/femme lesbians no longer dominated the scene in the bars. The new lesbo-look was defiantly androgynous. Butches and femmes were stigmatized again, this time not by the sexologists, but by those women they might otherwise regard as their closest allies. Many of them withdrew from the feminist movement. Apart from the tremendous disappointment this must have caused to individuals, their withdrawal from the movement should also be regarded as an important loss to the movement itself.

In 1981 Joan Nestle broke the Great Silence surrounding butch/femme relations with a pioneering article about the erotic and the political meaning of butch/femme relations in the fifties. She described butch/femme couples as women who played a highly complex erotic and social game. It was true that the butches generally bore the brunt of the open hostility and aggression directed at lesbians, but their role could only be seen in its true perspective by the support of their femmes. Nestle asserted that femmes were not merely passive women who could just as well have been heterosexual. Femmes helped to let the lesbian subculture survive in very unsafe times. They stood firm for their butches. In Nestle's view a butch was not merely a woman in male attire, but 'a woman who created an original style to signal to other women what she was capable of doing – taking erotic responsibility'.[19]

Her article met with a wide response. The Lesbian Herstory Archives which she founded with her lover became widely known, and her example was followed, also in Holland. In several places research on the meaning of butch/femme cultures was being done. Butch/femme was back. But had it really disappeared or had it only disappeared from the feminist point of view?[20]

Similar developments may be noted in various present-day third world countries. When in 1981 I came in contact with the Jakarta butch/femme scene I was struck by its rigid structure. But what moved me most was the enormous courage the women displayed, their brave defiance of the repressive, militarist society in which they lived. Today that culture is relatively untouched by feminism. In Peru and Argentina, on the other hand, countries in which there is a more or less (allowing for the great cultural differences between these countries) similarly rigid butch/femme bar scene, feminists are interfering. Consciousness-raising groups of feminist lesbians have been set up in which role playing is discussed. Feminists who had earlier shied away from supporting any lesbian demands now discuss political lesbianism. Lesbians are 'allowed' to enter the movement, but only on the conditions set by the present-day feminist political practice. Only very hesitantly are butch/femme relations being discussed for what they are.

Not only researchers discuss butch/femme relations nowadays. In various lesbian subcultures themselves, relationships based on the eroticization of role differences have become more accepted. But in a less rigid way, more playfully, changes of roles are now also allowed within these relationships – butches nowadays get laid.

LESBIANISM AND BIOLOGY

Constructionist theoreticians have instigated the debate on the various lesbian lifestyles. They are trying to locate 'the lesbian' within a social and historical context. In this way it has also become possible to analyze the socialization processes within lesbian cultures. Davis and Kennedy, for instance, have demonstrated how in the lesbian bars in Buffalo great pressure was exerted on those lesbians who had just come out. They had to adopt either of the two roles available, and were instructed by the older women, sometimes in a friendly fashion, at other times more roughly.

But constructionist theoreticians are not able to account for the transcultural continuities between various lesbian lifestyles. Both the berdaches and the butch/femme couples engage in polarized role playing. In both cases these women had to adopt their roles against sometimes considerable resistance from their environment. This indicates that there are also other factors which play a role. Is it possible to speak about a constitutional temperament which is determined individually by psychobiological factors? This is one of the questions essentialists are concerned about.

In this respect it is important to note that biological phenomena are not static. Several biologists have pointed to the interaction of social phenomena with biological factors.[21] Recent biological research on the interaction on physical characteristics and social processes indicates the dynamic and transformative character of this relation. The feminist biologists Birke and Vines have suggested we should speak of 'transformative processes', in relation both to social contexts and to physiological characteristics.[22] So we should not see the relationship between biology and social factors as a model of static interaction, but rather as a dynamic process. In this way the social may be seen as providing the niches in which the biological is acted out. But those niches in turn are constructed in a dialogue with biological factors.

In this respect I'd like to return to the berdaches. In what way did anatomical women decide they wanted to live the life of a berdache? In their early puberty girls were subjected to a ritual through which they were initiated to the status of a berdache. This ritual could not be reversed. Devereux has noted down the following story from the mouth of his Mohave informant Ñah-wera: 'When there is a desire in a child's heart to become a transvestite, that child will act different. It will let people become aware of that desire. They may insist on giving the child the garments and toys of its true sex, but the child will throw them away and do this every time there is a big gathering. Then people prepare a skirt of shredded bark for the boy or a breech clout for the girl. If they give them the garments worn by other members of their sex they will turn away from them. They do all they can to dissuade girls who show such inclinations. But if they fail to convince her they will realize that it cannot be helped. She will be chumming with men and be one of them. Then all those who have tried to change her conduct will gather and agree that they had done all that could be done and that the only thing for them to do was to give her the status of a 'transvestite'.[23]

So a girl needed a considerable amount of willpower to convince the other members of her tribe she wanted to adopt the status of berdache. How did she acquire that willpower?

Both of the most important feminist authors on the subject, Whitehead and Blackwood, limit their analysis to the statement that there was a social category intended for these women which they were able to make use of. While both writers acknowledge that girls often spoke of their desires after having had certain

dreams, they pursue the subject no further. They content themselves with assertions as '... girls achieve the cross-gender role in
each instance through accepted cultural channels'.[24] They do not
ask themselves why some girls do have these dreams and others
don't, nor are they concerned with the meaning of dreams on the
psychobiological level.

However, the Indians themselves do indicate certain psychobiological factors which are of influence upon the choice by certain individuals to adopt the status of berdache. Williams quotes
a Lakota shaman who, referring to a male berdache, made the
following remark: 'To us a man is what nature, or his dreams,
make him. We accept him for what he wants to be. That's up to
him....'[25] Whitehead gives us the following quotation of Forde
about the 'female inverts' among the Yuman: 'Female inverts
(*kwe'rhame*)... realize their character through a dream at puberty.
The characteristic dream is of men's weapons. As a small child
the *kwe'rhame* plays with boys' toys.'[26] And Devereux notes that
the Mohave feel that 'temperamental compulsions' play a decisive role.[27]

In most tribes the characteristic pattern therefore appears to
be the following: a girl or boy dreams that she or he belongs to
the opposite gender and manifests a behaviour belonging to
children of the opposite gender, defying resistance they meet
from other members of their tribe.

CONCLUSION

I have tried to present some dilemmas I was confronted with
when I began thinking about the meaning of 'the lesbian' in
various cultures and historical periods. In my presentation I have
focused on berdaches and butch/femme cultures. The great differences between berdaches and butches are apparent. The
butch/femme pattern of the fifties had a clear erotic connotation.
The identity of berdaches, on the other hand, is determined to
a large extent by their activities. Central concepts like gender,
sexuality and labour have different meanings for berdaches and
butch/femme couples. A constructionist approach offers some
scope for analyzing these differences, while also facilitating research into social elements of these same-sex lifestyles, such as the

process of socialization into butches or berdaches.

But some vital questions cannot be asked within a constructionist framework. The similarities between butch/femme couples and berdaches and their partners, that is, the polarized division of labour within the couple, do not fall within its scope of analysis. Nor do constructionist scientists concern themselves with the factors which play a role in the courage and willpower these women must possess to defy society the way they do. Constructionist theoreticians mainly concern themselves with the analysis of groups and social factors: lesbian subcultures, the historical development of same-sex lifestyles, et cetera. I suggest that we should also consider psychobiological factors in our attempts to understand 'the lesbian'. In this respect we will have to realize that physiological processes try to find ways within the dominant culture which may differ greatly: the psychobiological is always socially mediated. Essentialist scientists, especially those concerned with the dynamic character of the interaction between the social and the biological, can make important contributions toward analyzing how individuals live their lives within their culture.

Here it is important to analyze critically the language in which lesbian experiences are translated. The word *lesbian* has considerable political and scientific connotations. Precisely because within certain discourses the danger of censure of the 'lesbian' is so great, I feel it is imperative to discuss issues surrounding the 'lesbian' as openly and clearly as possible. In this way we may try to minimize the dangers of ethnocentrism and of the sociologization of sexuality.

I am afraid this presentation has not been able to give easy and handy tools for further research, but at least I hope it has posed certain questions in a different way, which may open up new areas for very careful analysis. There is so little known, for example, about the dynamics within lesbian couples transculturally, about the self-perception of butches and femmes, about sexuality in relation to gender. Indeed, about so many other aspects of our lives and the lives of our sisters all over the world who are not able to be here now, because mere survival in their major concern.

NOTES

Many of the points raised in this lecture are the result of discussions I had with Noor van Crevel. We prepared a paper together for the *Homosexuality, Which Homosexuality?* conference (Saskia Wieringa and Noor van Crevel, 'Beyond Feminism: the Butch/Femme Debate'. In *Conference Papers*, History. Amsterdam: Free University and Schorer Foundation, 1987) which formed the basis for the present essay.

1   The research project 'Women's Movements and Organizations in Historical Perspective' was carried out between 1981 and 1986 in five countries (India, Indonesia, Peru, Somalia, Sudan) and the Caribbean region. See Saskia Wieringa, *Women's Movements and Organizations in Historical Perspective: an Evaluation Report*. The Hague: Institute of Social Studies, 1987.

2   See Saskia Wieringa, *Uw Toegenegen Dora D*. Amsterdam, 1987.

3   See for literature on berdaches:
Evelyn Blackwood, 'Sexuality and Gender in Certain Northern Native American Tribes: the Case of Cross-Gender Females'. *Signs* 10:1 (1984);
Harriet Whitehead, 'The Bow and the Burden Strap: a New Look at Institutionalized Homosexuality in Native North America'. In Sherry B. Ortner and Harriet Whitehead (eds.), *Sexual Meanings. The Cultural Construction of Gender and Sexuality*. Cambridge: Cambridge University Press, 1981.
For literature on the Chinese sisterhoods:
M. Topley, 'Marriage Resistance in Rural Kwangtung'. In M. Wolf and R. Witke (eds.), *Women in Chinese Society*. Stanford, 1975.
And on woman-to-woman marriages:
I. Amadiume, *Male Daughters, Female Husbands, Gender and Sex in an African Society*. London, 1987;
M.J. Herskovits, 'Some Aspects of Dahomeyan Ethnology'. *Africa* 5 (1932);
E. Jensen Krige, 'Woman-Woman Marriage, with Special

Reference to the Lovedu. Its Significance for the Definition of Marriage'. *Africa* 44 (1974);

R.S. Oboler, 'Is the Female Husband a Man? Woman/ Woman Marriage among the Nandi of Kenya'. *Ethnology* 19:1 (1980);

D. O'Brien, 'Female Husbands in Southern Bantu Societies'. In Schlegel (ed.), *Sexual Stratification. A Cross-Cultural View.* New York, 1977.

4   See Joan Nestle, 'The Fem Question'. In Carole S. Vance (ed.), *Pleasure and Danger. Exploring Female Sexuality.* Boston, 1984.

Also, Anja van Kooten Niekerk and Sacha Wijmer, *Verkeerde Vriendschap* (Amsterdam: Sara, 1985); and Madeline Davis and Elisabeth Lapovsky Kennedy, 'Oral History and the Study of Sexuality in the Lesbian Community, Buffalo, New York, 1940-1960' (*Feminist Studies* 12:1, 1986) give some insights into the dynamics within butch/femme couples.

5   A *stone butch* is a butch who derives her satisfaction by giving her partner sexual pleasure, but who does not want to be touched by her partner in return.

6   Alfred C. Kinsey *et al.*, *Sexual Behavior in the Human Female.* Philadelphia: Saunders, 1953.

7   See Carole S. Vance, 'Social Construction Theory: Problems in the History of Sexuality', in this volume.

8   Recently a secret women's script was discovered in China. For hundreds of years Chinese women communicated their miseries and joys to each other and to themselves in this script, which was only taught to other women. Much of it was lost, as the women often took their diaries with them to their graves. There are indications that this women's script was also one of the means of communication between sisters in the Chinese vegetarian sisterhoods.

9   R. van Lier is a good example of an anthropologist who stopped doing research on female same-sex unions when he was confronted with societal disapproval of the direction his research was taking. See R. van Lier, *Tropische tribaden. Een verhandeling over homoseksualiteit en homoseksuele vrouwen in Suriname.* Dordrecht, 1986.

10   Amadiume, *op.cit.*, p. 7.

11   See for instance Van Lier, *op.cit.*; and Gloria Wekker, 'Matisma and Black Dykes'. In *Homosexuality, Which Homosexuality? Conference Papers, op.cit.*, Social Sciences, Vol. 2.

12   Amadiume, *op.cit.*, p. 47.

13   Ruth Landes, as quoted in Whitehead, *op.cit.*, p. 91.

14   F. Karsch-Haack, *Das gleichgeschlechtliche Leben der Naturvölker*. Hamburg, 1911, p. 511. (my translation)

15   David F. Greenberg, 'Why Was the Berdache Ridiculed?' In Blackwood (ed.), *op.cit.*, 1986.

16   A.L. Kroeber, *Handbook of the Indians of California*. Bureau of American Ethnology, *Bulletin*, 78 (1925);
     George Devereux, 'Institutionalized Homosexuality of the Mohave Indians'. *Human Biology*, no. 9, 1937.

17   Nestle, *op.cit.*, p. 233.

18   Anna Rüling, 'Welches Interesse hat die Frauenbewegung an der Lösung des homosexuellen Problems?' In *Jahrbuch für sexuelle Zwischenstufen. Auswahl aus den Jahrgängen 1899-1923*. Edited by Wolfgang Johann Schmidt. Frankfurt am Main: Qumran, 1984.

19   Nestle, *op.cit.*, p. 235.

20   As Joan Nestle pointed out at the *Homosexuality, Which Homosexuality?* conference, 'The butch/femme cultures did not die out. They existed alongside other lesbian subcultures, but they lost contact with the worlds of women.'

21   In his endocrinological studies, MacCullock, for example, concludes that there is no physiological basis for the larger part of human sexual behaviour, and certainly not for the choice of one's sexual object. See Malcolm MacCullock, 'Biological Origins of Homosexual Behaviour in Man'. *British Journal of Sexual Medicine* (February 1980).
     Likewise, the biologist Ruse points up the importance of an interaction between biological and social sciences, after concluding that genes do play a certain role in homosexual behaviour, but that social factors are important as well. Michael Ruse, 'Are There Gay Genes? Sociobiology and Homosexuality'. In Noretta Koertge (ed.), *Philosophy and Homosexuality*. New York: Harrington Press, 1985.

22   Linda Birke and Gail Vines, 'Beyond Nature versus Nurture: Process and Biology in the Development of Gender'.

Women's Studies International Forum 10:6 (1987).

23 Devereux, *op.cit.*, p. 503.
24 Whitehead, *op.cit.*, p. 30.
25 Fire and Erdoes, quoted in Walter L. Williams, 'Persistence and Change in the Berdache Tradition among Contemporary Lakota Indians'. In Blackwood (ed.), *op.cit.*, 1986, p. 192.
26 Forde, quoted in Whitehead, *op.cit.*, p. 92.
27 Devereux, *op.cit.*, p. 518.

ON THE SOCIAL CONTRACT

Monique Wittig

I have undertaken a difficult task: to measure and reevaluate the
notion of *social contract*, taken as a notion of political philosophy
– a notion born with the 17th and 18th centuries, and which is
also the title of a book by Jean-Jacques Rousseau.[1] Marx and
Engels criticized it as not relevant in terms of class struggle, and
therefore not of concern to the proletariat. In *The German Ideology*
they explain that the proletarian class, owing to its relation to
production and labour, can only confront the social order as an
ensemble, as a whole, and that it has no choice but to destroy the
state. In their opinion, the term 'social contract', which implies
a notion of individual choice and of voluntary association, could
possibly be applied to the serfs. For in the course of several centuries they liberated themselves one by one, running away from
the land to which they belonged. And it is also one by one that
the serfs associated to form cities, hence their name *bourgeois*
(people who have formed a bourg).[2] (It seems that as soon as
Rousseau had developed the idea of social contract as far as it has
ever been developed, history outdated it. But not before some of
his propositions were adopted without amendment by the
French Revolutionary Assembly.)

I always thought that women are a class very much structured
as was the class of serfs. I see now that they can tear themselves
away from the heterosexual order only by running away one by
one. This explains my concern for a pre-industrial notion as social
contract. For the structure of our class in terms of the whole world
is feudal in essence, maintaining both side by side and in the same
person forms of production and exploitation that are at once
capitalistic and pre-capitalistic.[3]

In broad terms that is one aspect of my task. Another aspect
has to do with language. For to a writer language offers a very
concrete matter to grasp. It seems to me that the first, the permanent, and the final social contract is language. The basic
agreement between human beings, indeed what makes them
human and makes them social, is language. The story of the

Tower of Babel is a perfect illustration of what happens when the agreement is broken.

Having used several times the term 'heterosexual contract'[4] in my past writings as well as having referred to the 'social contract as heterosexual', it has become my task to reflect on the notion of social contract. Why is this notion so compelling even though it has supposedly been given up by modern science and history? Why does it reverberate here and now far from its initial momentum, the Enlightenment of the 18th century? Why, at the same time, did I urge vehemently that we should break off the heterosexual social contract? The general question of the social contract, in so far as it encompasses all human activity, thought, and relations, is a philosophical question always current as long as 'humankind [that] was born free ... is everywhere in chains,' to quote Rousseau. Its promise of being achieved for the good of all and of everyone can still be the object of a philosophical examination, and since this promise has not been fulfilled by history, it retains its utopian dimension. Thus formulated in its general aspects, the question extends to all humankind. Now when I say let us break off the heterosexual contract per se, I designate the group 'women'. But I do not mean that we must break off the social contract per se, because that would be absurd. For we must break it off as *heterosexual*. Leaning upon a philosophical examination of what a well-established social contract could do for us, I want to confront the historical conditions and conflicts that can lead us to end the obligations that bind us without our consent, while we do not enjoy the reciprocal commitment that would be the necessary condition for our freedom (to paraphrase Rousseau).

The question of the social contract in the very terms of Jean-Jacques Rousseau is far from being obsolete, for in its philosophical dimension it was never developed further. The question of the sexes, which itself narrowly delineated the general design of society, if approached from a philosophical point of view encompasses and embodies the general idea of social contract. There are historical reasons as well to resuscitate the notion of social contract, and these have to do with the structures of the groups of sex and their particular situation among the relations of production and intercourse.

The main approach to the notion of social contract must be a philosophical one, in the sense that a philosophical point of view allows the possibility of synthesis, in contrast to the divided point of view of the social sciences.[5] And indeed, 'social contract' is a notion of political philosophy, the abstract idea that there is a pact, a compact, an agreement between individuals and the social order. The idea came into existence with the English philosophers of the 17th century, Thomas Hobbes (*Leviathan*) and John Locke (*Treatise of Government*), and the French philosophers of the Enlightenment, chiefly Rousseau with his *Social Contract*. The appearance of the idea, according to historians of ideas, was a result of the questioning of the old medieval theories concerning the state. These asserted that the state can only be a theocracy, since all authority emanates from god; and kings, being kings by divine right, rule to achieve a divine order.

Philosophers long before the social contract came into existence had committed their attention toward the composition of society. The philosophers were apprentice legislators and rulers. They thought about the best government and the ideal city. Political questions were then asked, taught, and discussed as philosophical questions, politics being a branch of philosophy. There was a narrow margin between their elaborations and utopia, since many of them had been confronted with practical problems: Plato was called to the court of Sicily by Dionysius the tyrant. Then later on he taught and educated his nephew who was to become a king – Aristotle was the preceptor of Alexander. Plotinus was given the means by another tyrant to construct and create the ideal city, a long-time object of speculation and hope. Being caught in such a close connection between speculation and ruling, the philosophers must have known that there was a utopian limit to their creations. I imagine it thus because of the trials they had to go through in reality when they approached the throne too closely. In *The Republic*, Ninth Book, Socrates and Glaucon discuss the perfect city and its ideal form:

> *Glaucon* 'But the city whose foundation we have been describing has its being only in words; there is no spot on earth where it exists.'
> *Socrates* 'No; but it is laid up in heaven as a pattern for him

who wills to see, and seeing, to found that city in himself. Whether it exists anywhere, of even will exist, is no matter.'

No wonder, then, that Rousseau in the foreword to his book the *Social Contract* addresses the reader thus: 'I may be asked whether I am prince or a legislator that I should be writing about politics.' And Rousseau, who wanted to distance himself from those he called with contempt 'the philosophers', says: 'I answer no.' But several of his propositions were adopted directly and without transformation by the revolutionary assembly. These direct connections of the philosophers to tyrants, kings, and political assemblies may seem to us to belong to the domain of the marvellous. However, we can remember how recently President Kennedy asked the members of his staff to elaborate upon the situation of women. And the initiative of these women gave birth to one of the first detachments of the women's liberation movement, instigated by persons all very near to the 'throne'.

But if, at the start of politics, a philosopher like Aristotle was aware that society was a 'combination', an 'association', a 'coming together', it was not so in terms of a voluntary associaton. For Aristotle, society could never be established with the agreement of its members and for their own good, but only as the result of a *coup de force*, an imposition of the clever upon the strong-bodied but feeble-minded. Indeed, for Aristotle the strong and powerful are those with intelligence; those possessing bodily strength fall into the category of the weak. In his words:

> "Essential is the combination of ruler and ruled, the purpose of their coming together being their common safety . For he that can by his intelligence foresee things needed is by nature ruler and master; while he whose bodily strength enables him to perform them is by nature a slave, one of these who are ruled. Thus there is a common interest uniting master and slave".[6]

Hobbes and Locke use the terms *covenant*, *compact*, and *agreement*; and after them so does Rousseau, while emphasizing a term much more politically rigorous: the *social contract*.

Covenant, compact, agreement refer to an initial covenant

establishing once and for all the binding of people together. According to Rousseau, the social contract is the sum of fundamental conventions which 'even though they might have never been formally enunciated, are nevertheless implied by living in society.' Clearly it is the existence of the social contract in terms of up-to-dateness that is particularly stimulating for me in what Rousseau says. Whatever its origin, it exists here and now and, as such, it is apt to be understood and acted upon. Each contractor has to renegotiate the contract in new terms for the contract to be in existence.

Only then does it become an instrumental notion, in the sense that the contractors are reminded by the term itself that they should reexamine their conditions. Society was not made once and for all. The social contract will yield to our action, to our words. Even if we say no more than Rousseau: 'I was born the citizen of a free state, and the very right to vote imposes on me the duty to instruct myself in public affairs, however little influence my voice may have in them.'

Rousseau is the first philosopher who does not take for granted that if there is such a thing as a social contract, its driving force is 'Might makes right' (and under other denominations belonging to the conscious or to the unconscious order, modern historians and anthropologists seem to yield to the inevitability of this principle in society in the name of science). Nothing is more enjoyable than his sarcasms about the 'right of the strongest', which he shows to be a contradiction in terms. In the *Social Contract* he says:

"The strongest man is never strong enough to be master all the time.... The 'right of the strongest' – a 'right' that sounds like something intended ironically, but which is actually laid down as a principle. To yield to force is an act of necessity, not of will; it is at best an act of prudence. In what sense can it be a moral duty? ... Once might is made to be right, cause and effect are reversed.... But what can be the validity of a right which perishes with the force on which it rests? If force compels obedience, there is no need to invoke a duty to obey, and if force ceases to compel obedience, there is no longer any obligation. Thus the word 'right' adds nothing to what is said by 'force', it is meaningless".

I come back to the historical situation women are in and which makes it at least appropriate for them to reflect upon what has borne upon their existence without their agreement. I am not a prince, I am not a legislator but an active member of society, and I consider it my duty to examine the set of rules, obligations, and constraints this society has placed upon me. That is, *if* rules and obligations provide me with a freedom I would not find in nature, or *if* it is not so that society has taken us in on the terms, as Rousseau puts it: 'I make a covenant with you which is wholly at your expense and wholly to my advantage; I will respect it as long as I please and you shall respect it as long as I wish.' (The term 'nature' is used here rhetorically, since everybody knows there is no way out of society.) But whether we want or not, we are living in society here and now, and proof is given that we say 'yes' to the social bond when we conform to conventions and rules never formally enunciated but nonetheless known and applied like magic by everyone. Proof is given that we say 'yes' to the social bond when we talk a common language as we do now. Most people would not use the term 'social contract' to describe their situation within the social order. However, they would agree there are a certain number of acts and things one 'must do'. 'Outlaw' and 'mad' are names for those who refuse to go by the rules and conventions, as well as for those who refuse to or cannot speak the common language. For this is what interests we when I talk of social contract: precisely those rules and conventions that have never been formally enunciated. The rules and conventions that go without saying for the scientific mind as well as for the common people. That which for them obviously makes life possible, exactly as for them one must have two legs and two arms, or one must breathe in order to live.

Being tied together by a social link, we can consider that each and every one of us stands within the social contract – the social contract being, then, the fact of having come together, of being together, of living as social beings. This notion is relevant for the philosophical mind, even if not instrumental anymore for the scientific mind, through the established fact that we live, function, talk, work, marry together. Indeed, conventions and language show on a dotted line the bulk of the social contract, which consists in *living in heterosexuality*. For to live in society is to live in heterosexuality. In fact, to my mind *social contract* and *heterosexuality* are two interchangeable notions.

The social contract I am talking about is heterosexuality.

The problem I am facing in trying to define the social contract is the same kind of problem I have when I try to define what heterosexuality is. I confront a nonexistent object, a fetish, an ideologial form which cannot be grasped in reality except through its effects, whose existence lies in the minds of people but in a way that affects their whole life, the way they act, the way they move, the way they think. So that we are dealing with an object both imaginary and real. If I try to look at the dotted line that delineates the bulk of the social contract, it moves, it shifts, and sometimes it produces something visible, and sometimes it disappears altogether. It looks like the Möbius strip. Now I see *this*, now I see something quite different. But this Möbius strip is fake, because only one aspect of the optical effect appears distinctly and massively – *heterosexuality*. Homosexuality appears like a ghost, only dimly and sometimes not at all.

What, then, is heterosexuality? As a term it was created as a counterpart to homosexuality in the beginning of this century; so much for the extent of its 'going without saying'. Jurists would not call it an institution; in other words, heterosexuality as an institution has no juridical existence (marriage legislation in France does not even mention that the partners to the contract must be of different sexes). Anthropologists, ethnologists, and sociologists *would* take it to be an institution, but an unwritten, an unspoken one. For they assume a preexistence, due to something exterior to the social order, of two groups: men and women. For them, the men are social beings, the women are natural beings. I compare it to the approach of psychoanalysts when they assume there is a pre-Oedipal relationship of the mother to the child, a pre-social relationship which in spite of its importance for humankind does not emerge from history. This view has for them the advantage, in terms of the social contract, of doing away with the problem of origins. They believe they are dealing with a diachrony instead of a synchrony. So does Lévi-Strauss with his famous notion of the exchange of women: he believes he is dealing with invariants. He, and all the other social scientists who do not see the problem I am trying to underline, would, of course, never speak in terms of 'social contract'. It is indeed much simpler to take what I call 'social contract' to be *status quo*, that is, to talk in terms of something that *has* not changed and *will* not change. Thus we have in their literature words like *fathers, mothers, brothers, sisters*, etc., relations that can be studied as though they must go on as such for ever.

Aristotle was much more cynical when he stated in *Politics* that things *must be* as he says. 'The first point is that those that are ineffective without each other *must be* united in a pair. For example, the union of male and female.' Notice that this point of the necessity of heterosexuality is the first point of *Politics* – and notice also that the second example of 'those ... that *must be* united as a pair' is found in 'the combination of ruler and ruled'. From that time on, male and female, the heterosexual relationship, has been the parameter of all hierarchical relationships. It is almost useless to underline that it is only the *dominated* members of the pair that are 'ineffective' by themselves. For 'ruler' and 'male' go very well without their counterparts.

Now I return to Lévi-Strauss, for I am not going to pass by the idea of the exchange of women which has had till now such good fortune with feminist theoreticians. And not by chance either, since with this theory we have revealed the whole plot, the whole conspiracy, of fathers, brothers, husbands, against half of humankind. Masters and slaves are certainly more transient than women in the use one can have for them. For women, 'the slaves of the poor' as Aristotle called them, are always at hand, they are the valuables that make life worthwhile, according to Lévi-Strauss. (Aristotle would have said it not very differently: they make for the 'good life'.) When Lévi-Strauss described what the exchange of women is and how it works, he was obviously drawing for us the broad lines of the social contract, but a social contract from which women are excluded, a social contract *between men*. Each time the exchange takes place it confirms between men a contract of appropriation of all women. For Lévi-Strauss, society cannot function or exist without this exchange. By showing it, he exposes heterosexuality not only as an institution but as *the* social contract, as a political regime. (You have noticed that sexual pleasure and sexual modes are not the issue here.) Lévi-Strauss answers the charges anti-feminism rewarded him with for producing such a theory. And although he concedes women cannot be completely interchangeable with the signs of language with which he compares them in terms of exchange, he has no reason to worry about the shocking effect such a theory can have upon women – no more than Aristotle had when he defined the necessity of slaves in the social order – because a scientific mind must not be embarrased and shy when dealing with crude reality: and this is crude reality indeed. There cannot be any fear of a rebellion in the case of women; better yet, they have been convinced that they *want* what they are forced to do and that they are part of the contract of society that excludes them. Because even if they, if we, do not consent, we cannot think outside of the mental categories of heterosexuality. Heterosexuality is always preexistent within all mental categories. It has sneaked into dialectical thought (the thought of differences) as its main category. For even abstract philosophical categories act to socialize the real. Language casts sheaves of reality upon the social body, stamping it and violenty shaping it. For example, the bodies of social actors are fashioned by abstract language (as well as by non-abstract ones). There is a plasticity of the real to language.

Thus heterosexuality, whose characterstics appear and then disappear when the mind tries to grasp it, is visible and obvious in the categories of the heterosexual contract. One of them which I tried to deconstruct in a short essay is the *category of sex*. And it is clear that we are dealing here with a *political* category. A category which, stated flatly, makes us understand the terms of the social contract for women. I quote from this paper called 'The Category of Sex':

> "The perenniality of the sexes and the perenniality of slaves and masters proceed from the same belief. And as there are no slaves without masters, there are no women without men. The *ideology of sexual difference* functions as censorship in our culture by masking, on the ground of nature, the *social opposition between men and women*. Masculine/feminine, male/ female are the categories which serve to conceal the fact that the difference is social.
>
> The primacy of difference so constitutes our thought that

it prevents turning inward on itself in order to question itself, no matter how necessary that may be to apprehend the bases of that which precisely constitutes it.

The category of sex is the political category that founds society as heterosexual. As such it does not concern being but relationship (for women and men are the result of relationships), although the two aspects are always confused when they are discussed. The category of sex is the one that rules as 'natural' the relation that is at the base of (heterosexual) society and through which half of the population, women, are 'heterosexualized' (the making of women is like the making of eunuchs, the breeding of slaves, of animals) and submitted to a heterosexual economy.

For heterosexuality is a totalitarian order which to prove true has its inquisitions, its courts, its tribunals, its body of laws, its terrors, its tortures, its mutilations, its executions, its police. It shapes the mind as well as the body since it controls all mental production. It grips our minds in such a way that we cannot think outside of it.

Its main category, the category of *sex works specifically, as 'black' does through an operation of reduction, by taking the part for the whole, a part (color, sex) through which the whole human group has to pass as through a screen*".[7]

When Adrienne Rich said 'heterosexuality is compulsory', it was a step forward in comprehending the kind of social contract we are dealing with. Nicole Mathieu, a French anthropologist, in a remarkable essay on consciousness made clear that it is not because we remain silent that we consent.[8] And how can we consent to a social contract that reduces us by obligation to sexual beings meaningful only through their reproductive activities or, to cite the French writer Glaucon, to beings in whom everything, even their minds, is sex?

In conclusion I will say that only by running away from their class can women enter the social contract (that is a new one), even if they have to do it like the fugitive serfs, one by one. We are doing it. Lesbians are runaways, just like maroon slaves and runaway wives, and they exist in all countries because the political regime of heterosexuality represents all cultures. So that breaking off the heterosexual social contract is a necessity for those who do not consent to it. For if there is something real in the ideas of Rousseau, it is that we can form 'voluntary associations' here and now, and here and now reformulate the social contract as a new one, even though we are not princes or legislators. Is this mere utopia? Then I will stay with Socrates's view and also Glaucon's: If ultimately we are denied a new social order, which thereiore can exist only in words, I will find it in myself.

NOTES

1   *The Social Contract, or Principles of Political Right*, by J.J. Rousseau, citizen of Geneva.

2   Colette Guillaumin, 'The Practice of Power and Belief in Nature'. *Feminist Issues* 1:2 (1981).

3   Colette Capitan Peter, 'A Historical Precedent for Patriarchal Oppression: "The Old Regime" and the French Revolution'. *Feminist Issues* 4:1 (1984).

4   Monique Wittig, 'The Straight Mind'. *Feminist Issues* 1:1 (1980); and
    'One Is Not Born A Woman'. *Feminist Issues* 1:2 (1981).

5   This statement by Marx and Engels is particulary relevant to the modern situation.

6   Cf. Aristotle, *Politics*.

7   Monique Wittig, 'The Category of Sex'. *Feminist Issues* 2:2 (1982).

8   Nicole-Claude Mathieu, 'De la Conscience Dominée'. In *L'Arraisonnement des Femmes*. Paris: Edition de l'Ecole des Hautes Etudes en Sciences Sociales, 1985.

NOTES ON CONTRIBUTORS

Dennis Altman (AUS) is the author of six books, including *The Homosexualization of America* and *AIDS in the Mind of America*. He teaches Politics at La Trobe University, Melbourne, and is Vice President of the Victorian AIDS Council.

Henk van den Boogaard (NL) finished his Political Science studies at the University of Nijmegen in 1982. Published books on homosexuality in Cuba (1982) and anti-gay violence (1986). Works now at the Department of Gay and Lesbian Studies at the University of Nijmegen and as a researcher at the Schorer Foundation in Amsterdam.

Liana Borghi (IT) teaches Anglo-American (women's) literature at the University of Bologna. She is a founding member of the Libreria delle Donne in Florence and of the lesbian group 'L'amando(r)la'. She runs, with a partner, the lesbian publishing house Estro. Although she has written on a lot of topics/themes/issues, she says what really matters is that she has translated Adrienne Rich into Italian.

Ingrid Foeken (NL, 1947) is a social scientist (MA) and a social worker (MA). She is a feminist therapist, supervisor and trainer on issues of lesbianism and sexual abuse/incest. Co-founder of several women's therapy centres in the Netherlands. Works at Stichting De Maan, a feminist mental health care centre in Amsterdam.

Mary E. Hunt (USA) is a Catholic feminist theologian. She is the co-director of Women's Alliance for Theology, Ethics and Ritual (WATER) in Silver Spring, Maryland, USA. She is finishing a book on women's friendship.

Anja van Kooten Niekerk (NL, 1953) works as an assistant director and programme coordinator at the Schorer Foundation in Amsterdam. She is the editor in chief of the Schorer imprint (An Dekker Publishing House) and is a member of the Editorial Board of the Journal of Homosexuality. She published a book in

1985 on lesbian lifestyles in the Netherlands between 1920-1960 together with Sacha Wijmer.

Maurice van Lieshout (NL, 1953) has published several articles on gay history and literature and homosexuality. He is the co-author of a book on pioneers of homosexual emancipation (Amsterdam, 1988). He is currently editor of *Jeugd en Samenleving* (Youth and Society) and lecturer in gay and lesbian literary studies at the University of Amsterdam, Department of Modern Dutch Literature.

Theo van der Meer (NL, 1950) is research fellow of the Netherlands Organization for Scientific Research at the Faculty of Law, Free University of Amsterdam. He is preparing a dissertation on 17th and 18th century sodomitical subcultures in Holland. Has also published on subjects as the persecution of sodomites.

Guy Ménard (CAN) is Professor of Religious Studies at the Université du Québec à Montréal.

Jan Schippers (NL, 1952) studies Clinical Psychology at the Free University of Amsterdam. Works as a therapist and coordinator at the Schorer Foundation. He has specialized on the topics of psychosocial help and counselling for gay men. This year he will publish a book on therapies for gay men.

Randolph Trumbach (USA) was trained at the Johns Hopkins University, and is Professor of History, Baruch College, City University of New York. He is the author of *The Rise of the Egalitarian Family: Aristocratic Kinship and Domestic Relations in 18th Century London*. He has also written a number of preliminary studies for a forthcoming work on *The Sexual Life of 18th Century London*.

Martha Vicinus (USA) is Professor of English and Women's Studies at the University of Michigan, Ann Arbor. She is the author of *Independent Women: Work and Community for Single Women, 1850-1920* (1985), and the editor of two collections of essays on Victorian women. She is also the co-editor of the forthcoming *Reclaiming the Past: The New Social History of Homosexuality* with Martin

Baum Duberman and George Chauncey, Jr.

Carole S. Vance (USA), an anthropologist, writes about gender and sexuality. She edited *Pleasure and Danger: Exploring Female Sexuality* (1984). She is working on a book about the Meese Commission on Pornography in the United States, and teaches at Columbia University in New York City.

Jeffrey Weeks (UK) is a social historian and sociologist whose major work has been concerned with the social organization of sexuality and the historical emergence of the modern homosexual identities. He works in academic administration in London, and is a visiting research fellow at the Universities of Kent and Southampton.

Saskia Wieringa (NL) is an anthropologist, working at the Institute of Social Studies, The Hague. She carried out research mainly in Indonesia and Peru. She has published a novel on those experiences.

Monique Wittig (USA) teaches literature and political theory at Duke University in Durham, North Carolina. In addition to the books *L'Opoponax* (1964), *Les Guérillères* (1969), *Le Corps lesbien* (1973) and *Virgile, non* (1985), Wittig has also published short stories, plays, literary reviews, and essays.